THE PULSE OF THE EARTH

Seismograph recording from an eruption of Merapi volcano, November 23–24, 1930.
Vulkanologische en Seismologische Mededeelingen 12 (1933): 138.

ADAM BOBBETTE

THE PULSE OF
THE EARTH

Political Geology in Java

DUKE UNIVERSITY PRESS · DURHAM AND LONDON · 2023

Project Editor: Ihsan Taylor
Designed by Matthew Tauch
Typeset in Alegreya and Comma Base by
Westchester Publishing Services

Library of Congress Cataloging-in-Publication Data
Names: Bobbette, Adam, [date] author.
Title: The pulse of the earth : political geology in Java / Adam Bobbette.
Description: Durham : Duke University Press, 2023. |
Includes bibliographical references and index.
Identifiers: LCCN 2022055559 (print)
LCCN 2022055560 (ebook)
ISBN 9781478025054 (paperback)
ISBN 9781478020073 (hardcover)
ISBN 9781478027089 (ebook)
Subjects: LCSH: Historical geology—Indonesia—Java. | Religion and science—
Indonesia—Java—History—19th century. | Geology—Indonesia—Java—History—
19th century. | BISAC: SOCIAL SCIENCE / Human Geography | SOCIAL SCIENCE /
Ethnic Studies / Asian Studies
Classification: LCC QE28.3 .B633 2023 (print) | LCC QE28.3 (ebook) |
DDC 555.98—dc23/eng/20230519
LC record available at https://lccn.loc.gov/2022055559
LC ebook record available at https://lccn.loc.gov/2022055560

Cover art: Mount Merapi, Indonesia, ca. 1930. Courtesy
of Balai Penyelidikan dan Pengembangan Teknologi
Kebencanaan Geologi archive.

Thank you Giyono, Suparno, and Sukidi

CONTENTS

————

PREFACE

———

THE MODERN EARTH WAS MADE IN JAVA · We—as in the *we* who believe that the earth is broken into tectonic plates that glide across the surface of the earth and grind into each other, and that the ocean floors are bisected with massive trenches that ooze the stuff that makes continents—*we* inherited these stories from Java. Our orthodoxy, the taken-for-granted scientific picture of the history and structure of the earth, was forged on the slopes of Javanese volcanoes as scientists watched them shudder, explode, crumble, turn to dust and ash, and wash into the oceans. Scientists photographed the remains of houses cracked by earthquakes, then they circled smoking calderas in airplanes, hid in bunkers, peered from prison lookout towers, trekked through forests of giant ferns and pine trees growing from volcanic soils. It was in these volatile, rambunctious landscapes that a new, modern story of the earth was forged; a story that stressed how the earth was formed under duress, a system of creative destruction, a surface remaking itself in deep time—buckling, crushing, and reemerging from its own split seams.

Java has been, for more than a century, an intellectual center for earth narratives. These narratives were built not only by Western scientists conducting work in Indonesia but through uneasy and complicated collaborations between mystics, colonial Christians and Muslims, Sanskritists, ethnologists, antiquarians, occultists, postcolonial revolutionaries, and ethnonationalist animists. Earth stories were cosmic stories, told with one foot on a caldera and the other on the ruins of a Hindu temple. Volcanologists carried binoculars and tilt meters, guns and oblations;

they prayed to ocean goddesses and mythical jihadist serpents in craters. We inherit this past, it made the earth *we* now know.

When we imagine that the Anthropocene is an unprecedented moment, shocking because humans are now acknowledged to be participating in processes as ancient and soundly inhuman as geology, we actually *should* be surprised by how little we have understood of geology and how late many of us are to the game. The Anthropocene is revolutionary only for a small few, often scientists and humanists in Western metropolitan circuits. But the core problem of the Anthropocene has been central to modern geology for more than a century, and it was crucial from the beginning in Java. How humans are or are not implicated, and to what degree of profundity (how ontologically deep), in geological processes was the prevailing metaphysical riddle for geologists there. The question was asked with a special intensity even before colonial geologists began extensively mapping the island for the first time in the late nineteenth century. Societies in Java were traditionally ordered on the principle that geology was social, that social history was geological history, and that volcanoes were societies. Modern European geophysics was built amid this expansive conception of the sociality of geology, and European colonists were fascinated by it; they learned how to understand the relationship between geology and society from it. Standard Western geological science was not simply imposed on a prior indigenous geology; instead, Native and colonial geological knowledges produced each other, even if the process was uneven, indirect, and sometimes violent. And now they contain each other. The Anthropocene was theorized with profound intellectual and political intensity in Java long before it became of interest to contemporary Western scholars.

Acknowledging that society was considered geological in the Javanese geological sciences goes some way to pluralizing the intellectual traditions that have helped shape contemporary theories of the Anthropocene. Much Anthropocene theory remains unfortunately bound up with histories that continue to center Western science at the expense of its much more plural and cosmopolitan origins. While geological theory is currently seeking to identify the material markers of the Anthropocene, there is also an opportunity for us to expand our appreciation of geological thought beyond the conventional focus on the West and toward traditions that have often been suppressed in conventional narratives.

Javanese geology helps us understand how thoroughly contemporary discussions of the Anthropocene are a spiritual project. It is often assumed that the earth sciences could not be further from theology, that geological narratives are the result of a secularizing society shirking the grasp of its Christian narratives. Java shows us otherwise. It was not only Christianity that was at stake in geological narratives, it was also Islam, Hinduism, Buddhism, and animism. Deep time was contrived in a space crowded with temporalities—catastrophic, circular, rhythmic, spiraling, linear. And it adapted to them, incorporated them, and sometimes sought to repress them. Geological time—and, in particular, Anthropocene time—thus remains religious time, the inheritance of struggles with religious traditions. It is strange to think that geology was ever secular, or that secularism ever succeeded, or that the Anthropocene is a secular science. Instead, Javanese geologists learned from and leaned on Hindu temporal narratives, ancient Greek myths, and Islamic saints and ancestors to build their modern science that shaped the very standard modern earth stories that we have inherited, even the theory of plate tectonics. This book is about these pedagogies, these messy intercalations from paranoid praying mapmakers to scientist mystics with seismographs; it is about how they created "our" modern earth on the slopes of Javanese volcanoes.

LIVING WITH VOLATILE GEOLOGY · I first learned about Javanese geology after turning a corner. I was in a taxi on the way to the airport in Surakarta, a medium-sized city in Central Java. As the taxi driver took a left turn, the road suddenly pointed in the direction of a cone emerging from the land, the summit was jagged, stone gray, half obscured by clouds.

"What is that?" I asked the taxi driver. "That? Oh, that is Merapi."

I soon learned that Merapi was a volcano, that it was active, and inhabited. Some people were saying that nearly one million people lived there. I also learned that a few years earlier, in 2010, it had erupted and killed a so-called gatekeeper who lived in a village close to the caldera. I read in the *Guardian* that there was a conflict between scientists and the gatekeeper because he had refused to leave the volcano during the eruption. The article referred to him as the volcano's "spiritual guardian."

My intuition told me that the people who lived on Merapi had things to teach those of us who did not live there. My hunch was that the extreme and unpredictable environment on Merapi was the future many of us are headed for as the climate crisis produces ever more uncertainty in natural systems. Merapi, too, is all about unpredictability, and people have been living with it for centuries. It seemed to me that this was what people there could share wisdom about.

On my first trip up the flanks to the village of Deles, I met a man named Sukiman. He had an anarchist ethos and celebrated the volcano, with its caldera smoking only a few kilometers away. He embraced an ecological ethic of mutual aid between people, nonhumans, and the volcano. We discussed how he was caring for persecuted monkey communities that lived on the flanks of the volcano and provided early warning signals for eruptions when they fled before humans even sensed danger. He also advocated pesticide-free farming and planting native crops. Sukiman was well known in the region as an outspoken critic of government and as an advocate for disaster management reform. He even presented his case to the United Nations.

I came to understand that villagers in Deles, with Sukiman's encouragement, were self-managing their own disaster risk reduction and preparedness. They took advantage of their proximity to the caldera to take videos and photos of eruptions and later sell them to international media outlets, keeping the proceeds in a collective community pot dedicated for disaster relief. Communal savings were also created from voluntary contributions from villagers' harvests. Evacuations, Sukiman told me, were pitched as holidays, periods of reprieve from the boredom of everyday labor. The villagers were trying to build a communitarian ethos of mutual aid to manage the uncertainty of the volcano. Rather than fear the volcano, they shared an ecology, a cosmology even, of mutualism. This seemed promising—inspiring actually. Perhaps we, too, could learn how to thrive with the radical uncertainty of nature, even in its most extreme circumstances. Perhaps we could transform uncertainty into a vehicle for creating deeper forms of interdependence between society and nature. Maybe that is what residents on Merapi could teach us.

On that same trip, I also visited the village of Kinaredjo, where Maridjan, the "spiritual guardian" from the *Guardian* article, had died in the eruption of 2010. The destroyed parts of the village had been rebuilt, including a new mosque in the traditional wooden Javanese style. I met Maridjan's son, Asih, who had taken over the job from his father and who explained to me that he was continuing his father's work of undertaking annual pilgrimages to the volcano to give it offerings. In the village, a disaster tourism business had sprung up, taking curious passengers on Jeep rides to the hard, dusty, dried lava flows nearby. Kiosks were selling Kinaredjo tea, souvenirs, and T-shirts with Maridjan's face emblazoned on them. I was told that the Jeep business was so lucrative that some of the drivers had made enough money to open their own restaurants. The eruption had been devastating, but it also provided new economic opportunities and chances for regrowth.

It was on this visit that I learned of the richness of the stories about the volcano, the expansive pantheon of gods and goddesses and ghosts that live inside it and on its flanks. Keeping these stories alive and meaningful was crucial to Maridjan's and Asih's work as well as to devoted followers in the village and across Indonesia. Many Javanese men saw that Maridjan, before he died, upheld a tradition of so-called local wisdom, a quintessentially Javanese form of mysticism in which volcanic activity was inseparable from social and political orders and volcanic tremors and explosions signaled not just nature but also a society in duress.

Later, I began to spend time on leafy Cendana Street in north Yogyakarta, in the government volcano observatory. The observatory had its origins and mandate in the early twentieth century, when Indonesia was a Dutch colony, to monitor the volcano and warn the population of eruptions. Today, it is a high-tech, well-respected scientific volcano observatory. As scientists monitor the volcano from Cendana Street, there are also six outposts on the slopes and dozens of smaller, unmanned, transmitting stations. In the main observatory, there are nearly one hundred staffers. Some of them are on twelve-hour rotations, reading seismographs and overseeing television monitors. Tilt meters measure the deformations of the ground, and an assortment of other instruments surveil and record the volcano's every move and breath. During the eruption in 2010, observations went all the way from the slope of Merapi to Yogyakarta, Bandung, the presidential palace in Bogor, and the United States Geological Survey (USGS).

There were not only farmers constructing multispecies mutual-aid communities but also Javanese mystics, enterprising disaster victims, and scientists, each trying to make sense of the unpredictability of Merapi. Each of these groups often had very different stories to tell about the volcano. Scientists understood that it was part of the global plate tectonic system. South of Java, they reasoned, about five hundred kilometers away in the Indian Ocean, was a continental subduction zone, where the Australian plate was driving below Java and resurfacing on land through volcanic outbursts. They not only thought Merapi was the result of planetary evolution; they were also representatives of the state and public health officials dedicated to protecting the population. Yet, in Kinaredjo, where Maridjan died, many villagers celebrated narratives that had been transmitted from before the colonial era and the establishment of any scientific observatory. For many residents on the upper slopes, volcanic activity was made sense of through references to stories connected to the founding of the sultanate in Yogyakarta in the eighteenth century; these stories suggested that the first sultan to rise to power and establish a kingdom in the sixteenth century had done so through arrangements (marriage and treaties) with deities in the volcano and the Indian Ocean. Living with the volcano demanded offerings and rituals because volcanic activity was connected to human moral and ethical behavior. What animated nature, according to stories in the observatory and in the villages, were different, seemingly exclusive, and contradictory forces. Sometimes those incompatible visions were held together in a fragile assemblage, sometimes by one person. I met Indonesian scientists who prayed to Allah in the observatory between meetings about the most recent seismograph readings. I met a white French seismologist who spoke excellent Javanese and fluent Indonesian, and who joined Javanese rituals with his Javanese partner. I met scientists who held that the theory of plate tectonics confirmed the origin stories of the Central Javanese sultanates. I drank tea with Javanese mystics trained as seismologists and with seismologists who meditated on the meaning of nothingness. One afternoon, I had a conversation with an observatory technician who had seen ghosts wandering around the observatory the night before. It is no surprise that people hold seemingly contradictory and inconsistent views, nor is it world-shattering to encounter it in Indonesia. It has long been a prevailing interpretation by Western and Indonesian intellectuals that Indonesian culture emerges from a long history of stitching together diverse cosmologies from centuries of cosmopolitan contact.

I began to split my time between the observatory and the village of Keningar on the western slope, a village high up the slope, similar to Deles. Keningar is subject to intense, widespread, and mainly illegal sand mining, where local and Indonesian migrant laborers dig at the residue of past eruptions, deposits of sand, ash, and stones. The mining was causing profound ecological destruction to the river valleys, agricultural land, and the water supply. It also gave rise to social conflicts and sometimes violence between environmentalists, farmers, and miners. Village activists responded with litigation and pushed hard and ambitiously on what they saw as a stressed and dysfunctional legal system. On top of that, they were also practicing spiritual activism, performing rituals, mysticism, magic, and spirit possession to fight corruption and drive the miners away.

Volcano scientists had a difficult time gaining respect in these circumstances. Many people in Keningar were suspicious of government officials, including scientists, suspecting that they represented, or were directly implicated in, government corruption—the same government that also failed to protect their rivers and landscapes from mining. Some scientists saw the "traditional practices" of ritual, magic, and spirit possession in Keningar as forms of folk culture, which they dismissed as voodoo and peasant superstition. At the worst of times, scientists, mystics, and activists were locked in holding patterns of mutual misrecognition.

I met a farmer in Keningar, Sukidi, a man in his eighties, who mediated local spirits. The spirits, he told me, were enraged by the mining, and if it continued there was sure to be an eruption, or at least a landslide. The volcano was talking back to the miners; it was in solidarity with activists and farmers. Sukidi told me that his friends often encountered volcano spirits in their dreams; when people died, their spirits went into the volcano. The mountain was social history materialized. Eruptions and landslides, the shuddering of volcanic earthquakes, were the gestures of rage-filled intercessions. Merapi had much to say; it was a matter of learning how to hear it.

This was what interested me in Keningar—Sukidi and his friends could help us live in the Anthropocene, an age of volatile and unpredictable nature constitutive of human agency, a period in which geology is woven with human culture, not only imprinted and inscribed by human efforts—cities, roads, and mines—but also haunted to its core in the very categories that describe geology and the sciences that study it. Anthropocene geology is also on the move, destabilizing the conventional boundaries between culture and lithos in an unceasing geological undermining. The animate geology of Keningar seemed to offer a new way into thinking the present more broadly by resolutely denying the conventional distinctions between stones and persons, human sociality and lithic substrate, politics and geology, and replacing them with a form of geological thought that is also always social thought, in other words, a political geology.

Making sense of the uncertainty of the volcano was inseparable from navigating ways of knowing, which in turn meant navigating multiple, sometimes competing, practices of mediation. Merapi was multiple indeed. Yet its fragments were bound together. What was certain was the common magic of conjuring the hidden interior of the volcano and earth. As Bernard Siegert has argued, the often-assumed distinction between high-tech and folk-tech is condescending; they both, in their different ways, share the magic of conjuring invisible worlds.[1] The technologies of modern Javanese volcanology and mysticism conjure from felt tremors the constant churning of a plate tectonic earth renewing itself and the voices of restless spirits. What the magic of volcano science makes clear is just how flawed our contemporary narratives are about the disillusionment and disenchantment of the modern sciences. The earth sciences, in fact, have their ontological feet, as it were, in the magical act of conjuring hidden worlds such as the processes buried deep inside volcanic mountains or their gurgling magma chambers. And a volcano observatory is an utterly enchanted space, replete with idols (photos of volcanoes), daily rituals (reading seismographs or tilt meters), and an acknowledgment among volcanologists that they are witnesses to the utter mysteriousness of the earth's processes. Such acknowledgment runs counter to traditions of critical social theory that berate the sciences for banishing mystery from the world through rationalization, alienation, and instrumentalization. Contemporary attempts to revive the mysteries of geology through poetically inflected reflections on nature or poetic experiments with social theory often reproduce this misunderstanding: volcanology, and specifically volcanology in Java, has never been disenchanted; it has always been in magic-making collusion with mystical Islam, geological animism, socialized geology, possession play, ancestral obsessions, and other techniques of living with and through invisible worlds. This book is about these uneven, shifting boundaries, piggybacking, and unexpected collaborations. When we try to imagine how to live in a new geological epoch in which lithic and human processes seem uniquely conjoined, we are actually inheriting a much older conception of the earth. The rest of this book shows how that conception came to be and what it can tell us about living with the earth.

PLAN OF THE BOOK · Chapter 1 outlines the core ambition of political geology, which is to explore the intersections of politics, the geological sciences, cosmology, and culture. Political geology was inspired in part by discussions surrounding the Anthropocene and a turn across the humanities to grappling with geological agency. Yet, as the chapter shows, political geology, with its attention on the history of geological and earth knowledges, reveals how the Anthropocene debate in the geosciences was prefigured by Javanese spiritual geographies and volcanology for at least a century. The Anthropocene debate, in fact, belongs to the much older ambition in the geological sciences to question the boundaries between society and the earth, between *bios* and *geos*. The Anthropocene debate also signals a moment in which modern scientists are implicitly engaging much older ideas that have long been central to Javanese political philosophy, including the notion that politics is foundationally geological. The chapter then explores three significant volcanic eruptions and the colonial-political milieu that brought about the formation of volcanology as a modern science of governance in Indonesia.

Chapter 2 examines four geological maps of Java and the contexts of their production to explore how geological narratives of Java have changed since the late nineteenth century. The chapter traces how these maps represented Javanese volcanism and were tied to shifting scientific narratives of the earth's history. The chapter shows that geologists transformed their vision of Java as an island of natural and cultural antiquities in which volcanoes were the ruins of once great mountains, to a vision of Java as a young island in the violent throes of youthful earth-building. Adopting and adapting ideas of continental drift before many other geologists around the world did were key to this transformation. Combining oceanography with terrestrial geology was crucial to this new view, which later set the stage for the development of the theory of plate tectonics in the 1970s. The maps examined in this chapter were turning points in this new earth history.

Chapter 3 shows how the theory of plate tectonics landed on Mount Merapi. The chapter explores how the contemporary theory of the relationship between ocean and land was prefigured and enabled by Javanese spiritual geographies. The Central Javanese sultanates emerged through an acknowledgment that deities in the ocean and volcanoes were related to the sultans. Political power was made possible through these associations with chthonic deities. The theory of plate tectonics mirrored this belief structure. It was based on a radical shift in geological thought to understanding the exchanges between oceans and volcanoes as related. This chapter explores how these two visions fit together and the politics of their clashing and melding. It follows both the mystics and sultans as they gave offerings to volcano and ocean deities and the geologists as they, in turn, considered the mystical foundations of plate tectonics. The chapter describes these intersections in terms of *intercalation*.

Chapter 4 turns to the beginning of volcanology in the Netherlands East Indies and the anxieties of late colonialism. It traces the fate of the idea that medieval Javanese Hindu-Buddhist civilization was destroyed by a cataclysmic eruption of Merapi in AD 1006. This idea became a way to naturalize the end of a culture and to explain the rise of Islam. Colonial scientists in the twilight years of their own empire explored imaginaries of radical environmental change and cultural impermanence. Theosophists, Javanese nationalists, aristocrats, Sanskritists, philologists, and volcano scientists trudged up and down the slopes of Merapi looking for mystical communion with the earth.

Chapter 5 traces the origins of geopoetics in the work of the largely forgotten geologist Johannes Umbgrove in Java in the 1920s. The chapter shows how Umbgrove developed an aesthetic conception of geologizing that became an expansive notion of cosmic and terrestrial evolution. In his book *The Pulse of the Earth*, published in 1942, Umbgrove developed *geopoetics* as a means to describe his scientific method that connected the psyche to the galaxy. The earth, mind, and cosmos were understood as structured by polyphonic rhythms and cycles; geopoetics had nothing to do with poetry about rocks. This chapter explores how Umbgrove developed geopoetics not only on Javanese volcanoes but also in conversation with orientalists such as Paul Deussen, a friend of Nietzsche's and translator of the *Upanishads*. Umbgrove's influence went on to shape the early formulations of the theory of sea-floor spreading and plate tectonics in the 1960s. When Umbrgove's geopoetics became plate tectonics, it sought to create a vision of the earth as a system of creative destruction.

Chapter 6 considers the significance of volcano observatories as contact zones between volcanology, geopolitics, and the Javanese ethno-nationalist mystical movement Kejawen (Javanism). The chapter explores the development and evolution of one observatory on Merapi that acted as a place where new technologies contributed to shifting conceptions of the human body, the earth, and communication. The chapter also examines how observatories were places through which the Indonesian, French, and other states could operate at rural frontiers to manage political crises. Kejawen had its roots in the late colonial spiritual geographies of Central Java, theosophy, and mystical Islam; and observatories became sites at which Kejawen practitioners struggled with imaginaries of the Republic, infrastructure, and volcanism. As much as observatories were architectures of the state, they were also places where scientists' and mystics' ideas about spatial and temporal proximity transformed each other.

ACKNOWLEDGMENTS

———

THIS PROJECT HAS MOVED AROUND A LOT · I have carried it, and it, in turn, has carried me. Parts of it were written in notebooks in Singapore, in a room in Jakarta, at a temporary desk with piles of old photobooks in the volcano observatory in Jogja, with final read-throughs in Central Sulawesi. There was the pleasant library with the quiet transistor radio at the Geological Survey in Bandung, and there were the rainy days on the deck by the cashew grove in Lombok. Many hours were spent in a *gubuk* on the edge of Mount Merapi getting away from the project, listening to the forest, and hanging out with Giyono. Cambridge, Sydney, Jogja, Malang, Surakarta, Kuala Lumpur, Hong Kong, London, Amsterdam, Tasmania, Glasgow, and the South Downs were some other places where bits and pieces or entire chapters were written, jettisoned, and rewritten. And on volcanoes, most often Merapi, but also Tangkunban Perahu, Idjen, Kelud, Merbabu, Rinjani, Vesuvius. All these topographies nourished this book and deserve thanks.

The conversations, friendships, and support (material and spiritual) that made this book possible are no less dispersed and long range. I will proceed chronologically. In Cambridge, where the project was conceived, it was nourished, challenged, and inspired by Ash Amin, Clive Oppenheimer, Michael Bravo, Simon Schaffer, and Andrew Barry. In Jogja, thank you to the Kunci community for the front-porch and dinner-table conversations. Elizabeth Inandiak offered me the little room on columns. Thank you, Sophia Hornbacher-Schönleber, for conversations and motorbike rides. Thank you, Mes 56. Thank you, Farid Rakun and Ening Nurjanah, for the best of Jakarta all the time. I send warm grat-itude to the following: the volcanologists who let me follow them around and join at their dinner tables, and all the people of Keningar for wel-coming me and the long evenings on porches sharing stories and lessons in enchantment. In Sydney, Alison Bashford, Emily Kern, Jarrod Hore, and Naomi Parkinson helped guide the project in new directions. Three years with the New Earth Histories research program at the University of New South Wales (UNSW) were invaluable. Kasia Jezowska criticized and encouraged. Zeynep Oguz, Mira Asriningtyas, and Dito Yuwono cham-pioned the project, giving it energy when it seemed like it was going no-where. Francesca Hughes and Jonathan Meyer welcomed us in London and provided escape in the hills of the Southdowns, away from a pandemic, to finish a final draft. Thank you, Nigel Clark, for encouraging the project from the very beginning at the Political Geology workshop at Cambridge in 2018 and for providing sage guidance through all its twists and turns. Jeffrey Malecki gave much needed copy-editing help. Courtney Berger at Duke University Press stuck with this and kindly guided it into the world. Anonymous reader two encouraged me to clarify the contributions of the project. Thank you to the production team at Duke for all of your careful work. Thank you, Seth Denizen, for—in one way or another—being in this conversation since the beginning when I told you about gatekeepers on Merapi while we sat on a stoop in front of a Hong Kong 7-Eleven. Fin-ishing a book can be tiring and living with someone finishing a book even more so, not to mention frequently boring; thank you, Candice Chung, for your patience and, even more, your nourishment.

Earlier versions of some of the arguments in this book have appeared in different forms in the following: "Processions: How the Spiritual Ge-ographies of Central Java Shaped Modern Volcano Science," *Indonesia* 113 (April 2022): 51–66; "A Javanese Anthropocene?," HKW *Anthropocene Curriculum*, April 22, 2022, https://www.anthropocene-curriculum.org /contribution/a-javanese-anthropocene; and "The Spiritual Geographies of Plate Tectonics: Javanese Islam, Volcanology, and Earth's New History," *New Earth Histories*, ed. Alison Bashford, Emily Kern, and Adam Bobbette (Chicago: University of Chicago Press, 2023).

. . . .

Unless otherwise noted, all translations are my own.

CHAPTER ONE

POLITICAL GEOLOGY
AS METHOD

POLITICAL GEOLOGY · Political geology was created to bring together geology and politics in new ways. It developed largely within a milieu of geographers and was, in part, inspired by discussions surrounding the Anthropocene.[1] But political geology also resonated with conversations across the humanities with shared interests in the social life of geology and the geology of social life. Political geology attempted to extend those interests by foregrounding the *geos* in the geopolitical at the very moment when many contemporary geopolitical analyses had forgotten that the *geos* of politics was actual material: grounded geological processes.[2] Turning to a concerted analysis of the ways that the earth and geological matter became politicized dovetailed with emerging critical analyses of extractivism and modern state politics, which showed that the transformation of nature into a resource was a process that coupled epistemology and technology.[3] Political geology could then foreground the ways in which the geological sciences were perhaps some of the most profoundly significant sciences in shaping the modern world because they provided the knowledge that drove extractivism. There would be no carbon capitalism, in other words, if not for the geological sciences. It would therefore be a mistake to try to give an account of the history of that earth-transforming capitalism without explaining how the sciences helped to define, prospect, and extract minerals, ores, and fuels. The political geology that is explained in this book, therefore, provides an expansive account of extractivism by explaining the social production of deep geological time, its context and controversies, and how it has been wrapped up with theology and cosmology. Extractivism, it might be said, is a cosmology. Providing such an account means acknowledging that the geological sciences were tools of European empire.

Yet, less obviously, those tools were also shaped or transformed by world knowledge traditions. This fact is rarely sufficiently acknowledged in critical literature on extractivism or the Anthropocene, where diffusionist models of scientific knowledge ("from the West to the Rest") are commonplace. The geological sciences are, in reality, cosmopolitan not only in the sense that they were developed by scientists acting in many parts of the world but also in the sense that there were (and continue to be) global traditions of geological knowledge independent of European or North American science. Moreover, those traditions helped author the standard European geological sciences. Modern geology, then, including the extractive sciences, is the product of global intelligence: encounters, brokering, and negotiation shaped them, not a linear dissemination.[4] While histories of the geological sciences have been amply told from the perspective of European and US scientists, it is less well understood how they were authored by actors conventionally understood as marginal, or peripheral, and then fed back to transform metropolitan ways of thinking. A multicentered vision of the movement of geological knowledge, with attention to the encounters, brokering, thefts, and gifts that produced it, can help complicate narratives that try to find redemption in local or indigenous counter-knowledges as resistance to extractivist modernity. Instead, the political geology in this book demonstrates just how long and winding the paths have been for many commonplace geological concepts; in fact, much global geological knowledge is local knowledge made planetary. The same ways of thinking about geology that Dutch colonial geologists encountered in Indonesia in the early twentieth century, for instance, then went on to create new Western scientific narratives about the entire earth. They were, in fact, even redeployed in new theoretical contexts to form the basis for the theory of plate tectonics while the local origins of the theory (and Indonesian intellectuals) were written out of the story. Part of the method of political geology is tracing these erasures, shifts of scale, and unexpected influences of geological knowledge to follow their transmission and how they end up enabling extractivist practices.

Much of the geology in this book is on the move and in the making. Unlike many other extractivist contexts in which the sciences stabilize and fix geology in place—turning it into a resource through quantification, spatialization, and mapping—volcanoes are completely different. They explode and melt and rumble. They cannot be approached or hacked away at like a gold or nickel deposit. Therefore, volcanic political geology is a different kind of politics and a different kind of geological knowledge. The core relationship to volcanoes in colonial Indonesia, as we will see, was not a form of extraction through stabilization—it was not about mining underground or scraping the surface—instead, it was about the management of volatile, unpredictable matter in space and time, of negotiating flows and rhythms and pulses to protect an extractive plantation economy. The thrust of geological knowledge about volcanism was not how to identify profitable ores, minerals, and fuels but, instead, how to anticipate a disaster, identify cycles and patterns of eruptions, and predict the future to protect plantation labor and better organize plantation land. Geologists thought about geology not as stable and fixed objects, nor according to the long and slowly transforming processes of geological evolution, but as a material that flows. Their goal was not to take geological material and transform it into a commodity but to negotiate its ability to suddenly move and destroy an already immensely profitable plantation economy; it was a political geology of choreography. They sought to bring society together with a mobile nature.

This eruptive political geology was often troubled by the porosity of the *geos* and *bios*. As Kathryn Yusoff and Elizabeth Povinelli have shown in their analyses of extractivist capitalism, the very categories—*geos* and *bios*, geology and biology, the living and the dead—are the product of a fundamentally cultural, political, and historical process. The geological sciences played a key role in shaping that distinction.[5] The drawing of the dividing line between *geos* and *bios* was not only a product of modern scientific categorization; it was also a profound political maneuver. By separating *biological life* from *dead matter*, things could be ordered into new hierarchies: mere *matter* could become extractable, exploitable, and fungible, while what was endowed with *life*, the organic, could be placed above and endowed with uniquely respectable values. The solidification of these categories lent ballast to imagined hierarchies between humans and geological material; there could be no human exceptionalism without the privileging of the *bios* over the *geos*. (Some) humans were seen as uniquely different from and above the lowly matter of inorganic (dead) geological material. However, the political geology of Javanese volcanology since the late nineteenth century tells a more complicated story. The relationship between *bios* and *geos* in Java has consistently been seen as horizontal, porous, and fundamentally destabilizing. One reason for this was the relentless vibrancy of volcanoes; they seemed to express the liveliness of the earth itself. It was difficult for scientists and earth theorists on volcanoes to neatly parse out and privilege biological matter from dead, inorganic material. Were the volcanoes not alive? How could you not acknowledge the vibrant agency of a liquefying mountain? Indeed, even the geologist Johannes Umbgrove came to understand in the 1930s that the line between the *geos* and *bios* was porous, always on the move, and fundamentally elusive. He saw, too, that this realization was consistent with the cosmology outlined in the *Upanishads*, which in turn shaped the knowledge systems of the early Javanese kingdoms built on the volcanic plains where he had come to question the distinction between *geos* and *bios*. Hindu cosmology, Umbgrove thought, already showed that life was geological. The modern sciences, he argued, were only now catching up to that insight. Colonial volcanologists like Umbgrove were therefore ready to imagine a different kind of nature, one not burdened by the hierarchies of extractivism. Umbgrove's work belongs to an undercurrent in the modern geological sciences that has been generally ignored or forgotten by contemporary researchers interested in the Anthropocene and in the history of the geological sciences. Revealing this undercurrent can help complicate our narratives of the history of geology because it foregrounds scientists who were interested not in separating the living from the dead but instead in troubling their distinctions, in operating in the ambiguous spaces between biological and lithic life, where volcanoes could become persons and persons could transform into cold, petrified slabs hanging on the side of crater and known as lava tongues.

ATTENTION AND INDIFFERENCE TO JAVANESE VOLCANOLOGY · Given its significance to the history of geological thought, Indonesian volcanology has been surprisingly absent from global histories of geology. Martin Rudwick's pathbreaking histories of deep time zoom over the Indonesian archipelago and acknowledge the contributions of a few Dutch colonial geologists.[6] The large body of mostly well-known popular literature on the history of Indonesian volcanoes mostly omits the context, history, or politics of the science.[7] These omissions are less the case in the sociology and anthropology of volcanic disasters, where there is a larger body of literature on the social production of volcanic risk; yet, that scholarship rarely takes a long view, nor does it contextualize the political history of the geological sciences in Indonesia. Many scholars have recently turned to traditional and folk ideas about risk in Java in an attempt to question stadial, and often neocolonial, developmentalist approaches to disaster science; but it is still common to separate out science from Javanese spiritual traditions and set them in opposition to each other, as if their histories have been independent of one another.[8] No one has brought together the modern history of volcano science with Javanese spiritual traditions or shown how they made each other or depended on each other. The assumed divide between modern science and local knowledge is tenacious, even though it is not real. It is therefore not well understood how science and local knowledge not only shaped each other but also went on to inform broader geological narratives of the earth's history outside of Java. The comprehensive scholarship of Naomi Oreskes and Henry Frankel, for instance, on the history of the theory of continental drift and plate tectonics, acknowledges the work of "the Dutch School"—colonial geologists in the Netherlands East Indies in the 1920s and 1930s—but excludes almost entirely the role of Indonesians.[9] Their histories, like so many others in the history of the geological sciences, begin and end in Europe and North America, giving the impression that it is primarily people in those places who have shaped the global narrative of the history, structure, and origin of the earth. Excluding Indonesians from this story is not a minor omission; it is a familiar, Eurocentric move. Indonesia is the fourth most populous country in the world, in a region nearly the size of continental Europe; it was undoubtedly a crucial site for the development of the postwar geological sciences. Lewis Pyenson has been one of the few historians of science to appreciate the earth sciences in Indonesia, but his *Empire of Reason: Exact Sciences in Indonesia, 1840–1940* curiously excludes an account of volcanology, even though it was one of the "crown jewels" of colonial science.[10] Jean Gelman Taylor's *The Social World of Batavia: Europeans and Eurasians in Colonial Indonesia* gives an account of the role of science and *mestizo* cultures in Batavia, but only up to the turn of the twentieth century and also with scarce attention to geology and volcanology.[11] Rudolf Mrázek's masterful study of the existential crises of engineers in the late colonial Indies, *Engineers of Happy Land*, focuses mainly on the period after Taylor's book ends, but it too only glances at volcanology.[12]

The scholarship on the history of volcano science in Indonesia, therefore, has largely been left to scientists to write. From the late colonial period, Georg L. L. Kemmerling, Reinout van Bemmelen, H. Albert Brouwer, Newman van Padang, and Johannes Umbgrove stand out for their efforts to document the history of their pioneering science. They published in technical journals, bulletins, obituaries, and scholarly monographs. In the postcolonial period, John A. Katili, Adjat Sudrajat, and Surjo stand out. The Badan Geologi Kementerian Energi dan Sumber Daya Mineral (Geological Agency of the Ministry of Energy and Mineral Resources) has also compiled a small number of excellent resources on the history of volcano science.[13] The aforementioned works were crucial sources for this book. In addition to this literature, a number of popular works by Indonesian volcano scientists were equally useful: Adjat Sudrajat wrote a hagiographic biography of the Dutch colonial geologist Reinout van Bemmelen, who also appears in chapters 2 and 4 of this book.[14] Sudrajat was perhaps the first volcanologist anywhere to write a popular novel in which a volcano played a leading role, *Prahara Gunung Galunggung*, which was published by the Badan Geologi (Geological Agency).[15] Sudrajat also wrote an introductory history of Indonesian volcano science.[16] One of the most prominent geologists of the postcolonial period was John A. Katili, who from 1952 to 1955 was also a columnist for the nationalist magazine *Mimbar Indonesia* (Indonesian platform), in which he discussed geological issues for a new postcolonial readership.[17] He later published several books in Indonesian and English on scientific issues and connected geology with national development. Between 1951 and 2008 he published more than 250 articles.[18] Sudrajat and Katili collaborated on a monograph about the eruption of Galunggung, near Bandung, in 1982–83.[19] Since the establishment of the Vulkaanbewakingsdient (Volcano Monitoring Service) by the colonial government in 1920, later renamed Vulkanologisch Onderzoek (Volcanological Survey), volcanologists have been some of Indonesia's most famous and outspoken scientists; their writings have helped establish the science at the heart of modern scientific culture and have engaged with the most pressing issues in the country. It is even more surprising, then, that English- and Indonesian-language scholars have paid little attention to this work. The marginalization of the volcano sciences is especially stark when compared with the overwhelming number of studies on the botanical and agricultural sciences in Indonesia. As one of the most volcanically active and densely populated places on earth, with one of the most influential traditions of earth sciences, this is a major oversight that this book attempts to rectify.

The line that now frequently separates geology from anthropology is a recent invention in Indonesia. When in 1931, Felix A. Vening Meinesz presented to the Royal Geographical Society in London his discovery of an ocean trench nearly eight thousand miles long, south of the Indonesian archipelago, he dedicated an entire lecture to his studies of Indonesian culture as seen from his submarine.[20] Philip Kuenen, a collaborator of Vening Meinesz's, was a geologist on the pathbreaking Snellius oceanographic expedition in 1929–30 to the eastern part of the archipelago. In 1941, he published *Kruistochten over de indische diepzeebekkens* (Crusades over the Indian deep sea basins); his "crusades," in this case, included his ethnographic studies of Indonesian culture, which he undertook when he was not measuring or taking samples from the ocean floor.[21] When Georg Kemmerling, one of the founders of the Volcanological Survey, undertook fieldwork to investigate volcanic craters in Java, Bali, and the Moluccas in the 1910s and 1920s, he repeatedly included descriptions of sacred sites, rituals, and prayers in his scientific papers.[22] Geologists prospecting for exploitable ores and minerals likewise wrote accounts of Indonesian culture that blurred the meaning of prospecting as a purely economic concern and that constituted a form of ethnology; finding sites for extraction was entangled with describing cultures. In some cases, geologists' work merged with travelogue and tourist diary, but it nevertheless indicated a familiarity and fascination with Javanese culture. Ideas about volcanoes and ideas about culture created each other in colonial Java.

In contrast to histories of Javanese volcano science, scholarship on Indonesian spirituality and religion is immense. No doubt, this has to do with the fact that Java and Indonesia have belonged to the cannon of western English-language anthropological fieldwork sites at least since Margaret Mead and Gregory Bateson landed in Bali in 1936. Later, the creation of Southeast Asian studies grew, in part, out of geopolitical fears over the spread of "Asian communism" and further established the Indonesian archipelago in the network of anthropologists' field sites. More recently, though, Indonesian anthropologists have begun to take over this role of studying Indonesian culture and belief systems. This book leans heavily on English-, Dutch-, and Indonesian-language accounts of spiritual and religious movements in Java from the early twentieth century up to the present. The exhaustive work of historian Merle Ricklefs on the Central Javanese sultanates has been indispensable for this. I largely agree with Ricklefs's diagnosis that Central Javanese Islam was a "mystic synthesis" that brought together mysticism, local deities, a strong Muslim identity, and the imperatives of dynastic rule in a volatile volcanic landscape.[23] What I contribute to that frequently inspiring (and often intimidating) canon of Central Javanese historiography is to show how the mystic synthesis influenced, and in turn was transformed by, volcanology and modern scientific conceptions of the earth system.

This leads to my penultimate point about political geology as a method. As I mentioned above, one of the ambitions of political geology is to center the *geo* in geopolitics. In recent years, geographers have tended to engage with the agency of a multitude of nongeological nonhumans. This aligned with contemporary turns in geography, such as new materialisms and the emergence of the Anthropocene debates, that placed geological concerns at the center of the discipline but that less frequently considered geological processes themselves or the history of geological knowledges. I aim here instead for a political geology that not only contributes to a better understanding of geological material but also grapples with the culture of geological knowledge and the history of the geological sciences and their role in social life and the formation of political power. Undertaking this means historicizing and situating scientific concepts about the history of the earth, which are otherwise frequently taken for granted in current critical discourses about geology. Likewise, political geology may be able to address some geographers' perennial lamentations about the divide between human and physical geography. The gulf between the two could, perhaps, be mended by better understanding the production and social effects of the earth sciences.

Such ambitions for political geology were always, in some ways, running parallel to the venerable tradition of political ecology, which has one of its roots in the 1970s and 1980s in the work of Piers Blaikie, who among others, worked on the politics of geology—through soil erosion and land degradation in the "Third World."[24] The vast world of political ecology has not since lost sight of the politics of earthly material.[25] Yet, in the Indonesian context, scholarship has, I reiterate, not comprehensively considered the history of volcanology, the politics of the geological sciences, or their intersections with Indonesian knowledge traditions. Instead, political ecology in Java has tended to focus on the connections between botanical and political processes; and, because of this, political geology, as I imagine it, complements rather than eclipses—or worse, competes with—this tradition of political ecology.

A JAVANESE ANTHROPOCENE · The recent proposal to name the current geological epoch the Anthropocene signaled that geologists were recognizing that the border between geology and society had become porous. For many geologists, this was unprecedented. In the history of Javanese volcanology, however, it came as no surprise. As I mentioned above, blurring the boundary between geology and society has been crucial for Javanese volcanologists for more than a century. As volcanologist Reinout van Bemmelen put it in 1954, after more than two decades studying volcanoes, "Mountain building provides the very basis of our existence on earth."[26] He developed a form of volcanological determinism that placed volcanic processes at the center of cultural processes. Civilizations, he argued, could not be understood without also understanding the dynamism of the earth. Van Bemmelen's friend and colleague, Umbgrove, came to develop his complementary theory that sought to bring together civilizations, species differentiation, and consciousness with volcanic processes in *The Pulse of the Earth* (1942). Umbgrove drew on the term *Psychozoic*, as used by Joseph Le Conte, a geologist and physician, who in 1877 stated that he based the term on "the fact that Man, the specialist of spiritual and intellectual differentiation, appeared on the stage and began to extend his supremacy over the world."[27] Le Conte continued, "The geological importance of the appearance of man is not due only or chiefly to his transcendent dignity, but to his importance as an agent which has already very greatly, and must hereafter still more profoundly, modify the whole fauna and flora of the earth."[28] Umbgrove's use of the *Psychozoic* not only anticipated Anthropocene debates, it was also one example of how volcanologists in Java sought to account for the multiple directions of influence between geology and society. As both Umbgrove and van Bemmelen knew well, even the Holocene was so named in the first place because it reflected the emergence of human agriculture.[29] In Java, volcanology has long been social history.

The spiritual traditions of Central Java also acknowledged these blurry boundaries. The sultanates of Central Java, some of them formed in the sixteenth century, were understood to have been founded upon associations between sultans and deities in volcanoes through sex, marriage, or friendship and acknowledged that sovereignty was conditional upon geology. Ritual processions and the giving of offerings to volcanic peaks by sultans, mystics, and scholars reflected the debts that society owed to geological deities. Not only was society dependent on geology for its existence; it owed debts to geology for its sustainability. Polities came into being through geological alliances. The relationship was not unidirectional, from nature to society, or through society imprinting itself on nature; rather, geology subtended society while social events persistently resulted in natural effects such as earthquakes and eruptions. Dutch colonial volcanologists were aware of these traditions; many were fascinated and even influenced by them. In fact, we know of many of these traditions because of the ethnologists, scientists, and geologists who recorded them.

The coproduction of sovereignty and geology persisted into the postcolonial period and became uniquely potent in the New Order between 1965 and 1998. This era was presided over by the dictator Suharto, who fashioned himself after the same Central Javanese sultans whom Dutch colonial administrators and ethnologists documented as having had sex with chthonic deities. When power was slipping from Suharto's grasp in the 1990s, for instance, he was rumored to have had a network of nearly fifty spirit mediums and magicians working for him.[30] He was also known to give offerings to the goddess of the Indian Ocean, Nyai Ratu Kidul, and to deities in Mount Agung in Bali.[31] He held, for instance, a ritual at Prambanan temple beside Merapi in which he buried a *kris* dagger in the ground to stabilize his political future; when the cosmos was out of order, so too was the political world.[32] When Kelud in East Java erupted in 1991, the tabloid magazine *Misteri*, which supported the regime, exclaimed that it was a sign that Suharto was coming as a "just king" in the time of the apocalypse to save the poor.[33] In the New Order, authoritarian political power was mystical and geological, and natural catastrophe was the result of social catastrophe. It is commonplace today to say that there is no such thing as a natural disaster; this was axiomatic for New Order authoritarianism.

Scholars have drawn attention to the contemporary legacies of this conflation of the social and the geological. Nils Bubandt has shown how the eruption of a mud volcano outside of Surabaya caused by exploratory drilling exemplified the Javanese Anthropocene.[34] Lapindo Brantas, an Indonesian oil and gas company, was prospecting for natural gas in 2006 when they caused an explosion. The explosion turned into an eruption of a mud volcano that inundated and buried the village of Balongnongo before earth berm walls could be hastily built to contain the leak. But the government, courts, and the walls were all ineffective, and the villagers became refugees when the company refused to acknowledge their responsibility. Supporters from all over Indonesia held protests and rituals, and Balinese priests ordered the provisioning of offerings. Jars of mud became souvenirs, and stones from the muck became potent objects. As Bubandt puts it, "The strange life of stones and mud speaks to a spectral moment in Indonesia in which geology is political, politics is corrupt, and corruption is haunted by spirits."[35] These intersections recalled how volcanoes in Java, whether spewing mud or lava, shuddering with earthquakes, studied by scientists, or proffered offerings by dictators, have long been sites at which the boundaries blur between the *anthropos, bios,* and *geos.* In fact, they have long constituted each other. Seen in this light, Java has much to teach those of us who are trying now to come to terms with how to live in an Anthropocene.

THE BEGINNINGS OF VOLCANOLOGY IN JAVA · Modern scientific volcanology has its roots, no doubt, in the global scientific interest in Javanese volcanism of the late nineteenth century. This is obviously because Java was (and still is) one of the most densely inhabited, volcanically active regions on earth. The spine of volcanoes at the center of the island had erupted hundreds of times between the late nineteenth century and early twentieth.[36] Some of the most famous eruptions of the last two centuries happened in Indonesia: Tambora in 1815 and Krakatoa in 1883. Unsurprisingly, Java was understood to be an important place to go to understand volcanoes.

Colonial Java at the turn of the twentieth century was also a plantation economy that relied on eruptions to fertilize the soil; yet, these same plantations also needed protection. The Netherlands East Indies grew and exported botanical products (spices, rice, tea, tobacco, medicine, rubber, teak, and cinchona) to European markets and made the Netherlands one of the wealthiest places in Europe. The natural sciences were also largely driven by efforts to manage and improve the local plantation economy, and because of this, Java was a world center for botanical knowledge.[37] The research stations and gardens at Buitenzorg and Bandung were at the forefront of plantation technologies, tightly networked with botanical centers in cities of the British and Dutch empires such as Amsterdam, Kew, Singapore, Ceylon, Sydney, Calcutta, and beyond. In the 1910s, cinchona experimentation in Bogor was at the vanguard for its use in treating malaria, and Europeans throughout tropical colonies relied on it to not die. So too, rubber plantations were expanding across the island and fulfilling burgeoning industrial demand for rubber products, and palm oil was being newly experimented with as a lubricant for machine parts and a component in candles. The Pacific Science Congress was held in Batavia and Bogor in 1920, with more than two hundred scientists from the Pacific region learning about the state of science and engineering in the Indies. But plantations inevitably extended up the verdant slopes of volcanoes, where the higher altitude and cooler air provided excellent conditions for the cultivation of tea, tobacco, and teak. It was not only the crops that grew there that brought people into proximity with the volcanoes but the rivers too that threaded down from the craters and carried water into the lowlands and out into the oceans, connecting the tops of volcanoes to the flat lands. As Clifford Geertz succinctly put it, "Java [is] . . . a set of small-scale, richly alluvial galleries hemmed in by volcanic mountains."[38] The proximity of gallery to crater meant that eruptions were bound to have significant local and global costs.

Three eruptions around this time were significant. The first was that of Krakatoa in 1883, which was so huge and loud that it registered across the world. The volcano was in the strait between Java and Sumatra, at a distance from inland plantations but nevertheless so powerful that it destroyed many of them. More significant, at least for the authorities, was the interruption of trade from the Netherlands East Indies to Europe and Asia.[39] Ships stopped sailing and goods stopped moving. The possibility that such threats could recur spurred attempts by geologist Rogier Verbeek to systematically map for the first time all the volcanoes and their geological contexts in Java and Sumatra in an effort to diagnose future eruptions.

The second event was the eruption of Kelud in East Java, thirty-six years later, in 1919. A lake had formed in the middle of the caldera; it exploded out of the top and rushed down the slopes (figure 1.1).[40] A wall of mud and debris spilled into the market town of Blitar and overturned houses, lifted cars, and intercepted a train trying to escape the town. Corpses with their clothes torn off were later exhumed from the mud.[41] More than 5,000 people died, 135 square kilometers of plantations were destroyed, and 9,000 houses were ruined.[42] After expeditions to the crater to understand what happened, government engineers vowed to drill a tunnel into the caldera to drain the crater lake.[43] Such an undertaking required mining, rail, and road engineering expertise (figure 1.2). Drilling

FIGURE 1.1 Kelud, showing its crater lake after an eruption in 1901. Georg L. L. Kemmerling, "De uitbarsting van den G. Keloet in den nacht van den 19^{den} op den 20sten Mei 1919," *Vulkanologische Mededeelingen* 2 (1921): 105.

FIGURE 1.2 Expedition to Kelud, hot lahar (pyroclastic mudflow) in the background. Georg L. L. Kemmerling, "De uitbarsting van den G. Keloet in den nacht van den 19^{den} op den 20sten Mei 1919," *Vulkanologische Mededeelingen* 2 (1921): foto 4.

into the wall of a volcano had never been undertaken in the Netherlands East Indies (or perhaps anywhere, for that matter), and it presented a series of challenges, not least the heat inside the crater walls and the danger of drilling into a hot lake from below it. It was also the first time the authorities had attempted to directly intervene in volcanic processes to shape an outcome favorable to their plantation economy.

Another consequence of the Kelud eruption was the establishment of a government-run Volcano Monitoring Service dedicated to monitoring the islands' most disruptive volcanoes.[44] The authorities resolved to incorporate modern scientific monitoring and communications with the populace into colonial government policy, which motivated a recognizably modern, cosmopolitan form of volcanology. The small group of scientists who participated in this were mainly mining or military engineers and geologists. They began to publish bulletins of their observations and studies that soon circulated among geologists trying to define volcanology as a new and modern science in the United States, Japan, and Europe. The formation of the Volcano Monitoring Service, later the Volcanological Survey of the Netherlands East Indies, institutionalized volcanology in the East Indies. Volcanologists such as Berend G. Escher, Charles E. Stehn, Georg L. L. Kemmerling, Reinout van Bemmelen, Johannes Umbgrove, Maur Neuman van Padang, Louis Rutten, Gustaf Molengraff, and others were often not only volcanologists (the term was not even greatly in circulation at the time); they were also economic geologists, prospectors, engineers, or stratigraphers. Volcanism, though, became the prism through which they came to understand a broad range of geological problems. For many of them, their principal theoretical preoccupations became the origins of volcanoes and, in turn, the planetary and historical processes that created them. In other words, they were fascinated with *orogeny*—mountain building. They frequently understood volcanic processes as the engine of lithospheric evolution, which placed them at the vanguard of European and US debates about geological history because they were sympathetic to notions of drifting continents proposed by Alfred Wegener in 1912. Most American or European scientists were dismissive of "continental drift," but geologists in the Netherlands East Indies developed innovative concepts to rethink planetary history. In other words, Javanese volcanoes became the model through which scientists understood the entire earth. For this they would retrospectively be called the Dutch School.

The third important eruption was that of Merapi in 1930. Volcanologists had built a permanent watch station there after the eruption at

Kelud, an effort of the Volcanological Survey. It was a flimsy hut located on a hill called Maron and included telescopes and what appears to have been the first seismometer on a volcano in the East Indies (figure 1.3). The massive eruption washed the hut away, buried the seismometer, displaced thousands of people, and destroyed nearly forty villages (figure 1.4).[45] In response, scientists regrouped and planned a much more durable observation station at Babadan, to the west of the caldera, which included a bunker that could withstand the clouds of superheated gasses and flying boulders. The bunker contained a new seismograph and soon became part of an expanding network of observatories on Merapi's southern and southwestern flanks. What was new was the installation of telephone and telegraph cables linking the observatories to the lowland market towns. The communications network was far more extensive than at other observatories, and it accelerated communication from the top of the caldera to urban centers while also importing lowland technologies into rural, often impoverished, villages. Observatories thus became architectural outposts of the state and contact zones between colonial scientists and rural cultures.

Volcanology emerged in Java because of these three eruptions, and it then became an established mechanism of colonial governance. As volcanologists frequently put it, their aim was to protect people and property. But the new interest in monitoring helped volcano scientists acquire resources—offices, transportation, assistants, funding—to greatly extend their efforts. And the first generation of state volcanologists used all the techniques at their disposal; they wrote detailed case studies of eruptions based on observatory records and site visits, and they drew on eyewitness accounts and photographed, measured, sketched, and described eruptions. Whole new apparatuses of knowledge-construction were brought to bear. After the eruption at Kelud, for instance, Kemmerling compiled a report of nearly 120 pages for the Dienst van het Mijnwezen in Nederlandsch Oost-Indië, Vulkanologische Mededeelingen (Bureau of mines in the Netherlands East Indies, Volcanological Reports), with engineering diagrams and exquisite photographs by Kurkdjian studios, one of the Netherlands East Indies' most prolific photography studios that also made landscape portraits for tourists. By the 1920s, the volcanologists had support from the military to fly airplanes and conduct aerial surveys of eruptions and their effects, compiling vast archives of aerial caldera photos from every angle (figures 1.5, 1.6, and 1.7). As Susie Protchsky has observed, aerial photography brought together military with scientific

FIGURE 1.3 The first monitoring post on Mount Merapi at Maron hill, beside Blongkeng River, March 1920. *Post Maron bij K. Blongkeng, Maart 1920.* Courtesy Balai Penyelidikan dan Pengembangan Teknologi Kebencanaan Geologi archive.

FIGURE 1.4 Photograph from 1931, surveying the destruction of Demong village from the Merapi eruption of 1930. *Kroon verwoeste dessa Demong met graven en vliegenhuisje.* Courtesy Balai Penyelidikan dan Pengembangan Teknologi Kebencanaan Geologi archive.

FIGURE 1.5 Military aerial survey of Mount Merapi, December 22, 1930. *Militaire luchtvaart, afd. top en zuidflank G. Merapi.* Courtesy Balai Penyelidikan dan Pengembangan Teknologi Kebencanaan Geologi archive.

FIGURE 1.6 Military aerial survey of Mount Merapi, December 1930. *Militaire luchtvaart, afd. bovengedeelte van het gloedwolkgebied met de groote bocht in het Blongkeng ravijn.* Courtesy Balai Penyelidikan dan Pengembangan Teknologi Kebencanaan Geologi archive.

FIGURE 1.7 Lieutenant Wegner at Tidar airfield, Magelang, 1933. *Lt. Wegner voor het vliegtuig op het vliegterein tidar bij Magelang.* Courtesy Balai Penyelidikan dan Pengembangan Teknologi Kebencanaan Geologi archive.

modes seeing, and volcanology became an integral form of territorial knowledge and control.[46] By the closing years of the Dutch colony in the late 1930s, volcanologists had constructed a visual culture of volcanoes, established modes of practicing fieldwork, and pursued ambitious theoretical frameworks that were uniquely integrated with the plantation economy but extended to the entire history of the earth.

As materially grounded as colonial volcanology was, it was also mythical, theological, and cosmic. Answering why a volcano erupted eventually led to questions that expanded beyond the visible to bigger questions about the region and, often enough, about the cosmos. Indeed, the most theoretically ambitious volcanologists, who often became the most influential, coupled observation with attempts to situate Indonesian volcanism in the history of the evolution of earth. Brouwer, Kemmerling, van Bemmelen, and Umbgrove engaged with prevailing geological theories that suggested volcanoes were created by a cooling, shrinking earth that buckled at the surface and created explosions. But many questioned this orthodox narrative and wondered whether volcanism was the result of the surface of the earth sliding horizontally. Perhaps, they asked, drift caused mountains to build and magma to emerge from below. Engaging these debates put Dutch colonial volcanologists at the heart of European geological controversies, and Vening Meinesz, van Bemmelen, and Umbgrove (as we will see in chapters 2, 4, and 5) developed complementary yet unorthodox positions. Van Bemmelen developed a theory of *undation*, which posited huge waves traveling through the earth's surface, that he vigorously defended until his death in 1983, even though there was very little uptake of the idea by his contemporaries. Meanwhile, Umbgrove posited cosmic rhythms of mountain building, climate change, and species diversification that recurred in 250-million-year cycles, corresponding to the time it takes earth's galaxy to rotate. Umbgrove and van Bemmelen wondered whether geologic and biological time was cyclical, occurring in rhythmic "pulses," and if so, whether pulses could be predicted like seasons but in deep time. For both, volcanology was a science that made cosmic order and disorder, crisis, and catastrophe legible in the landscape. At the same time, at the foreground of their cosmic geology was the question of the place of humans and geological determinism. They wondered to what extent humans were a product of geological processes, and whether the coming into being and passing away of civilizations was rooted in planetary-wide processes of mountain building. Were cultures also tectonic?

Indonesian volcanoes taught colonial scientists to see the earth in new ways. And so did Indonesians; Javanese political geology enabled European scientists to think differently about the relationship between culture and the lithosphere. The purpose of political geology as a method, therefore, is to stay close to these acts of translation, movement, and transformation in earth knowledges and to map the ripples of their political effects. Not only does political geology place Indonesian knowledge at the center of modern earth knowledges; it also enables us to destabilize conventional narratives about the geological sciences.

———

CHAPTER TWO

THE ORIGINS OF JAVA IN FOUR MAPS

From an Island of Ruins to Youthful Throes

———

GEOLOGICAL MAPS AND ORIGIN STORIES · This chapter traces how geological narratives of Java have changed since the late nineteenth century by examining four maps. I have chosen these four maps because they are synoptic and complete, unlike many other geological maps that came before or after. Another reason is because they are consequential: these maps transformed the understanding not only of Java but of the earth itself; they established new narratives of Java's geological and even social history, and they helped create the theory of plate tectonics that radically re-narrated the earth's history and structure in the 1960s. What began, for the map makers, as an attempt to understand Javanese volcanism developed into a reimagining of the origins and destinies of continents, the mechanisms by which they moved across the lithosphere, and how they tore apart and reemerged remade on the surface. Volcanoes came to be seen as expressions of an earth in a state of creative self-destruction. Javanese volcanoes are at the heart of the current orthodox conception of the earth; and the origin stories taught in most schools about how continents came to be and how land separated from water had their first drafts in these maps.

Each of the four maps took nearly a decade to create. Their makers traversed a landscape equivalent in distance to that between Paris and Vienna. They crossed mountains, forests, cities, rice paddies, plantations, shorelines, and volcanoes. One map was the result of submarine voyages from the Netherlands to the East Indies and grueling months spent at sea wrestling with faulty instruments and extreme heat. The maps were drawn through hot and cold wars, local and global conflicts that constrained or enabled geologists in their fieldwork. Some of the technologies that were used—airplanes, ships, bunkers—were adopted after their deployment in battle. Volcanic disasters in 1883, 1919, and 1930 compelled the drawing of new maps, while other disasters—floods and mudslides—interrupted work in the field. The Indonesian revolution in 1945 put an end to the colonial geological offices; their mapmaking departments closed, and no maps of significance were produced in Java until 1979. The four maps here, then, represent the transition between two states: the Netherlands East Indies and the Republic of Indonesia. They even carry us through to the third era of Indonesian postcolonial history, the New Order, which fell in 1998, nearly two decades after the theory of plate tectonics was first applied to the region. Changing ideas about where the state stops and the earth starts can be read across the lines and colors of these maps. Rogier Verbeek and Reinder Fennema's first map, completed in 1896, for instance, was the result of, or even provided the evidence for, a firm belief that the continents were permanently fixed in place and that the earth was shrinking. Later maps of the 1920s and 1930s were instead imbued with enthusiasm for theories of continental drift, when few other geologists around the world were convinced of it. Colonial geologists thought that the vigorous shaking of the land and exploding mountains perhaps suggested that ocean floors were crashing into rigid continental structures. In 1970s New Order Indonesia, when the theory of plate tectonics was convincingly applied to the archipelago, the oceans became invested with dreamy visions of new and unprecedented mineral wealth for the young country. These maps are inscribed with these epistemic reorientations; through them we can read the evolution of narratives not only about how Java came to be but about how it came to stand in for the earth as a whole. As for the geologists who made the maps, we can see how they, too, came to understand that Java was not a periphery but instead exemplified fundamental planetary processes everywhere.

Volcanoes were crucial actors in these new cartographic narratives. Devastating volcanic eruptions across Java sent geologists in search of their causes. This search required maps that would show the extent of volcanism, how deep and how far they ranged, the shape of their craters, and the matter they were made of. It also meant understanding the broader tectonic structures of the island and its history. Comprehending volcanism was almost immediately metaphysical; it meant theorizing the invisible, the subterranean, that which could not be measured or touched in the field; it meant creating narratives of an inaccessible underworld, its history, and its protagonists. Geologists asked whether volcanoes connected underground in vast plutonic rhizomes or whether they were individual, acting independently of one another? Asking such questions led them to scrutinize assumptions about Java as an island with fixed boundaries and instead open their minds to the active role of the ocean floor. Perhaps Java was just the ocean reconfigured? Volcanoes became windows, then, into the deep structures of the earth. Mapping the edge of a volcanic crater was to glimpse into the whole earth. These maps represent four visions of what geologists saw from those edges and how they assembled them into the modern theory of the earth.

VERBEEK AND FENNEMA: THE GEOLOGY OF JAVA AND MADURA · Rogier Verbeek, a geologist and mining engineer, was the first to complete a geological map of Sumatra in the 1870s. There was an emerging colonial excitement about the prospects for exploiting coal, oil, and tin, and the colonial government had engaged Verbeek to complete the survey. Based on his success, he was immediately engaged by a government eager to continue the project on neighboring Java. One of the government's motives was to identify the extent of Java's known but undeveloped coal and oil deposits. Verbeek had found plenty of coal and oil in Sumatra and hoped to do the same in Java; so beginning in 1880, he focused on West Java's well-known coal in the hills of Preanger, near Bandung. The project was soon derailed by volcanic eruptions; in 1883, Krakatoa exploded in one of the largest and most famous eruptions in modern history. Crops experienced widespread failure, ships were moored, some were even scattered deep inland by the powerful tsunami the resulted from the eruption.[1] The sun went dark in Europe, and the sound waves from the explosion were so powerful that they blew down walls in Semarang and Surabaya in Central Java. Tsunami waves crashed on beaches in South Africa and Sri Lanka, and shipping between the East Indies and the rest of the world ground to a halt. Suddenly the economy of the Netherlands was in hiatus. The governor general called on Verbeek to stop his mapping and devote his energies instead to comprehending the extent of the devastation and the cause of the explosion. Verbeek spent the following year working on it. His results, later published in *Nature* and abbreviated or quoted in major newspapers around the world, were widely read by a public fascinated with the grim details and supernatural aesthetics of the spectacle.[2] When he returned to work on the Java map, he had become a world-famous geologist with an emboldened interest in volcanism and situating it within the broader context of Java and a theory of the earth. Java was, after all, riddled with volcanoes that could explode like Krakatoa, and many of them were in even closer proximity to cities or the plantation system on which the Netherlands relied. As soon as he had begun mapping, however, he was again interrupted. In 1885, Semeru in East Java exploded, and members of his team were sent there to compile a report of the devastation.[3] Reinder Fennema, Verbeek's collaborator who had drafted many of the maps for publication, was also sent away for nine months to map parts of Sumatra, and after that, for two more years, to survey for oil and potable water for the development of a new mining town (also in Sumatra), based on Verbeek's initial mapping years before. Verbeek nevertheless managed to survey Java for six years, traveling with a reduced crew, from volcanic crater to crater, and coast to coast. He would meet with colonial officers, Javanese locals, and plantation workers to interview them about any sightings of profitable ores and minerals, which he would then track down to include on his map. Once Fennema and the others had rejoined him, Verbeek spent two more years writing the report and drawing the maps before finally publishing the two-volume work in French in 1896, which included the most comprehensive geological maps of Java to that date (figure 2.1).

Before analyzing Verbeek's map, it is useful to grapple first with his studies of Krakatoa (figure 2.2). These showed his understanding of the lithosphere that he would later apply to all of Java. He saw volcanoes as disconnected "hearths" on a shrinking earth, and this understanding would, for subsequent geologists, become a theory to contend with. He was convinced that a recent surge of earthquakes had caused ocean water to infiltrate through "a rent or fissure in the crust," into the "molten substances below."[4] The water was then, in his view, pressurized into a volatile mixture until it exploded. He drew cross sections of the lithosphere that depicted ghostly outlines of the vanished Krakatoa protruding above a drain-like hole in the surface and a cross section that depicted four

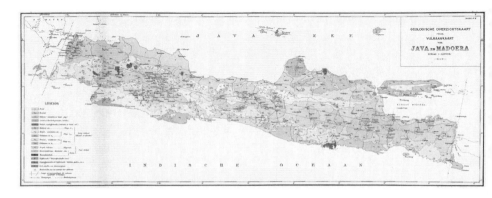

FIGURE 2.1 "Geologische overzichtskaart tevens vulkaankaart van Java en Madoera" (Geological overview and volcano map of Java and Madoura). Rogier D. M. Verbeek and Reinder Fennema, *Description géologique de Java et Madoura*, vol. 3, *Atlas* (Amsterdam: Joh. G. Stemler, 1896), bijlage II, kaart II.

hundred meters below sea level, though the useful details ended at nearly two hundred meters, about a quarter as deep as the volcano extended above the sea level. The other drawings were flat, plan views (as if seen from above), or perspectives (as if seen from the ground). His images indicated that his understanding of Krakatoa was constrained to the surface and that the volcano was a nearly self-contained, vertically linear unit.

The chapters of Verbeek and Fennema's *Description géologique de Java et Madoura* (Geological Description of Java and Madoura) were structured according to Dutch colonial political divisions called residencies.[5] Each chapter subdivided the residency structure further into stratigraphy that represented the geological history of each residency. This structuring of the book allowed it and its accompanying maps to be used as a field guide to the geological history and mineral contents of each residency; it made the landscape newly legible according to their stratigraphic divisions that themselves functioned like chapters in a narrative, beginning with the Cretaceous, Old Tertiary, and Young Tertiary, and ending in the near present, which Verbeek and Fennema called New or Modern.[6] Political boundaries were overlaid onto these stratigraphic boundaries, which in turn were ordered into loosely historical sequences of earth's history.

These stratigraphic sequences, it is important to note, did not correspond to absolute dates. The Cretaceous, for instance, did not have a year or period of years associated with it. This was not only the case in Verbeek's work; in the late nineteenth century, virtually no geologist anywhere associated years with stratigraphic sequences. Strata simply signi-

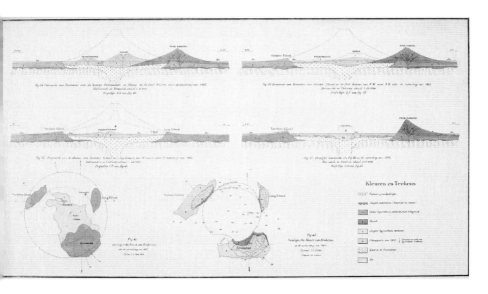

FIGURE 2.2 Plans and sections of Krakatoa. Rogier D. M. Verbeek, *Krakatau: Album* (Brussels: Institut National de Géographie, 1886). Royal Collection Trust.

fied the material found in the strata and matched a loosely chronological ordering of what was "older" and "younger." Verbeek was also, apparently, uninterested in speculating about the age of the earth or in identifying the exact age of stones. When Verbeek and Fennema were writing, other European geologists frequently argued about the age of the earth, but their speculations ranged widely.[7] In the seventeenth century James Ussher dated the earth's origin to 4,004 years before Jesus was born. By the mid-nineteenth century, the view had changed dramatically. Darwin, a student of Charles Lyell's stratigraphy, suggested in early editions of *On the Origin of Species* that the earth was perhaps more than 300 million years old, or at least more than 100 million.[8] Such vast ranges were due in part to the lack of agreed-upon methods for measuring geological time. In 1863, William Thomson (later Lord Kelvin) argued that the earth was between 100 and 200 million years old based on his theories of thermodynamics and the rate of the cooling of the earth.[9] A contemporary of Verbeek and Fennema's, Eduard Suess (who also used some of Verbeek and Fennema's work) balked at proposing absolute dates but in his *Face of the Earth* read the biblical flood and other ancient texts as historical descriptions of actual events that could be explained by geological process. The exact age of the earth was contested, but the majority of geologists were certain that it was at least in the millions of years, if not much more.[10] Stratigraphy, though, did not need absolute dates to reconstruct past worlds; it worked with successive periods and with subdivisions based on the fossil record. For Verbeek and Fennema, known history in the region began with the Cretaceous—the age of the first fossil deposits in Java—which were characterized by orbitolines, ancient single-celled organisms found across the region. As John Phillips put it in his "Geological Scale of Time" from 1860, the Cretaceous was a period of "marsupials and mammals."[11] In other words, for Verbeek and Fennema, primordial Java was inhabited. The next stage, the Eocene, was identified by nummulites, lentil-shaped fossils smaller than a fingernail, and once-thriving single-celled ocean protozoans. The Eocene was also characterized by foraminifera, a vast class of porous, spongy, single-celled sea creatures.[12] The description of Java's history was, perhaps because of this, as spatial as it was temporal. The past was legible through the fossils and deposits that corresponded to those discovered and defined by geologists working across the island. When Verbeek and Fennema turned to calculating the ages of Java's strata, they found that a mere 1 percent of Java's deposits had persisted since these "earliest times." Thirty-seven percent had been deposited in the Miocene and Pliocene; 33 percent of the land was from the Quaternary, or modern period, and the remaining deposits—27 percent—were "new volcanic."[13] Java, in other words, was young.

Java's recent history, in geological terms, was not uneventful; it was defined by catastrophes and cycles of change that were old enough that Verbeek and Fennema could envision volcanoes as uniquely antique ruins, which coincided with their understanding of Javanese culture as belonging to that antique past. In the most ancient periods, Verbeek and Fennema argued, the seas were low, and Java was connected to Asia by land bridges. Fossils found on Borneo and Peninsular Malaysia showed that animals had once migrated between them, and Verbeek and Fennema agreed with Suess that the earth was cooling, shrinking, and warping the crust like an aging apple.[14] Verbeek imagined that Java was being uplifted by this process, exerting pressure on adjacent areas and forcing them to fold as sediments eroded downward. Later in the Cretaceous, Verbeek believed, parts of Java had sunk, and water inundated and interrupted the land bridges that connected it to the mainland. Then, massive subsidence and displacement of the crust and cracks in the surface appeared, much like he had seen at Krakatoa, and the surface sagged as vast quantities of molten matter emerged, growing, and spilling into lateral folds and building mountains.[15] Verbeek and Fennema imagined that "several tens of thousands of cubic kilometers of erupted material" caused deposits 3,000 to 6,000 meters deep.[16] "It would require," they wrote, "for the release of such a mass, more than 2,000 eruptions equivalent to Krakatoa in 1883."[17] Modern Java, therefore, began in vast cataclysms of a magnitude never seen before; the devastation of Krakatoa was hardly even a glimpse into the eruptions that brought Java into being. The sea remained high well into the Young Tertiary, as the massive eruptions continued to build up and finally broke the sea's surface as eight separate volcanic islands. They found the evidence for this in river sediments and corals located high up on hills and mountains that could only have been there, they reasoned, due to high seas. When the ocean retreated, rivers drained the fossils and deposited them farther afield and revealed the massive volume of newly erupted material in the shape of the island, elongated from east to west, narrow from north to south, with a spine of volcanoes running lengthwise down its center.

Land, though, continued to be uplifted by the compression of the earth, perhaps up to 180 meters high, and land bridges reappeared between Java and Borneo, Sumatra, and mainland Asia; mammals migrated, this time from as far as Siam (present-day Thailand) and British India.[18] Then, as before, the cycle repeated; the ground sank under the tremendous volume of new material, and the islands separated once more. Modern volcanoes, they noted, were remnants from this time of unprecedented upheaval of 2,000 eruptions: "It follows from the above," Verbeek wrote, "that for the most part volcanoes are ruins of mountains, by collapse the cones have lost their summits which in the past were significantly higher."[19] Ancient volcanic complexes would have been sublime masses. For Verbeek, volcanoes did not explode, they collapsed; they were not the result of magma issuing forth from deep in the lithosphere where tectonic plates crashed into each other; they were instead ruins of deep time. Once fallen, their material eroded and weighed down the ground, forcing it to fold and uplift into new ridges and hills as the seas rose and fell around them. Volcanoes, Verbeek and Fennema wrote, "do not all issue from one single space full of lava but they are rather openings from small, separated hearths which enclose a state of fusion."[20]

Verbeek and Fennema's conception of volcanoes as ruins coincided with an enthusiasm for Javanese antiquities. Archaeologists and ethnologists had only since the 1840s begun to compile statistics on archaeological sites, and the project had remained provisional and haphazard until the 1890s, when a shift in attitude about Java's past occurred.[21] Ruins had come to represent forgotten histories and evidence of powerful empires and cultures that predated the arrival of Islam and, later, European colonization. Even if Verbeek and Fennema thought that Java was relatively young in geological terms, they nevertheless understood that volcanoes were antiquities in a land of ruins. The Bataviaasch Genootschap van Kunsten en Wetenschappen (Batavian Society for Arts and Sciences) asked Verbeek—before he had begun his *Description géologique de Java et Madoura*—to also catalog, map, and date every ruin he encountered during his survey.[22] While Verbeek was collecting fossils and hunting for coal seams with locals, he was also querying them about the location of local ruins. His remit was wide—*candis* (including mausoleums, bathing places, temples), temple caves, stairs carved into mountain sides leading to sacred sites, stone inscriptions, stelae, portals, walls, terraces, brick constructs, images, ancient stones, graves, or otherwise anything that remained from the early Islamic and pre-Islamic period. He published his results as *Oudheden van Java* (Antiquities of Java) in 1891, which included 671 entries with locations and descriptions of the geology and stratigraphy of the ruins; and thus, stratigraphic history became cultural history. He also compiled a list of 229 ancient stone inscriptions (of the 400 that were known) that included dates and locations so as to establish a cursory, but at the time the most complete, chronology of the political geography of early modern empires in Java up to the thirteenth century.[23] Verbeek's fascination with ruins was connected to broader ambitions, which I explore in greater detail in chapters 4 and 5, to connect Javanese culture with a pre-Islamic history and with notions of cultural decline and progress. But what is important to bear in mind here is that, for Verbeek, constructing geological history was a practice closely aligned with the reconstruction of lost social and political worlds. Understanding volcanoes as ruins coincided with understanding Javanese culture as a ruin. His imaginary of volcanic cataclysm, cycles of rise and fall in the land, connection to and separation from the mainland, and natural history as a history of destruction would also inform conceptions of the social history of the Javanese.

Verbeek and Fennema ultimately hoped that their catastrophic histories would lead them to exploitable materials; dividing history according to its stratigraphic chapters was a way to prospect for ores by imposing a grid of intelligibility on the landscape. Oligocene and Miocene strata, for instance, contained lignite coal; Miocene strata, they hoped, contained oil; and in the hills south of Surabaya, there would be, perhaps, salt and iodine.[24] But Verbeek and Fennema noted that after nearly a decade of piecing together the story of Java's rocks and culture, climbing its volcanoes, and measuring its shorelines, their chapter on exploitable matter "will be unfortunately very short because, except oil and some building stones, one does not encounter in Java a single mineral species worthy of exploitation; the diverse deposits of mineral and coal offer absolutely no technical value."[25] Plus, the oil deposits they found were minor. The largest extraction operations had already been established near Surabaya, and they came upon nothing that compared to the deposits in Sumatra, which was quickly becoming the most productive site for petroleum extraction in the East Indies. They came to understand, after all their efforts, that a land created by volcanoes created little worth extracting.

The *Description géologique de Java et Madoura* also included the "Kaart van den Oost-Indischen Archipel" that depicted not the stratigraphy of Java but rather its volcanoes in relationship to the sea (figure 2.3). The map revealed a fundamental theoretical problem whose resolution would later have an impact on new theories of the earth. The map situated Java and its volcanoes on a continuous underwater shelf with Asia. As they depicted it, the East Indian archipelago was the southeastern-most edge of the Eurasian continent. Significantly, they also depicted the dark spine of volcanoes cutting through the archipelago. To the south, they showed very shallow bathymetry, indicating the dearth of ship soundings. Verbeek wrote, though, that surveys for telegraph cables had begun to show that the Indian Ocean was impressively deep, perhaps more than three and a half kilometers.[26] Those telegraph lines were meant to connect Europe with the colonies, and the Dutch had long sought to develop their own telegraph connections in order to limit their reliance on British cables.[27] But the sounding evidence created a mystery; Verbeek was unable to explain the surprising drop in the ocean floor. He called it the "tearing." "We are completely uncertain," he wrote, "and this uncertainty will always persist, because we can never collect rock samples from the Indian Ocean."[28] It was too deep. He betrayed his northern and Western fixation; the south was beyond the limit of what could be known. The edge and depth of Java was defined by the ancient underwater land bridges with the Eurasian continent. His coordinates would be reoriented in the coming decades as the ocean floor emerged with greater resolution and as the dark arc of volcanoes came to represent a wholly different causal relationship between Java and the Indian Ocean; Java would no longer originate in the

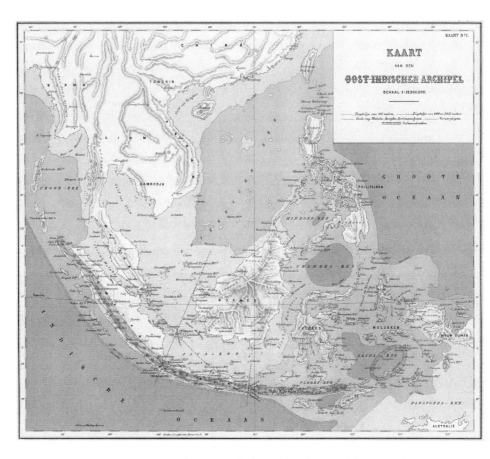

FIGURE 2.3 "Kaart van den Oost-Indischen Archipel" (Map of the East Indian archipelago). Rogier D. M. Verbeek and Reinder Fennema, *Description géologique de Java et Madoura*, vol. 3, *Atlas* (Amsterdam: Joh. G. Stemler, 1896), bijlage I, kaart I.

rising and falling of land and sea but would instead be seen as an extension of the "tearing."

VENING MEINESZ: GRAVITY ANOMALIES IN THE EASTERN ARCHIPELAGO · The next map to narrate a new origin story of Java was not a geological map defined by stratigraphy. Instead, it was a map of gravity. It depicted Java not as a ruin but as a fold in the ocean floor. Felix Vening Meinesz completed it in nearly eight years for the Nederlandse Commissie voor Geodesie (Netherlands Geodetic Commission), in part to map the ocean floor for the purpose of laying telegraph cables to the colony.[29] Historian

Peter Boomgaard has shown that Vening Meinesz's project was also the result, during the "heyday of the late colonial state," of a turn to greater interest in pure sciences. Funding investigative science was seen to align with colonial ambitions to educate the colonies and place them in scientific competition with other European colonies.[30] Science, it was also thought, would foster a gentlemanly culture of inquiry.[31] Lewis Pyenson has also noted that Vening Meinesz's wealth and the tense relationship between the Dutch Royal Navy and the colony after the First World War allowed him to convince the navy to lend him a submarine as a diplomatic gesture of goodwill.[32] Vening Meinesz stated his purpose as follows: to "investigate the gravity field in one of the most extensive regions of tectonic activity on Earth."[33]

Vening Meinesz graduated as a civil engineer at the Technical University of Delft in 1910 and soon after joined the gravimetric survey of the Netherlands. For his PhD research, he sought to overcome the problems of measuring gravity with pendulums. Pendulums had been used to determine the distributions of gravity and, hence, the mass of the earth's surface. The technique had been applied to mountains, rivers, and sedimentary basins, too, and it was becoming newly useful in measuring the mass of continents. Gravity measurements were compelling to scientists trying to understand if continents sat in equilibrium with the oceans, a theory called isostatic equilibrium, which was central to *fixist* geological theories because it explained how the continents and oceans remained horizontally stable. Gravity measurements could go a long way toward explaining the shape and weight of the edges of continents and how they connected to the ocean floor. Vening Meinesz applied the methods to the soggy, estuarine Netherlands but noticed that the waterlogged soil caused his instrument to tilt before he could make an accurate measurement. He devised instead, for the first time, a system that used four pendulums at once to counteract the movement, and between their rotations he could deduce the force of gravity. He speculated that the gravity meter was even accurate enough that it might work at sea, where such measurements had been elusive until then because of the instability of ships in waves.[34] He proposed to map the *geoid*, the mathematical model of the shape of the earth, by taking the gravity meter to sea. He suspected he might find that the earth's surface was lumpier than conventionally thought. "Besides local deviations," he wrote, "there probably exist deviations of some hundred meters elevation or more, extending over great parts of the Earth's surface." The problem, he reflected, was "to determine these deviations"—in other words, to accurately map the ocean floor for the first time.[35]

Vening Meinesz's earliest experiments failed when he set up the apparatus on a ship's deck that rocked in the waves so greatly his results were scrambled. He then shifted the apparatus to a submarine because it could submerge deep into the water column below the surface waves.[36] After successful experiments off the shores of the Netherlands, the navy loaned him a submarine and crew, and he undertook his first expedition to the East Indies in 1923. By 1939, sixteen years later, he had spent nearly three years under water undertaking a monumental and unprecedented number of measurements in the Atlantic, Pacific, and Indian Oceans.[37] In 1923 he went to Java from the Netherlands by way of the Suez Canal; in 1923, from Holland to Alexandria; in 1926, beginning in the Netherlands, he traveled through the Panama Canal to Java; between 1928 to 1930, he made several passes through the East Indies; and in 1932, he undertook measurements in the Caribbean. Between 1935 and 1939, he traveled from the Netherlands to Java by way of South Africa and western Australia, then returned to Holland. The distance he covered was remarkable not least because of the duration of the voyages and the sheer number of measurements and gravity stations he and his crew established but also because of the general discomfort to Vening Meinesz, who was six feet, six inches tall in the cramped space of a submarine. The work was also notoriously boring and hot. To take measurements, the crew had to halt the engines on board to reduce interference, which in turn raised the temperature in the submarine. On three voyages between 1926 and 1927, they covered more than 25,000 kilometers and established nearly 300 *gravity stations* (sites where measurements were taken); they submerged three or four times every twenty-four hours, once or twice per night. Vening Meinesz reported dryly that "during the first voyage of two months continuous rough weather was experienced; this did not tend to alleviate life on board."[38]

In 1930, he delivered two lectures at the Geographical Society in London about his preliminary findings. The publication that accompanied his talks included what would later become a widely distributed map of his results (figure 2.4). Two things were striking about the map: the extensive tracks of his four voyages and the dark line of "negative gravity anomalies," where the force of gravity on the seabed suggested a vast underwater trench. The submarine had revealed a continuous furrow more than 8,000 kilometers long and nearly 160 kilometers wide. South of Java, these anomalies followed the ridge of "tearing" that Verbeek knew about.[39] Vening Meinesz said that it ran "beside the ocean deeps."[40] In some places it coincided with submarine ridges or island chains, but not in others. Never had it been imagined that the entire archipelago was bordered to the south by an invisible, massive, valley.

What was also remarkable was that the discovery of the trench coincided with a new idea about the source of earthquakes. Working in the Royal Magnetic and Meteorological Observatory outside of Batavia, Simon W. Visser had begun to understand that earthquakes were issuing from far deeper in the earth than had been previously understood, as far as six hundred kilometers underground.[41] Previously, many geologists had thought that earthquakes were shallow products, or that they issued from the inside of bursting volcanoes. However, when Visser plotted their origins with the use of new seismographs, he found that their origins corresponded almost exactly with the trench in the ocean. Vening Meinesz pointed out that the depression "shows a curious correlation with the distribution of volcanoes in this region"; it also ran almost exactly parallel to the dark line of volcanoes on Verbeek and Fennema's "Kaart van den Oost-Indischen Archipel."[42] The two spines of peak and valley, it was

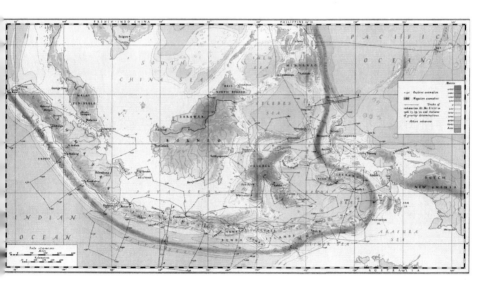

FIGURE 2.4 Map illustrating gravity anomalies in the East Indian archipelago. F. A. Vening Meinesz, "Gravity Anomalies in the East Indian Archipelago," *Geographical Journal* 77, no. 4 (April 1931).

becoming clear, must be related. Vening Meinesz was uncertain what caused the belt and was reluctant to propose theories, but he suggested that it was a giant fold; he imagined that the crust was flowing into it in a way that caused stresses and cracks and resulted in volcanoes and earthquakes.[43] The accepted notion that the continents sat in equilibrium with each other was unable to explain such a fold. Verbeek's vision of volcanoes as discrete units was giving way to an ocean-centered understanding.

The fact that Vening Meinesz imagined that the crust was flowing into the fold indicated his sympathy with theories of continental drift first proposed by Alfred Wegener in 1912 and then again in 1915. Wegener suggested that the continents moved horizontally by driving through the ocean floor.[44] Vening Meinesz's discovery of the trench and the increasing certainty that it was structurally related to seismicity and volcanism added to the plausibility of vast horizontal movements between land and the sea. Vening Meinesz and others seeking to connect these elements did not become wholesale Wegenerian drifters, though. Instead, they developed a vibrant local culture of theoretical debate and instrumental innovation to explain what seemed drift-like in their own terms. While theories of drift were rejected by many US and European geologists, it remained at the center of theoretical speculation in Java for the next four decades, in part because of Vening Meinesz's mapping.

After he presented his map in London, Vening Meinesz continued surveying the seabed throughout the 1930s with his four-pendulum gravimeter, which had by then been dubbed the "golden calf" by his crew. Its color was gold, but the sailors also received a bonus for sailing with it because of the added hardship.[45] The sailors' name was appropriate for other reasons too: what better analogy for the worship of an idol that promised to lead them to the hidden world of the ocean floor and reveal to them the workings of the earth.

Between 1932 and 1948, the Netherlands Geodetic Commission published Vening Meinesz's results in a four-volume set, *Gravity Expeditions at Sea*. In volume 2, published in 1934, Vening Meinesz's occasional collaborator Johannes Umbgrove contributed a chapter pointing out that the formation of the fold seemed to have been in the Miocene and corresponded with Verbeek's definition of the period of cataclysmic eruptions.[46] Umbgrove departed from Verbeek, though, by suggesting that the fold was the result of the "sinking of the crust of the earth until the limit of elasticity has been passed and folding downwards occurs." It was, he wrote, "supported by the surface structures and the geological history of these areas" and provided a portrait of a new tectonic structure of Java and the entire archipelago.[47]

In volume 4, from 1948, Vening Meinesz included a photograph from an experiment by Philip Kuenen that explained the trench (figure 2.5). Kuenen was a geologist and had been on the Snellius Expedition between 1929 and 1930, the most extensive marine expedition in the eastern Netherlands Indies, which revealed unparalleled detail about the ocean floor. He was also a keen advocate of theories of continental drift and engaged Vening Meinesz and Umbgrove in debate about how to account for the origin of Java. To test Vening Meinesz's conception of downward folding, Kuenen built a model of the earth's surface with a container filled with water with a layer of Vaseline on top; one side had a vise to compress it.[48] The components represented their assumptions about the earth: the bottom layer of water represented the mantle and was denser but relatively plastic; the Vaseline represented earth's crust and was lighter, floating, and more rigid. The vise, meanwhile, represented the horizontal "compressive stress" that caused the folding.[49] As the vise compressed the content, the Vaseline folded downward and remained unbroken. As the fold deepened, the lighter surface materials converged and bulged on top (the men imagined this would be mud, sand, and clay as well as buckling and uplifting surface matter). The result, the men considered, was a suggestive re-creation of the fold in the ocean floor. Satisfied, Vening Meinesz wrote, "The plastic deformation of the crust is well illustrated by the beautiful experiments of Kuenen."[50] The remaining baffling question was where exactly the compressive stress came from. While the mechanics of the folding was beginning to become understood, the mechanism that caused the vise to move was still a mystery. It was the same question that critics had raised against Wegener's theory decades earlier: What was the mechanism that drove drift? If the sea floor was truly moving into the southeast Asian continental mass, what was the force? It was a question that led Vening Meinesz to speculate about earth's evolutionary history and the origin of land as emerging from a primordial catastrophic event.

Meinesz proposed to build on the work of the American geologist David T. Griggs, who was a proponent of drift and an outlier among US geologists because of it, to venture a provisional answer: giant convection currents. Convection currents meant that the crust or mantle was in in a semiliquid state and driven by the circulation of heat in the earth. In the beginning, Vening Meinesz imagined that the primordial crust was "sucked" into the earth by a vortex of convection rising and falling near

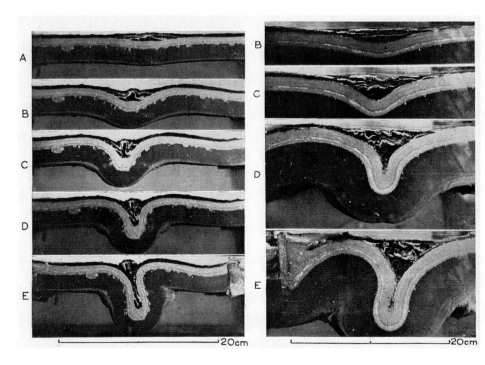

FIGURE 2.5 Experiment results. Ph. H. Kuenen, "Negative Isostatic Anomalies in the East Indies," *Leidse Geologische Mededelingen* 8, no. 2 (January 1937): 186–87.

the site of the fold. The currents drove the surface to flow into the fold, and as it buckled downward, hot material rose, cooled, and then sank underneath the basins.[51] The convection currents, he thought, pushed not from the edges like the vise in the experiment but rather at the site of the fold itself. The idea was developed into a new, expansive earth origin myth in "The Origin of Continents and Oceans," in 1952.[52] Vening Meinesz conjectured that in the primordial earth, before the nickel-iron core completely formed, a large convective flow emerged from the depths and radiated heat into the cosmos. The crust hardened and thickened and formed the first *protocontinent*, a whole, united continent, covering one-third of the earth's surface. The primordial differentiation that it created between core and crust then created a tipping point, an irreversible change that sped up the bifurcation between the hot nickel-iron core and the cold crust, trapping heat inside the earth and exacerbating the difference between the thickness of continents and the thinner ocean floor.[53] Then the current somehow multiplied and tore apart the massive protocontinent, dragging fragments across the earth through the thinner ocean floor. This originary catastrophe, a shattering of the one into the many, an irreversible self-differentiation into fragmentation, explained why continents were roughly of the same basic composition: they were formed from a single source and then migrated across the surface. This process of shattering also explained the geography of continents: "Continental antipodes," he wrote, "[are] generally an ocean; only six percent of the earth's surface does not conform to this rule."[54] Vening Meinesz imagined the broken, Vaseline-like buoyant, protocontinent torn into near equal parts; and all continents pointed back to the protocontinent, a time when all land was once unified. What he found in Indonesia was a story that explained all continents, a story of a catastrophic fall, an earth of fragmentation. The furrow in the ocean floor in the distant waters of the colony was in fact a model for the origin of the drift of all land; it was at the center of the earth's evolution. His origin story explained the trench, but it also used the trench to explain the earth.

In 1928, Vening Meinesz was invited by the US Navy to bring his "golden calf" (his four-pendulum gravimeter) to the West Indies. He recorded a strip of anomalies off Puerto Rico and Haiti that was nearly a mirror image of the furrow in the East Indies. In 1932, he was invited to join the US Navy–Princeton Gravity Expedition on the USS *Chewink* to teach US scientists how to use the four-pendulum gravimeter. His assistants were Thomas T. Brown and Harry H. Hess. Hess would later work at Princeton University and become a leading theoretician of plate tectonics based on his extensive work at sea and the skills he was taught by Vening Meinesz. Hess and Vening Meinesz maintained a long-standing correspondence, and in the early days and especially during the time of his work with Vening Meinesz, Hess was willing to challenge the US fixist orthodoxy with theories of drift.[55] The aim of the *Chewink* voyage was to investigate the anomalies Vening Meinesz had found in the Caribbean in 1928 and to explain the tectonic structure of the Bahamas island chain.[56] Drawing conclusions from Vening Meinesz's tutelage, Hess explained in a 1933 report that there is "a direct correlation between the seismic phenomena, faulting, and volcanic activities," the same as that which had been found off Java.[57] The following year, the Geodetic Committee of Japan imported a four-pendulum gravimeter to investigate the origins of earthquakes and tsunamis in the region. They found a third belt of gravity anomalies in another mirror image of the trench in the East Indies.[58] Through the discovery of folds at continental margins, which were always associated with highly volcanic and seismically active island arcs, Vening Meinesz and the four-pendulum gravimeter revealed a problem that conventional theories of a cooling earth and hydrostatic equilibrium could no longer adequately explain.

After 1945, four-pendulum gravimeters were beckoning scientists into the depths on at least twenty-seven submarines around the world.[59] In 1948 and 1949, J. Lamar Worzel and Maurice Ewing used a modified version of the "golden calf" on US Navy submarines to make almost 900 observations off the Pacific and Atlantic coasts of North America, Hawaii and Guam, Australia, and in the Bering and Chukchi Seas. By 1965, Worzel had published his account of nearly 4,000 gravity measurement stations at sea between 1936 and 1959.[60] The British were likewise invested in gravity measurements, and by the 1960s, Vening Meinesz's apparatus was in use by most Western states with an interest in seafloor exploration and geodesy, propelled largely by Cold War interests in submarine warfare and communications infrastructure.[61] Vening Meinesz's 1958 book with Veikko A. Heiskanen, *The Earth and Its Gravity Field*, was an essential resource for gravity measurement and theory by students at the Lamont Geological Observatory at Columbia University.[62] The book not only revealed new and unforeseen complexity in the ocean floor but helped to place its processes at the center of terrestrial evolution and what came to be called the new global tectonics, or plate tectonics. US and European geologists decisively adopted the theory in the late 1960s and early 1970s as the mechanism of lithospheric evolution and the trenches that Vening Meinesz found in the East Indies and then the West Indies became evidence for a new vision of how oceans met land and of the catastrophic history of the earth.

Before moving on with the details of how the theory of plate tectonics reshaped visions of the Indonesian archipelago, it is first necessary to understand another mapping project, Reinout van Bemmelen's rather reactionary *The Geology of Indonesia*, published in 1949. It was the next complete survey and history of the region, and it rejected Vening Meinesz's hypotheses in a return to a Verbeekian vision of a shrinking earth. But it was nevertheless a crucial intermediary study that ushered in new postcolonial geological stories about Java.

VAN BEMMELEN: THE GEOLOGY OF INDONESIA · Reinout van Bemmelen's magnum opus, *The Geology of Indonesia*, was not a single map. Volume 1 contained 378 figures and 124 tables in 732 pages. It was not merely *a* geological map but a synthesis of an ever-growing, unwieldy, nearly impossibly large archive of geological data that had been collected in Indonesia since the early twentieth century.

Van Bemmelen was born in Batavia to Willem van Bemmelen, the director of the Royal Magnetic and Meteorological Observatory in Batavia between 1905 and 1922. Van Bemmelen Sr. was the director of the same observatory that Visser later worked at when he discovered the depths from which earthquakes emanate. Willem van Bemmelen Sr. was a champion of scientific knowledge for its own sake and cultivated an aesthetic appreciation of nature. The young van Bemmelen spent many hours trekking up Javanese volcanoes with his father.[63] It was on those trips that van Bemmelen Jr. was encouraged to think about the processes driving landscape formation; it was also where he had his earliest aspirations to become a volcanologist.[64] Like many of the colonial elite, van Bemmelen Jr. studied in the Netherlands, where he trained as a mining engineer at the Technical University of Delft under Hendrik A. Brouwer and Gustav A. Molengraaff, who were early sympathizers, though not without skepticism and criticism, of Wegener's theories of continental drift.[65] Van Bemmelen once joined a seminar in which Wegener presented continental drift, but van Bemmelen rejected the theory and continued to criticize Wegener even when the European establishment began to accept the theory. After working in the Dienst van de Mijnbouw (Department of Mines), he was appointed chief of the Vulkanologisch Onderzoek (Volcanological Survey) in 1940, a post he held until his imprisonment during the Japanese occupation of Indonesia in 1942; he later repatriated to the Netherlands. His work on Javanese volcanoes taught him to consider that their formative processes could explain planetary evolution, and he developed a new origin story of the earth based on volcanically driven tectonics, or what he called *undation*.[66] Like Vening Meinesz, van Bemmelen took what he saw in Indonesia and applied it to the entire earth.

He worked on the manuscript of *The Geology of Indonesia* between 1937 and 1941 with the ambition of synthesizing the growing volume of new data about the region. Geological work in the Indies had accelerated since the turn of the twentieth century because of several factors. The Dutch colonial government had allowed foreign-owned private mining firms to prospect, which increased the number of geologists undertaking work for private enterprises; the use of fossil fuels to power the First World War greatly expanded geological exploration throughout the region. Peripheral areas in the East Indies were newly subject to intensified exploration. Borneo and Sumatra were exploited by the recently created Dutch and

British joint company Royal-Dutch Shell. There was also an expansion of opportunistic companies seeking to profit from economic liberalization.[67] Private mining companies were prospecting in New Guinea and on the islands to the west of Sumatra: Eastern Celebes, Timor, and Sumba. The work of synthesizing the volumes of new data, private records, and scientific papers into a coherent picture of the region was no small effort. By 1932, the Geologisch Mijnbouwkundig Genootschap (Geological Mining Society) had published a bibliography related to recent mining and geology in the Netherlands East Indies comprising over five thousand titles.[68] Not only had Vening Meinesz revealed the new geographies of the ocean floor; the Snellius Expedition of 1929–30 to the east of the archipelago released huge volumes of new bathymetric data. Kuenen, who had built the Vaseline model of Vening Meinesz's fold, participated in the Snellius Expedition and published papers synthesizing its results. Brouwer, Wilhelm H. Hetzel, and Henri E. G. Straeter undertook new expeditions to Celebes in 1929 and to the lesser Sunda Islands in 1937. Expeditions were also undertaken to Portuguese Timor in 1936 and to New Guinea in 1936–39. Paleobotanic expeditions went to Sumatra in 1925, and the findings of Louis Rutten and Walter Hotz's expeditions to Ceram in 1917–19 were also published.[69]

In 1942, before he could complete the synthesis of this material, van Bemmelen was taken as a prisoner of war by the Japanese military. On the way to prison, he apparently entrusted the manuscript of *The Geology of Indonesia* to an assistant, who later refused to return it to him after the liberation of Java in 1945. The stolen manuscript, according to van Bemmelen, was transferred to Yogyakarta where the seat of the new republican government was located. We can assume that if the manuscript had indeed been stolen, it was because it included precious details about the resources of the fledgling postcolonial state. The manuscript, however, never resurfaced and following van Bemmelen's return to the Netherlands after the war, he rewrote it over a period of four years. Some doubt has been cast as to his ability to complete such a massive work from scratch in such a short time, and it is well known that van Bemmelen's wife, Lusi van Bemmelen, helped prepare his published work but was never acknowledged.[70] The final version of *The Geology of Indonesia*, written at great speed and at a great distance from its source, was likely a result of her unrecognized labor.

The vision of *The Geology of Indonesia* was the application of the theory of undation to the Indonesian archipelago. The theory resisted the drift hypothesis of Wegener and the convection currents of Vening Meinesz and instead recalled Verbeek's model of a cooling, shrinking earth. For van Bemmelen, cooling created massive undating waves throughout the crust that formed mountains, volcanoes, and ocean trenches in great horizontal petrified pulsations. He organized his first volume according to an exhaustive description of the physiography of each region, followed by the stratigraphy and dating of geological periods of each region, and then descriptions of volcanism, its geology, eruption styles, and periodicity. This was succeeded by geophysics, including earthquakes, gravity measurements, and magnetism and by the application of the foregoing to the evolution of each physiographic unit; and finally, he laid out his grand theory of geological evolution according to undation.

It is worth recalling the key differences between van Bemmelen's and Verbeek's maps. Verbeek's map was organized according to the *political* boundaries of the residencies and *stratigraphic* units at a time when stratigraphy, as mentioned, corresponded neither to absolute dates nor to agreed-upon ages of the periods. When van Bemmelen was writing, nearly forty years later, stratigraphy had become significantly more subdivided; numerous novel ages had been defined, and identifying absolute geological time using radiometric dating was increasingly seen as legitimate. Arthur Holmes, in *The Age of the Earth: An Introduction to Geological Ideas* from 1927, used radiometric arguments to show that the earth was between 1.6 and 3 billion years old.[71] Van Bemmelen thought that the oldest strata in the archipelago were more than 300 million years old, still comparatively young in earth's history, just as Verbeek had also thought.[72] Van Bemmelen also agreed with Verbeek that the fossil evidence in the region was overwhelmingly from between the Tertiary and the present.[73] He confirmed Verbeek's picture of a submerged and reemerging land connected via land bridges to mainland Southeast Asia. Uplift, too, he thought, was crucial. The theory of undation pulled Verbeek's narrative into the twentieth century. For van Bemmelen, the history of Java and much of the archipelago could be explained by a cooling planet that created massive terrestrial bulges, volcanoes, and tremendously slow waves coursing through its surface. In short, the origins of continents and oceans was in an energy-depleting earth that crinkled as it cooled and shrunk into itself.

According to the theory of undation, epicenters known as *megaundations*— massive bulges created by the expulsion of energy from the earth's interior out into the cosmos—radiated waves from their centers like those from rocks dropped in a pond.[74] Java and Sumatra, for instance, islands made by folds in the ocean surface, were the effects of these ripples. But the waves spread across the entire surface of the earth, with multiple undating centers sending waves crashing into each other. Volcanoes were sites in the undations where the subsurface reached the exterior and released the ever-depleting energy from inside the earth. Volcanoes also drifted, plowed onward by the lithospheric waves, exploding and ultimately dying. Van Bemmelen departed from Vening Meinesz and any idea of primary convection; instead, convection currents were the product of undations; set into motion by the loss of energy, they were eddies of heat spinning like the vortices in the wake of a ship. Most likely referencing Vening Meinesz's reliance on Kuenen's Vaseline model, he wrote that he "denies the narrowing of the geosynclinal basins and the squeezing out of its contents by lateral shifts of the rigid framework, like the jaws of a bench-vice." By this, van Bemmelen simply meant that he did not agree with Vening Meinesz's vision of the mechanism of drift as convection currents. He went on to insist that "the Undation theory is opposed to all theories of crustal buckling or continental drift."[75] Instead, he revived the model of a shrinking earth and its disturbances of equilibria at the surface. For him, the evolution of the earth's surface was driven by cosmic burnout; his was a melancholic vision of an earth set in motion through energy loss.[76] As we will see in chapter 4, van Bemmelen, like Verbeek, was also interested in ruins; his Java was created through catastrophes, and the earth was defined by loss.

The *Orogenic Evolution of West Java* (figure 2.6) depicts the undation theory of Java. The north side (right-hand side) represents the coastal plain of Batavia and the Java Sea, in the direction of the Eurasian continent. The southern edge (left) ends thirty kilometers in the Indian Ocean, nearly into the region of the gravity anomalies depicted by Vening Meinesz. The first cross section at the top represents the Oligocene, a period in which Verbeek and Fennema noted a silence in the fossil record. In van Bemmelen's rendering, it is the time of an undation; West Java was sinking, the surface a "rigid crust" of limestone deposits. As the viewer proceeds down, from one cross section to the next, they progress in time toward the present and see the transformation of a simple landscape to a complex one in which vertical volcanic intrusions infiltrate from the south and ripple northward. The origins of this wave were as deep as seven and a half kilometers below the ground, about ten times deeper than Verbeek's map of Krakatoa from 1885. While van Bemmelen was attempting to justify his orogenic origin story with these diagrams, one of the consequences was that he represented Java

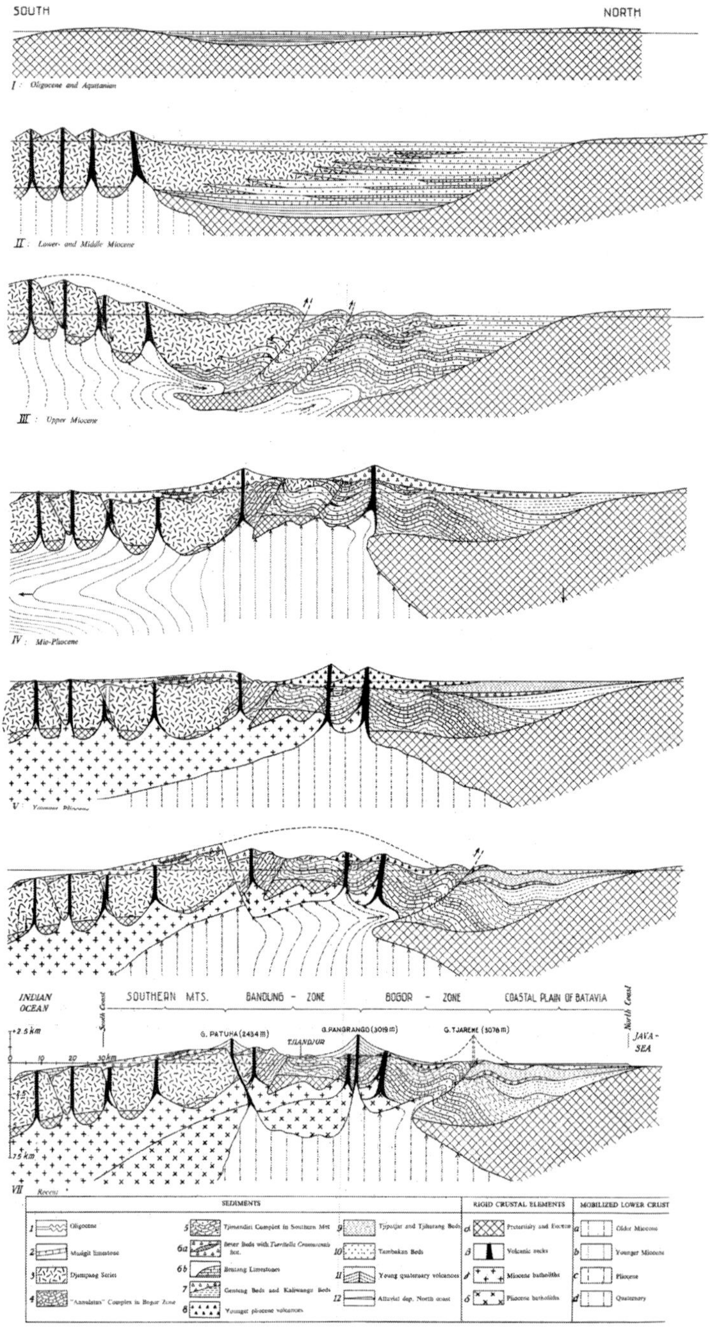

FIGURE 2.6 Cross sections through West Java. Reinout van Bemmelen, "The Orogenic Evolution of West Java," *Geology of Indonesia*, vol. 1B (The Hague: Government Printing Office, 1949), plate 37.

with a cross-sectional depth that had probably never been seen before. However much his history would later be contested, it not only contributed an unprecedented synthesis of existing data but also represented Java and Indonesia with a denser and more dynamic underground space than his predecessors had shown, while also creating some of the first sequential images of the evolution of Java over deep time. His filmstrip style of sequential cross sections made dynamism and speed visible for Indonesian geologists in unprecedented ways.

Van Bemmelen's history of Java, like others, bore little value for the resource geography of Indonesia. The second volume of his *Geology of Indonesia*, dedicated to economic geology, drew few direct parallels to his undation theory. Undation did little for finding valuable ores or locating new areas to prospect. In 1939, he remarked that 29 percent of total export value for the Indies came from minerals, the bulk of which was in petroleum products. He argued that his history was not reducible to the vulgar exigencies of economic geology. Rather, it was about cosmic principles, identifying "dynamic harmony," the codependence and mutual production of chaos and consonance that structured the universe. His introduction to the volume on economic geology warned against over-exploiting natural resources and the destructive effects of modern machinery, calling instead for the wise use of geology and for resisting the exploitation of the earth's finite volume of minerals.[77] The theory of undation was an illustration of a natural order that, he thought, humanity had to learn to live with; it was a guide to eternal laws that nevertheless, in their actualization, were as unpredictable as the surface of the earth.

The legacy of undation theory was to be eclipsed by plate tectonics and became little more than a footnote in the history of geological thought. Van Bemmelen's peers thought that megaundating centers could not sufficiently explain the conveyor belt–like movements of the ocean floors and their contact zones with the continents that geologists had begun to see everywhere.[78] Van Bemmelen was barely read outside of Indonesia. *The Geology of Indonesia* was nevertheless foundational. It formed the basis of future work in Indonesia and the training of volcanologists.

HAMILTON: TECTONICS OF THE INDONESIAN REGION · Indonesian geologist John Katili most decisively applied the language and concepts of plate tectonics, updated from Wegener's language of drift, to the region. Whereas Vening Meinesz shaped the theory of plate tectonics for European and US geologists based on his experiences with the fold south of Java, the theory returned to Indonesia in modified form through Katili, this time to create a new, hypnotic vision of fabulous Indonesian mineral wealth. Katili was the first person to graduate with a doctorate in geology from the Institute of Technology Bandung (Institut Teknologi Bandung; ITB) in 1960.[79] He was trained by Dutch colonial geologist Theodor Klompe, who was the patriarch of the geology program at ITB, a place with many revolutionary, anticolonial nationalist students, including the first president Sukarno, who studied engineering there in the 1920s (it was to Sukarno's revolutionary government in Yogyakarta that van Bemmelen's manuscript was likely delivered). Klompe stayed on through the tumultuous transition from colonial to postcolonial regimes and taught a generation of Indonesian geologists the methods of colonial geology. Likely because of this education, Katili was an admirer of van Bemmelen; he even contributed a revisionist essay to a commemorative issue of *Geologie en Mijnbouw* in 1979 in which he argued that van Bemmelen's undation theory set the groundwork for plate tectonics.[80] Katili was so successful at aligning his geological training with the ambitions of the new republic that he later became a close adviser and associate of Suharto and was given a late-career appointment as ambassador to Moscow. Katili's application of plate tectonics to Indonesia was also, as we will see, politically strategic; it allowed him to generate an optimism about the new resource potentials for the fledgling, poor, "Third World" republic desperate for optimistic imaginaries of growth and wealth.

Katili produced several of the first analyses that applied the language of plate tectonics to explaining the region; but given his commitments as adviser to the National Survey and Mapping Agency (Badan Koordinasi Survey dan Pemetaan Nasional) and, later, as director general of the national Department of Mining and Energy (Departemen Pertambangan dan Energi), he was unable to complete a new mapping project himself. Instead, he invited the geologist Warren Hamilton from the United States Geological Survey in 1970 to apply the new language and technologies to the entire region. Hamilton took more than eight years to complete this task, circulating between the geological offices in Bandung, the United States, and around Southeast Asia. He relied on consultations and the private papers of twenty-nine oil companies, including Pertamina, the national Indonesian oil company; he also leaned on agencies in Papua New Guinea, Australia, Thailand, Malaysia, and the Philippines as well as on the Lamont-Doherty Geological Observatory at Columbia University, with its 70,000 kilometers of continuous seismic reflection profiles made by the schooner *Vema*, which also carried a four-pendulum gravimeter and was a project driven by Maurice Ewing. The Scripps Oceanographic Institute and scores of other public and private institutions also supplied him with data.

Hamilton relied on this vast network to compile the base of information from which to draw the map for "Tectonics of the Indonesian Region" (figure 2.7). Like van Bemmelen's, Hamilton's monograph was synoptic but resulted in a single image (plus a monograph-length argument nearly four hundred pages long). He stated that his purpose was to transform the narrative of Indonesia, and like others before him, his goal was only secondarily economic. As he put it in 1970, before completing the work, "Although the tectonic map project is not directly concerned with economic geology, it is hoped that the final map will call attention to favorable terranes in which to search for metals or petroleum."[81]

He made a concerted effort to reject his predecessors. Verbeek's map was not even cited (likely because his work had already been incorporated and transformed into later maps). He lumped van Bemmelen and Umbgrove together as geosynclinists, that is, as fixists who thought that a shrinking earth caused folding and cracking of the crust. Hamilton declared with conviction that "there is no 'geosynclinal cycle,'" boldly brushing away a half century of geological thought.[82] Nor, he insisted, were

FIGURE 2.7 Warren Hamilton, "Tectonics of the Indonesian Region," US Geological Survey, Professional Paper 1078 (Washington, DC: U.S. Geological Survey, 1979), plate 1.

mountain-building processes cyclical or periodic, as van Bemmelen, Umbgrove, and many others had thought. Dismissing Vening Meinesz, he wrote that his gravity anomalies did not even measure actual conditions but the differences between the crust in the trench area and the assumptions of what his mathematical models said density *should* be.[83] According to Hamilton, it was Ewing, an American colleague who had also been taught by Vening Meinesz, who supplemented Vening Meinesz's "golden calf" with seismic refraction data and who corrected the theory.[84] There was much posturing in this dismissive slash-and-burn approach. But Hamilton's approach was also in line with the machismo of many US Cold War earth science theorists. By contrast, Katili took a much more conciliatory approach toward his predecessors, trying to bring them on board, even if they belonged to a fraught and difficult colonial past, a history that Hamilton did not even contend with.

Hamilton's cowboy straightforwardness was also applied to his Dutch predecessors' histories of the region. He wrote that Dutch geologists had erroneously assumed that the arc of volcanoes had not moved since the late Cretaceous. Hamilton thought the opposite: Java had moved; its current form had drifted south, and the continental boundary was once farther north. The Dutch, he thought, sloppily misidentified several of their samples, understanding them to be older than they were. Also, the same samples had likely been transported to where the Dutch found them, rather than being found at their originary locations, as was presumed.[85] He also argued that the Dutch mislabeled "old andesite" (volcanic material crucial to Verbeek's and van Bemmelen's histories) based solely on appearance rather than on chemical or other forms of modern analysis. They thought, too, that broken volcano cones were the oldest (as per Verbeek's vision of volcanoes as ruins) and that shapely cones were the most recent, but they overlooked studies of deposits that showed the contrary. In some cases, deposits had been labeled incorrectly: in South Java, colonial geologists mistook rock types and their ages and overlooked faults, folds, and unconformities between strata that indicated much more complex, multidimensional, and deeper temporal relationships. A deposit labeled Eocene was, in fact, from the Miocene.[86] At almost every turn that he invoked van Bemmelen in his text, it was to diminish him. The old story of Java was a result of poor methods but also a transformation in what counted as evidence. The surplus of errors, Hamilton showed, created the impression that Java had been stationary, but in fact it had *drifted*; it was the forefront of two tectonic plates whose contact zone moved over time;

the land that constituted Java and Indonesia, in the main, was the effect of these deep tectonic encounters.

Hamilton's new vision of the planetary story went as follows. The earth's crust was fragmented into seven large lithospheric plates with numerous shards and smaller fragments moving in relation to each other.[87] Indonesia was at the intersection of three megaplates, the relatively stable northwestern Eurasian plate, the westward-moving Indo-Australian plate to the south, and the Pacific plate to the east, moving inward. Mainland Southeast Asia was rotating clockwise, causing the Indonesian archipelago to be wedged and crushed—a shattered and fragmented front of the Eurasian plate. The contact zones between plates were defined by subduction zones such as the Indo-Australian plate that was driving underneath the Eurasian plate. To the east, where the line of Vening Meinesz's negative anomalies curled north, the Indo-Australian plate converged with the Pacific plate and bore down in a complex "strike-slip system" in which plates snapped past each other in sudden bursts or slowly ground one on top of the other.[88]

Hamilton did not disagree with Verbeek: Java had once been under the ocean. But Hamilton's history was revisionist. During the Cretaceous there was no continental material where Java currently sat. Verbeek understood that land bridges connected Borneo to Southeast Asia, allowing animals migrating between them. But for Hamilton, there was no island yet. The continental material was drifting, and by the Oligocene the material that would become north Java was still underwater; the belt of magma and volcanism was much farther south in contemporary terms. For Verbeek, this was the time when 2,000 eruptions the size of Krakatoa occurred. For Hamilton, periods of such intense volcanism did not occur until much later, in the Miocene and Pliocene. The key difference between their narratives was Hamilton's assertion that today's Java had drifted into place, and obviously, the mechanism for Hamilton was the contact between continental plates that defined island arcs and that had been described first by Vening Meinesz. There was no cosmic burnout.[89]

In a later paper in a special issue of *Geologi Indonesia* dedicated to Katili, Hamilton included a schematic diagram that clarified the subduction system of Sumatra and Java.[90] He imagined that the ocean was driven under Java, then reemerged through volcanic eruptions.[91] This was the plate tectonic history of Java: the ocean floor exploded through volcanoes, eroded into land, and then eroded back into the ocean floor once again. The process was broadly cyclical, volcanoes were the ocean floor becoming land, and Java was an extension of the Indian Ocean. Hamilton's vision was, however, not revolutionary; it built on the vision that Vening Meinesz, Umbgrove, and even to a certain extent van Bemmelen had proposed. That Java was a reconfigured ocean was a key idea that had been articulated, with more or less precision, since the early twentieth century. Katili, who was much more sympathetic to the Dutch colonial geologists, was more willing to consider plate tectonics as an extension of a much longer tradition of local geological theory, whereas Hamilton had simply erased the drifters as key theorists who prefigured and shaped his own narrative.

Working within Suharto's New Order as the minister for natural resources, Katili applied plate tectonics to identify sites for offshore oil extraction and, therefore, for national development. His biographers have even suggested that his willingness to apply geological theory to resource extraction and national development advanced his political maneuvering throughout the 1970s and 1980s, as he became one of the nation's most famous scientists.[92] His *Sumberdaya Alam untuk Pembangunan Nasional* (Natural resources for national development) from 1983 set the stakes of the new outlook. He began the book by acknowledging that the resources of the nation were given by Allah; they were the inheritance of the people, their natural capital. He then argued for the use of natural resources and technology for national development. Reflecting on discussions of the time about planetary resource limits, he argued that global inequality between rich and poor countries was a result of the distribution of resources. He argued for the necessity for internationalizing scientific cooperation between wealthy and developing states to equalize the distribution of resources. The theory of plate tectonics played a special role in his vision. He wrote:

> In the last decades there has been a revolutionary change in geological thinking as a result of the emergence of the concept of universal tectonics or plate tectonics. This new conception tries not only to give a comprehensive explanation of tectonic processes but also to explain the origin and distribution of mineral deposits, including petroleum. The effect is extraordinary, and the final picture is still rather difficult to imagine.[93]

In the Indonesian context it decisively oriented the search for national wealth to mineral and oil deposits away from land and into submarine basins north of Java, off Sumatra, and in the Banda Sea in the east, where plates smashed into each other. The very sites of plate tectonic activity discovered by Vening Meinesz were now seen as potential sources for oil and ores. "The geology and mineralization of each 'orogen,'" Katili wrote in 1984 "can now be resolved by the plate tectonic interpretation which links mineral provinces together in a more realistic way than was previously possible."[94] He continued, "In general there is an excellent correlation in Indonesia between plutonic arcs of various ages envisaged by the plate tectonic model and the occurrence of porphyry copper, manganese, gold-silver, lead-zinc-copper-silver veins, lead-zinc-copper-silver stratabound deposits, skarn deposits, and tin-tungsten-molybdenum deposits."[95] Such ores and minerals promised new wealth because they were linked to the growth of the new electronics industries and automobile-driven urbanization around the world; they offered the potential of supplying the increasingly electrified and siliconized world with materials for cables, microchips, batteries, steel, and metallic components. Katili drew a new map of Indonesia, compiling the new tectonic environment with its associated deposits; it was an aspirational map projecting a new wealthy future supplying Cold War growth.

The new plate tectonic reality also offered potential new international collaborations between Indonesia and technologically advanced states. New ocean drilling programs, because of the new theory, were already taking place in the deep ocean, and the International Program of Ocean Drilling saw states and companies investing in technical measures to access previously impossible-to-reach resources beneath the ocean bed. The Deep-Sea Drilling Project (coordinated by the Scripps Oceanographic Institute and the University of California), the International Decade of Ocean Exploration, Studies of East Asia Tectonics and Resources, and a host of other international collaborations attempted to build new technologies to mine the oceans at sites of tectonic convergence.[96]

CONCLUSION: JAVA AND PLATE TECTONICS · The theory of plate tectonics was born in the Indonesian archipelago. Katili's history of Java in the 1970s was the most recent chapter in a story that began with geologists seeking the correlation between Javanese volcanoes and the depths of the Indian Ocean in the early twentieth century. Scientists attempted to put the dark lines of Verbeek's and Vening Meinesz's maps together, and in doing so, they shaped the plate tectonic narrative of the earth, which was then further elaborated by Euro-American geologists during the Cold War. What was found in Java became a model for a new earth history. Vening Meinesz's invention of the four-pendulum gravimeter that US and European scientists then used to measure gravity in the ocean allowed scientists to locate more plate convergence zones in the Caribbean and Japan as well as mid-ocean ridges that reflected those already found in the Indonesian archipelago. In other words, the theorizing and measuring that began off the southern coast of Indonesia and on its volcanoes went on to change the modern narrative of the earth by contributing a new understanding of the relationship between the ocean floor and continents.

As Katili acknowledged in 1984,

> The impact of the geotectonic theories of Vening Meinesz (1934), Umbgrove (1949), Kuenen (1935), and Van Bemmelen (1949) can be understood only if one realizes that these scientists were the pioneers who for the first time recognized the importance of integrating land and marine geology to understand the complex nature of Indonesian geology, an approach which several decades later led to the development of concepts known as the new global tectonics.[97]

Java, its volcanoes, earthquakes, and submarine furrows enabled the emergence of the modern earth.

CHAPTER THREE

INTERCALATED

*The Political and Spiritual
Geographies of Plate Tectonics*

SCIENTISTS ON THE BEACH · In 1960, and then again in 1962, US research vessels from the Scripps Institution of Oceanography in California, the *Lusiad* and *Monsoon*, carried modified versions of Vening Meinesz's four-pendulum gravimeter (the "golden calf") a few hundred kilometers south of central Java. The crew dredged, trawled, and shot seismic signals at the ocean floor. The expeditions were part of the International Indian Ocean Expedition (IIOE) conducted between 1959 and 1965 (figure 3.1). In the words of the director Robert G. Snider, the Indian Ocean was "one of the last unknown areas of the globe."[1] More than forty-five research vessels from countries across the globe participated.[2] The *Lusiad* and *Monsoon* contributed samples and data from not only south of Java and Sumatra but also much farther afield.

The samples collected by the two vessels had two important destinies in our story of Java's role in shaping a new narrative of the earth. The first was that the samples were collated into early popular portrayals of the plate tectonic structure of the Indian Ocean. They contributed, for instance, to the *Physiographic Diagram of the Indian Ocean, the Red Sea, the South China Sea, the Sulu Sea and the Celebes Sea* (figure 3.2), which later formed the basis for a more popular depiction, the *Indian Ocean Floor*,

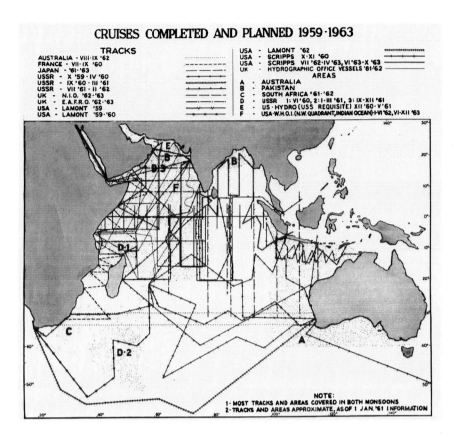

CRUISES COMPLETED AND PLANNED 1959·1963

FIGURE 3.1 "Cruises Completed and Planned 1959–1963." This map shows the ship trajectories and nation-states involved in the International Indian Ocean Expedition of 1959–1964. The *Lusiad*'s and the *Monsoon*'s tracks are visible south of Java and Sumatra and contributed to the data represented in Heezen and Tharp's *Physiographic Diagram of the Indian Ocean* (figure 3.2). Robert G. Snider, "The International Indian Ocean Expedition 1959–64," *Discovery* 22, no. 3 (March 1961): 114.

published in *National Geographic* in 1967. The *Physiographic Diagram* was drawn by Marie Tharp, who worked with Bruce Heezen at the Lamont-Doherty Geological Observatory at Columbia University to create a portrait of the never-before-seen structure of the ocean floor.[3] In the *National Geographic* version Heinrich Berran, a Swiss painter, applied his training as an impressionistic landscape painter of the Alps to the rendering of the vast terrain of underwater mountains and trenches, representing the fold that Vening Meinesz had discovered in the 1930s with the familiar drama of the Alps and confirming, even if implicitly, European scientists' understanding of the Indonesian archipelago as an Alps in the making. The *Indian Ocean Floor* was also an early popular representation of the hidden mechanism of plate convergences; where the earth's surface buckled, the ocean crust dove beneath continents and generated itself anew, as described by Warren Hamilton in "Tectonics of the Indonesian Region." It showed a new conception of the earth as defined by its deep structures—the ocean floor—that were themselves mobile. Yet, at the same time, this new vision for European and North American audiences was rendered in a way that made them as comfortably sublime as the Alps.

The samples from the *Lusiad* and *Monsoon* had a second destiny, too. They ended up in the hands of Warren Hamilton and on the pages of his "Tectonics of the Indonesian Region."[4] He used them as the basis for a diagram that showed an axis running from the Yogyakarta region directly south into the Java Trench, first mapped by Vening Meinesz. Using the samples from the *Lusiad* and *Monsoon* as evidence, Hamilton argued that the underwater trench was the result of *subduction*, a new term in geophysics that described a key process of plate tectonics whereby one plate was driven underneath another. The contact between two plates resulted in vast underwater trenches and valleys. Hamilton thought that these processes created the very materials that the *Lusiad* and *Monsoon* had collected. He went on to argue, in line with what many of his Dutch colonial geologist predecessors had argued, that as the southern Indo-Australian plate descended below the Eurasian plate it melted and liquefied into an arc of magma beneath Java and Sumatra, creating the spine of volcanoes. As one plate was crushed beneath the other, it melted, rose to the surface, and exploded. It was a circular relationship: as volcanoes blasted material through them, that material descended back down the slopes and into the trench. Java, therefore—as we saw in the previous chapter—was reconfigured ocean. For Hamilton, plate tectonics was a portrait of the horizontal cyclicity of Java, of an inseparable material relationship between the island and the Indian Ocean floor. As John Katili put it, the land was coming to be seen as the ocean, and the ocean as land.[5]

When the crews of the *Lusiad* and *Monsoon* took their samples, they very likely did not know that they were stealing them. The Indian Ocean was not, in fact, unknown. Such neocolonial narratives suggested that the ocean was a barren, empty space waiting for scientific knowledge to illuminate it. The scientists had, in fact, lifted their samples from the kingdom of Nyai Ratu Kidul, the goddess-queen of the Indian Ocean. For centuries before Hamilton or other US scientists appeared there, sultans,

FIGURE 3.2 Bruce Heezen and Marie Tharp, *Physiographic Diagram of the Indian Ocean, the Red Sea, the South China Sea, the Sulu Sea and the Celebes Sea* (New York: Geological Society of America, 1964). The Java trench is pictured (top right third) with exaggerated detail. The data this image was based on was derived, in part, from voyages in the Indian Ocean (see figure 3.1). The vast trench south of Java is one of the first depictions of Felix A. Vening Meinesz's "fold" and an early vision of the plate tectonic structure of the Indian Ocean. Image courtesy of Fiona Yacopino.

scholars, and mystics in Central Java gave offerings to her at nearly the same spot from which the samples were later pilfered. Pilgrims built bamboo rafts carrying gifts for the queen, which they released into the same waters that the *Lusiad* and *Monsoon* descended into. Some of those offerings may very well have been among the scientists' samples. When the Dutch geographer Pieter J. Veth wrote his monumental study of Java in 1882, *Java: Geographisch, ethnologisch, historisch* (Java: Geography, ethnology, history), he referred to the Indian Ocean as "the vast realm of Nyai Ratu Kidul."[6] In 1896, when the writer and former civil servant forester, H. A. van Hien, published *De Javaansche geestenwereld* (The Javanese spirit world), he wrote that Nyai Ratu Kidul "lashes Java's south coast with its high and heavy waves, and is the mighty protector of those who have settled in the fissures and caves of that inhospitable and precipitous coast."[7] He acknowledged the long-held Javanese understanding that the tsunamis, volcanoes, and frequent seismic activity that defined the southern coast were expressions of the queen's power. When Hamilton and Katili made claims about the revolutionary character of the theory of plate tectonics, they were, in truth, echoing these much older stories. Nyai Ratu Kidul had long been understood to have been in an alliance with the deities in Java's volcanoes, and earthquakes emanating from the ocean were often, in those stories, connected to eruptions. In other words, the ocean was understood to be land, and the two had to be understood together. When Hamilton argued that the ocean was where volcanoes originated, he was unknowingly making an argument that had long been central to Javanese spiritual geographies. In other words, plate tectonics was nothing new in Central Java. The spiritual geographies of Nyai Ratu Kidul prefigured it.

How does this change how we understand the theory of plate tectonics? This chapter shifts from chapter 2's largely internalist account of the history of geological mapping in Java to show how that science negotiated, mirrored, and was transformed by Javanese spiritual geographies. I explore how the spiritual geographies of Java and the theory of plate tectonics changed each other. While most contemporary accounts of the theory of plate tectonics have tended to show how Cold War militarism shaped the new narrative, in fact, it was completely bound up with much older Javanese concepts of the earth.

One of the terms Hamilton used to describe the space where ocean and land met was *intercalated*. It was a familiar term in geology used to describe hybrid geological conditions. For Hamilton, when the Indo-

Australian plate subducted, it mixed with the forefront of the Eurasian plate, dragging oceanic sedimentary rocks into a "mélange" and, in his words, "intercalated slices from oceanic plate."[8] Intercalations indicated intrusions of rock from different ages, whether sedimentary or volcanic, that came to mix or "interbed" and fuse with other rock textures. They were, in other words, fragments of time and space forced into new arrangements. Intercalations could be bands of different colors, textures, or chemical alliances, collaged together, untidy hybrids with rough edges. Broadly, intercalation was a way to think about patchworks of time-space, how they were assembled, and how differences were made to coexist. For Hamilton, this was what he found at those places where the US submarines descended into the ocean. Today, we can draw on the image of intercalation as a useful framework for understanding the relationship between the theory of plate tectonics and the spiritual geographies of Central Java. Intercalation gives us a way to conceptualize the convergences not just between geological matter of different ages and spaces but also between social worlds, how fragments of them were made to fit together and transform each other. To think about the intercalation of the spiritual geographies of Central Java with plate tectonics means attending to the mechanism that held them together, how they attached, however awkwardly. Modern volcano science did not simply replace an older spiritual geography, nor did it simply reproduce it; it in fact confirmed it, extended its reach and reality to the entire globe, and made it newly politically relevant. The intercalation of the two was always politically strategic, driven by the need to address highly local conditions; they were brought together to leverage social effects and to negotiate what it meant to live between a volatile, unpredictable ocean and volcanoes. What this says about the theory of plate tectonics as mythic and as Javanese—and as the local origins of a planetary narrative—is that we inherit Nyai Ratu Kidul, even if we do not live in Indonesia. When we invoke the theory of plate tectonics as a description of the earth we inhabit, we inherit the powers of Nyai Ratu Kidul. She changed us. This realization ought to remind us that the continued contemporary insistence on the revolutionary nature of the theory of plate tectonics in the 1960s has continually erased her significance as well as the significance of Indonesian thought, for that matter. It was Nyai Ratu Kidul who made the modern earth; we inhabit her plate-tectonic cosmos. As an intellectual framework, intercalation offers a more imaginative and pluralized vision of the genesis of modern earth theory.

SULTANS ON THE BEACH · Stories about Nyai Ratu Kidul are likely very ancient but became well documented in the eighteenth and nineteenth centuries. In many of the Central Javanese *babad* chronicles—stories and epic poems written mainly in Kawi, the old Javanese language, for the courts and held in their libraries—Ratu Kidul was a central character in the dynastic histories. Her significance was familiar not only to Javanese pilgrims and mystics but also, and increasingly so, to Dutch colonial scholars and ethnologists in the late nineteenth century. One well-known story about her was that she was a pivotal actor in the foundation of the sixteenth-century sultanate of Mataram, often revered by Central Javanese monarchs as one of the most powerful Islamic empires in Javanese history. She was said to have met with the founder of Mataram, Susuhunan Senopati, in the middle of the sixteenth century.[9] The basic outline of their meeting is as follows: Senopati was wandering through the warring states of Java looking for advice and for spiritual and secular political allies with whom to establish an Islamic sultanate. At the time, kingdoms were syncretized polities, and Islam was slowly penetrating from the north. Senopati's sultanate would not be the first, but it was an early, and perhaps the most extensive, Islamic kingdom in terms of its influence. The first Dutch ships had not yet arrived in Java, and the settlement of Batavia by Dutch traders was still half a century away. Senopati went to the shore of the Indian Ocean to meditate and encountered Nyai Ratu Kidul there.[10] She and Senopati slept together for three days; they then married and agreed that she would also marry and protect Senopati's descendants.

After the establishment of Dutch colonialism and its incursions into Central Java in the seventeenth century, the Mataram sultanate was made subservient to the Dutch East India Company. Through an increasingly disorganized and weakened court rife with corruption and internal competition, Mataram fractured into three smaller competing kingdoms under the Giyanti Treaty of 1755. One of those kingdoms was that of Mangkubumi, who established his kingdom at the site of present-day Yogyakarta and took on the name Sultan Hamengkubuwono I, or "Nail of the Cosmos I," so called because he held the earth and universe together. In the development of his palace complex, he acknowledged the founding myth of Senopati on the beach and the deities in the volcano by orienting his palace on a north-south axis and by including a room where the sultan could sleep with the queen. The main road from the palace pointed roughly north to Merapi and south to the ocean. The grounds were located nearly at the geographic middle point between the ocean and volcano, while also being, according to the sultan, the center of the cosmos. There is evidence that offerings had been given to Nyai Ratu Kidul by members of the royal family of the Yogyakarta sultanate at the turn of the nineteenth century, but the practice was surely much older and likely would have been contemporaneous with the founding of the sultanate in the eighteenth century.[11]

The tight-knit relationship between Nyai Ratu Kidul and the sultan of Yogyakarta was of particular interest to Dutch colonial ethnologists in the 1920s. The foundation of the Java Institute in 1919 in Yogyakarta and its journal, *Djåwå*, was a vehicle for reflecting on these geographies and the imbrications of spiritual geographies with politics. Contributors to the journal ranged from European scholars to educated colonial bureaucrats and Javanese translators, and they were often associated with the courts. A 1933 issue contained an article by R. Soedjana Tirtakoesoema, a Javanese translator and member of the institute, who described the process of the *labuhan*, a ritual he joined in 1921. It was an annual procession in which offerings were given by the sultan to Ratu Kidul, followed by an ascent up the southern slope of Merapi to provide offerings to deities in the volcano. The *labuhan* explicitly acknowledged that the spiritual geographies of the volcano and the ocean were bound together. By providing offerings to both topographies, the sultan recognized that his power was constituted by the deities in both locations and acknowledged that they were in relationships of exchange with each other. It was perhaps during a *labuhan* that offerings were released for Nyai Ratu Kidul on a bamboo raft, offerings that ended up in the samples later picked up by the *Lusiad* and *Monsoon*.

Tirtakoesoema explained in 1933 that the offerings given to Nyai Ratu Kidul consisted of fabrics and cloth such as sarongs and sashes printed with the patterns of the sultanate. People also offered her coins, perfumes, and incense, which suggests that the queen participated in the social life of the sultanate, and even donned the dress of a subject.[12] After providing offerings to the queen, Tirtakoesoema reported that the entourage then turned toward Merapi. They progressed first by train to Kalasan (near Prambanan), then to the administrative center at Kejambon, and finally to the village of Ngrangkah (Umbulharjo) on the southern slope of the volcano. The retinue progressed a few kilometers up the steep slope to the edge of the vegetation line to provide the final offerings. They then harvested slabs of sulfur for the palace; and the gatekeeper, or *juru kunci*—literally, key worker—responsible for conducting the ritual on behalf of the sultan said: "I have been dispatched by His highness the Sultan of Yogyakarta to present the royal clothing which is being offered to those who rule at the 'navel' of the land of Java, Mount Merapi."[13] The gatekeeper then named the following deities as those who ruled there: Sangyang Umar, Kyai Empu Permadi, Kyai Brama Kedhali, Gusti Eyang Panembahan Prabu Jagad, Kyai Sabuk Angin, Bok Nyai Gadhung Mlathi, and Gusti Panembahan Megantara.[14] These names were important to mention in part because of their honorifics, such as the "the highest" and the "greatest," and in part because they give titles and ranks such as king or *kyai* (a Muslim scholar). They were also significant because some deities were local ancestors, figures of historical importance, or deities of Islamic descent as well as members of Hindu genealogies. Kyai Empu Permadi, for instance, was a *wayang* character from the genealogy of Batara Guru, a variation on a character from the *Mahabharata*. In this instance, the character from the Hindu epic had metamorphosed into a *kyai*. Gusti Eyang Panembahan Prabu Jagad is also suggestive (*jagad* means "universe"), while other accounts of Merapi deities suggest that a similarly named deity, Kyai Sapu Jagat (meaning roughly "sweeper of the cosmos" or "cosmic cleaner"), lived there.[15] The invocation of *Jagad* or *Jagat* suggests a number of possible genealogies; perhaps it was Prince Dipasana, for instance, who died sometime around 1840 and who was said to have married the daughter of the ruling deity of Merapi, Raden Sapujagad.[16] Dipasana was also apparently skilled in magic and enlisted the solidarity of the spirit world to attempt a coup.[17] Sapu Jagad may also have been an Islamization of the much more ancient deity Juru Taman, or "guardian of the land."[18] There was also a cannon built for Sultan Agung, called Sapu Djagad, in the 1620s during his pious anticolonial campaign against the Dutch East India Company.[19] It was perhaps the Merapi deity who was named after the cannon, or perhaps the cannon was named after the deity. Whatever the direction of influence, Sapu Djagad's home in Merapi was considered a northern border of cosmic, spiritual, and political significance, while the queen of the Indian Ocean, Nyai Ratu Kidul, ruled the south. Together they constituted the foundational coordinates of the material-spiritual territory of Yogyakarta, from ocean to volcano, from the muddy depths of the ocean to the peak of the crater.

Merapi, then, was historical and genealogical, local and cosmic. The ritual pathways that connected the sultan to the Indian Ocean to the south and the peak to the north materialized those cosmic geographies. Part of governing the sultanate in 1921 was the maintenance of this physical and spiritual geography through rituals such as the *labuhan*. The realms of the ocean and volcano were understood as fundamentally and constitutionally connected; the rumblings and movements of one were understood to be implicated in the other. As Theodore Pigeaud explained in his 1927 analysis of the cryptic and often bewildering character of Baron von Sakender (the *babad* about him was likely written as recently as the mid- to late nineteenth century), for political orders to be established in Java, the prince or lord had to seek legitimacy with the deities in the mountains and with the queen of the ocean.[20] The volcanoes and the ocean constituted the foundations of political power; sovereignty was political geology.

When the *labuhan* ritual was recorded by Tirtakoesoema, the spiritual geography of Merapi was becoming familiar to an increasing number of colonial scientists. Georg Kemmerling, the head of the Vulkanologisch Onderzoek (Volcanological Survey,) undertook several fieldtrips to study the causes of Merapi's eruptions. He reported in 1922 that his colleagues had begun to understand that earthquakes after eruptions were being recorded in the Indian Ocean, 250 kilometers south of Yogyakarta, near where the *Lusiad* and *Monsoon* would later take their samples.[21] Kemmerling and his seismologist colleagues were beginning to suspect that volcanism in Merapi and earthquakes in the Indian Ocean were connected. He wrote, "After all, it seemed very possible that the imbalance occurring in the Indian Ocean creates an effect in Merapi."[22] He came to this conclusion while conducting fieldwork on what he called "an old ritual path" near Plawangan, the very same path that the *labuhan* had followed to the crater.[23] He ended his visit, like the *labuhan* had before him, in the exact field from which sulfur chunks had been harvested for the sultan.[24] It is very likely that Kemmerling had access to the *labuhan* path by way of the Javanese *mantris*, the assistants who accompanied scientists, conducted fieldwork, carried their equipment, and acted as translators with Javanese locals.[25] Kemmerling was coming to understand, on the *labuhan* trail, what the *labuhan* was designed to celebrate: the inseparability of volcanism from the Indian Ocean.

On that same expedition, Kemmerling also visited the crater from the north, traveling via the village of Selo to a plateau of large boulders called Pasar Bubar (also Pasarboebar or Pasar Bubrah) that abuts the crater wall. The name Pasar Bubar means "ruined market" in Javanese. Kemmerling's inclusion of the toponym in a "Vulkanologische Berichten" (Volcanological report) in 1922 was an early appearance of its usage in geologists' literature.[26]

Pasar Bubar was named as such because the boulders were understood to be market stalls for the pantheon of spirits in the volcano who would establish their night market there to trade goods with each other. At around the same time as Kemmerling's presence there, another toponym, this one for a large hill, also appeared in the vocabulary of colonial volcano scientists—Mesjidanlama, or "old mosque," so named because it was the mosque in which volcano deities were worshipped. Dutch attention to these terms not only bore witness to the existence of these spiritual geographies in the 1920s, they also recorded the presence of scientists in these places by way of the processional ritual infrastructures that brought them there. It was along those same paths that had long been taken to provide offerings or undertake pilgrimages that scientists undertook their fieldwork. Those paths were the only paths that would have led to such a high elevations; the landscape was too barren and dangerous to inhabit, so the only regular presence there would have been for spiritual purposes. The appearance of the spiritual geographies of the "ruined market" and "old mosque" on the scientists' maps indicates the direct manner in which the pathways of Merapi's spiritual geographies shaped how volcano scientists not only accessed the volcano but also understood it.

When the *Lusiad* and *Monsoon* dropped below the surface of the Indian Ocean nearly thirty years later, they were not at all entering an unknown space. They were not only descending into the ocean, they were descending into a thoroughly political realm that extended to the volcanoes. It was a social space—the Indian Ocean *and* Merapi—the foundation of political power and the polity. The samples they took were, truly, politicized geology, bits of stone and pebble and sand taken from the political geological assemblage of central Java. Those bits of politicized matter ended up in the unlikely place of shaping the images of the plate tectonic earth reproduced in *National Geographic* and put on the walls of schoolrooms.

NEW ORDER SPIRITUAL GEOGRAPHIES · Javanese sources documenting the connections between the spiritual geographies of Merapi and the Indian Ocean became rare for nearly half a century after the 1930s. This was not because the *labuhan* ceased; Sukarno and Suharto were both known to have participated in them throughout the 1950s and into the 1970s. It is certain, too, that the role of the gatekeeper in Umbulharjo was continuously held since Tirtakoesoema recorded his experiences in 1921. But ethnological, anthropological, and literary descriptions of the deities were scant until a resurgence of interest in the 1980s and the waning days of Suharto's New Order. I turn here to that moment and how the spiritual geographies of the region intersected with a military dictatorship and set the stage for a later, more contemporary, intercalation with plate tectonics that sought to intervene in political-spiritual discourses.

When the Indonesian anthropologist Lucas Sasongko Triyoga conducted fieldwork in 1984–85 with villagers on Merapi, he found that the idea that the volcano and Indian Ocean were connected continued to be profoundly important.[27] He recorded a spectral political geology:

> Residents on the flanks of Merapi hold the belief that other than humans, nature is also inhabited by spirits called the invisible nation (*bangsa halus*) or invisible creatures (*mahluk halus*). Just as with human life, the spirit world is organized according to a governmental hierarchy with separate functions and activities. One of these spiritual government hierarchies which is close to the hearts of residents is the Spiritual Kraton in Merapi.[28]

A decade later, and in part inspired by Triyoga's work, German anthropologist Judith Schlehe joined a *labuhan* in Umbulharjo and recorded that Kyai Sapu Jagad was still a high-ranking deity in the volcano; in this case, he was cast as a minister in the invisible nation, responsible for its invisible army and for the forests and fields on the slopes. For others, though, she found that Sapu Jagad was considered the ruler: "His particular task is to make sure that the lava never flows in a southbound direction toward the palace (*kraton*) of Yogyakarta." The *labuhan*, she continued, was "a reward" of food and garments.[29] Schlehe found, once again, that "The kingdom of Mount Merapi maintains strong ties to other kingdoms, primarily to the *kraton* Yogyakarta. . . . These kingdoms are connected by the major rivers."[30]

In 1998, a year before the fall of the dictator Suharto, the French-Indonesian journalist and author Elisabeth Prasetyo (later Elizabeth Inandiak) published *Lahirnya Kembali Beringin Putih* (*The White Banyan*), based in part on her experiences with the *labuhan* and friendship with the *juru kunci*, the gatekeeper. This gatekeeper, Maridjan, lived in a modest house in Umbulharjo, the same village mentioned in Tirtakoesoema's 1921 account. Maridjan had also been an important figure for Triyoga and Schlehe, who interviewed him and conducted fieldwork in his village. We will come back to Maridjan in more detail below, but for now it is sufficient to turn to a brief record, likely semifictionalized by Prasetyo in *The White Banyan*, that stresses the relationship between the volcano and ocean.

Prasetyo describes Maridjan's dreams, as recounted by him. One dream is from when he was young and not yet the gatekeeper. One day, he climbed the volcano and, after reaching the top, soon fell asleep. He awoke inside the crater, a vast room filled with orderly rows of chairs. "There was also a monumental green gate, the gate for the Merapi palace." He continued, "Access to the huge room was protected by an employee sitting on a chair in front of a table on which was lying a book."[31] The narrative then suddenly switches scene back to his walk up the volcano, and he remarks that it had been raining, pouring even, the entire time. "Seen through the eye of the heart [*mata batin*], this rain was the escort sent by the South Sea, by the palace of [Ratu] Kidul. It was as if this escort was protecting the river Krasak, a river through which the lava flows often." He switches scene again, back to dream space: "In the dream this river represented the main road which leads to the South Sea. And there, there was a sort of esplanade, on which stood a soaked army standing in orderly lines, like many people waiting in a camp. At that time, my father was still alive and he had burned incense there for the starved soldiers."[32]

It makes sense that this was a vision of the spirit army of Kyai Sapu Jagad; that they fed on incense was a sign that they were spirits. It seems, too, that they were guarding the path to the river and to the other invisible nation in the Indian Ocean. The gatekeeper's dream made clear that for him and for the political geology of the sultanate in 1998, the volcano was still inseparable from the Indian Ocean.

It is worth pausing to consider what was new in the imagery of the gatekeeper and other residents. When the gatekeeper's dreams were recorded, the idea of "invincible nations" (*bangsa halus*) no doubt resonated with the idea that the Indonesian state was also *bangsa*; the word means "nation," but it also can mean "race," or "people." It probably suggested both, an invisible race and nation, but also an invisible sultanate modeled on Yogyakarta, a nation in the sense of the Republic of Indonesia, and a hierarchy that mirrored that of the military dictatorship that then ruled the republic. The volcano and the Indian Ocean were mirrors of this nation. Nature was a sultanate, a postcolonial state, and a military dictatorship. But the other way around worked equally well, too: the sultanate and republic were mirror images of the spiritual state of nature; not only were they structured in the same way, equally hierarchical, with armies, a queen, and a sultan; they also traded with each other; there was diplomacy and geopolitical maneuvering. The *labuhan* was one moment when the Indonesian state traded with the authoritarian spirit nation. But the spirit nation traded also independently between its realms, from the Indian Ocean to the vast room with orderly chairs inside the volcano.

When Triyoga, Schlehe, and Prasetyo were spending time in Umbulharjo with Maridjan, it was the height of Indonesia's "New Order," presided over by Suharto, an autocrat who maintained his position as president for thirty-two years and whose military was an ever-present reality in the republic; many ministers in all political parties were former or current generals. Even some volcano scientists and geologists wore army fatigues, representing the established order. The regime had come into being through a violent military coup in 1965, and in the later years of his rule, Suharto increasingly fused his military style with that of a Central Javanese sultan.[33] He sent dignitaries on the *labuhan* to the South Sea, and one of his closest advisers (also a former general), Soedjono, was known to consort with Nyai Ratu Kidul.[34] What was more, the sultan of Yogyakarta was Suharto's vice president. Triyoga even recorded that the hill at Plawangan, where Kemmerling had joined with the "old ritual path," was considered a place haunted by Communist ghosts. Suharto had ordered the mass killing of Communist Party members across Indonesia, but around Merapi there had been a special operation called the Merapi-Merbabu Complex. Local villagers and those with only the slightest affiliation with the Communist Party were summarily executed and left in unmarked mass graves on the volcano. The hill at Plawangan became haunted by those ghosts, now incorporated in their own way into the pantheon of the volcano, as present as the military general—like Kyai Sapu Jagad.

We might consider this a magical-mystical military complex in which the function of the gatekeeper is to struggle to make some sense of it.[35] The *labuhan*, in these terms, not only recalled the founding of the Mataram sultanate, its break-up by the Dutch, and the establishment of the Yogyakarta sultanate but also drew a line of ancestry between the current sultan-minister in a republic governed by a military general-president who was perhaps the descendant of the Islamic revolutionary Senopati, who founded the very kingdom that the sultan had ruled. These jarring political orders, long temporalities, and hybridizations of monarchy, modern democracy, and Islamic, Hindu, and Buddhist politics were all colliding for the gatekeeper to negotiate through rituals such as the *labuhan*.

As John Pemberton understood from his fieldwork conducted during the waning days of this period, rituals like the *labuhan* tried to maintain an order, or safety (*slamet*), in a manner of doing politics by other means, a kind of state politics by way of ritualized spiritual practice.[36] The possibility of disorder, though, was always present, either as social violence, the eruption of the volcano, or earthquakes and tsunamis coming from the South Sea. The *labuhan*, as much as it negotiated the genealogies of the powerful, also negotiated the disorder that could emerge from the landscape itself. Moreover, the disorder of nature and the social were co-constitutive, they mirrored each other, nature was an army too.

When Triyoga completed his fieldwork in 1983, it was only four years after Hamilton published his plate tectonic map of Indonesia (in 1979) and during the time that Pemberton was beginning his studies of the politics of ritual in Java. By the middle of the 1980s, the language of plate tectonics became the definitive scientific language to be applied to Central Javanese volcanism; it was understood that Merapi was reconfigured ocean floor and that the relationship between the two was defined by subduction. The realm of Ratu Kidul was coming to be seen as subducting into the volcano; they were, indeed, communicating with each other. Suharto, soon after, promoted John Katili to director of the Ministry of Mining and Resources and personal adviser on matters related to national development and resource exploitation. However much Hamilton liked to claim otherwise, he did not invent a new way of thinking about Java—he was schooled by the queen of the ocean.

THE GATEKEEPER · Before examining more deeply how plate tectonics intersected with the ritual procession of the *labuhan*, it is necessary to consider another significant phase of the gatekeeper Maridjan's life, after he was studied by anthropologists in the 1980s. Maridjan was known as a *juru kunci*, a position occupied in many places in Java and associated not only with volcanoes but also with cemeteries and holy sites. Gatekeepers were tasked with cleaning graveyards, providing offerings, and opening and closing sites to visitors. In the realm of the sultan of Jogja, there were gatekeepers also at the South Sea; and, as we saw earlier, Maridjan was not the first gatekeeper of the volcano. He was appointed directly by the 9th Nail of the Cosmos, Sultan Hamengkubuwono IX, and was considered an *abdi dalem*, part of the sultan's retinue. He was given clothing with motifs that represented the sultanate, heirlooms, and a *kris* dagger. Elisabeth Inandiak recorded that his sitting room in the 1980s and 1990s contained a simple mat on the floor, no chairs, a cabinet with the heirlooms from the sultan, a photograph of the sultan during his coronation, and a photograph of Merapi's crater. Maridjan's other tasks were to look for lost hikers and provide spiritual advice to guests. He was, like other *juru kunci*, a representative of the *kraton* and the sultan—but at the northern border of the realm, in an impoverished remote area, and at the edge of the spirit world. We should not, however, conceive of Maridjan as a mere puppet of the sultan; his appointment, as we shall see, generated a kind of agency, as he could leverage his relationship with the spirit realms of the volcano and the sultanate. As much as he could buttress the sultan's power, as the gatekeeper, he could also intervene in it and close the gate between the two worlds.

The 10th Nail of the Cosmos, or Sultan Hamengkubuwono X, took the throne of Jogja in 1988, after the death of his father. After the fall of Suharto in 1998, and amid riots, fire, and blood, the new sultan soon began ambitious development projects on the slopes of Merapi. These included a golf course that diverted the Opak River, on which the spirits moved between the caldera and the sea. That river also connected Maridjan's village to the Indian Ocean. The sultan appended exquisite hotels to the golf course, which was watered by those rivers, and building restrictions in Yogyakarta were relaxed, which resulted in new housing towers and hotels being erected that blocked views of the volcano from within the city. As water was being diverted from the rivers to support the new developments, it created shortages in villages downstream. Sand mining took place on a larger scale and at a faster rate than ever before in the volcanic rivers, extracting valuable sand to support the new construction boom, which further interrupted village water supplies as rivers were diverted or backed up. Like many villages on the slopes, residents in Kinaredjo were continually encouraged (even harassed) under the watch of the sultan to *transmigrate*, a Suharto-era project of relocating people from overly populated Java to other islands in the archipelago. Villages on Merapi were especially subject to this because of the ongoing danger there. Before, during, and after eruptions local politicians (*bupati*) often pressured residents to relocate, promising them housing and security elsewhere.[37] The combined forces of the threat of eviction, damaged water supplies, crass commercialism, and an outright disregard for the spiritual geopolitics of the kingdom began to sour the relationship between Maridjan and the sultan.

In April 2006, Merapi began to erupt: clouds rose from the crater, and lava rolled down its south side. The observatory raised the warning status and began to ask that villagers prepare to evacuate. The activity increased throughout the month, and the military arrived to usher people to safety. Members of the Jogja observatory asked that Maridjan leave, and the sultan then requested that inhabitants evacuate to nearby shelters. But Maridjan refused and insisted on remaining in his home even as the threat of the eruption increased. The former president Abdurrahman Wahid telephoned Maridjan with the same request, but again he declined. In an article in the local press, Maridjan made a reference to Kyai Sapu Jagad doing his natural work of cleaning the slopes: "Merapi is waking up, expelling hot clouds and lava. That is a part of cleaning Merapi. There is no need to be anxious, for Cangkringan [Maridjan's area] it is safe. But for other areas I cannot be certain, so please evacuate."[38] The journalist who reported these comments suggested that Maridjan knew his village was safe because of the ritual exchanges with the spirit world that brought him so close to understanding the spiritual-material workings of the volcano. Maridjan also argued that the eruption was caused by the ongoing destruction of the volcano: "Don't return with backhoes again. . . . Merapi can be angered. Don't destroy this earth we all occupy."[39]

It was not only journalists visiting Maridjan at that time. Elizabeth Inandiak wrote that local mystics and paranormal groups looking for revelations and visions also arrived. "The more active Merapi became," she wrote "the busier the hearsay (kabar anginnya) until finally [Maridjan] refused to speak."[40] Vice President Jusuf Kalla then arrived in Jogja and threatened to pick Maridjan up from his village and cart him off to a five-star hotel in the city, likely one of the very hotels built under the sultan's watch that also blocked views of the volcano. Kalla was then reported to have vented: "Superstitious people! It's enough! End this matter!"[41] The tide of trust was shifting, and Maridjan's authority was competing with that of the scientists at the observatory and of the military leading evacuations. Local police were even expressing solidarity with Maridjan.[42]

When the sultan personally asked Maridjan to evacuate, Maridjan responded through the media that the current sultan was not *his* sultan, he was merely the governor. It was the previous sultan, Hamengkubuwono IX, who had appointed Maridjan, and it was to him that he was duty-bound. He said, moreover, that the previous sultan had never asked him to leave during an eruption. Maridjan had defected and, in Inandiak's interpretation, had abandoned his function as gatekeeper, meaning his duty to protect the spiritual geopolitics of the *kraton*, the Indian Ocean, and Merapi—the mirrors between the visible and invisible nations. By refusing to recognize the sitting sultan "the gatekeeper broke the mirrors," she wrote.[43] The volcano, Jogja, and the Indian Ocean were under threat of fragmentation, of each world becoming independent, walled, and inaccessible, their political geology disengaging from each other, becoming locked behind separate spheres.

On May 26, 2006, only weeks after Maridjan refused to recognize the sultan, a powerful earthquake, popularly understood to have originated in the Indian Ocean, devastated the south of Jogja. More than 60,000 houses were turned to rubble and more than 6,000 people were killed. The homeless were, in many cases, left helpless, with little support from the sultan to rebuild their villages; rage was directed at the sultan for his failure to take care of his people. Maridjan's defection was then seen by many as visionary: he had understood that the sultan no longer represented the people, and the earthquake was an expression of the political discord. One of the effects of this was an increasing stream of locals coming to visit Maridjan to seek his advice and wisdom. International journalists, too, took the road up to Maridjan's village, and stories about him began to emerge in the international press.

Another consequence of the earthquake was a massive increase in sand mining in the rivers on the upper slopes of Merapi.[44] The rebuilding effort required even more sand than before for concrete, and the massive volumes of sand ejected from the erupting volcano provided a much sought-after building material. But much of the sand was sourced through illegal means to which the sultan turned a blind eye and, many suspected, from which he directly profited. Maridjan's hope to see the end of the sand mining did not come to pass—in fact, backhoes and trucks crowded into the river valleys and carted sand away at all hours of the day to feed the building boom in the destroyed parts of the town below. A violent sand Mafia emerged to protect the operations with hired thugs.

IS THE IMAGE OF A PERSON WORTH A PIPE? · After the eruption and Maridjan's increasing local and international fame, the owner of an energy drink company came to visit. The owner had family connections to an old friend of Maridjan's who had helped to install a water main from the river to the village in the 1970s. This visit is recorded in Inandiak's *Babad Ngalor-Ngidul*, which is based on her long friendship with Maridjan and his family. She refers to the owner as Mr. Boss, and it is likely that it was Irwan Hidayat, the director of Sido Muncul, the health drink and herbal medicine conglomerate. Inandiak recounts that Mr. Boss asked Maridjan if he could photograph him for an advertisement for an energy drink called Kuku Bima—the "nail of Bima," based on a *wayang* character with a massive thumbnail who was said to have once sheltered a princess from the rays of the sun with it (it is also a fashion for working-class Indonesian men to keep one very long fingernail, often the thumbnail). "We don't sell anything here," Maridjan reportedly replied, as he often did. The Boss then went on to argue that Maridjan owed a favor to Hidayat's family for the water pipe that had been installed all those years ago. "Come to think of it," Mr. Boss apparently said, "is the image of one person so valuable compared with that pipe?"[45]

Inandiak suggests that the appeal to family and favor could not have been refused and that Maridjan was coerced to agree. The promise of profit, she intimates, could also have resolved the current problems with water that the village was experiencing due to the sand mining. Maridjan signed the contract. No one outside the immediate family had a chance to read it. Soon after, Maridjan's face was gracing city buses in Jakarta, selling the energy drink. More busloads of tourists began to appear in the village to see the traditional gatekeeper, and the funds from the energy-drink advertisements were used to build a new mega mosque and to pave the road between Maridjan's house and the gate to the spirit world inside the volcano. The water problems, however, were never fixed.[46]

Maridjan became referred to in the media as the "health drink star," and he was soon approached by Jusuf Kala, the same vice president who during the crisis of 2006 had referred to villagers as "superstitious." Kalla was making a bid for the presidency in 2007, representing Suharto's old party, Golkar, and Maridjan agreed to join as a kind of spokesperson for the party conference held at the Hyatt Regency Hotel—another five-star hotel that had been built on the volcano in 1995 as part of the sultan's business plan. The corrupt sultan, also a member of Golkar and who would also later make a bid for the presidency, was there to greet Maridjan. The sultan even acted as a translator from Javanese to Indonesian for Maridjan, literally speaking for him.[47] Kalla introduced Maridjan by saying he was a man who was "resolute and able to make decisions in any situation or risk."[48]

The reversal, in Inandiak's reading, was absolute. The link between the spiritual geography of the volcanic peak and the Indian Ocean had been severed. Maridjan had lost his moral authority and had been cynically co-opted by the very system he had criticized. In becoming a national celebrity, he was no longer the servant of Kyai Sapu Jagad but of Kuku Bima, the energy drink. What is certain is that he was increasingly transforming into a kind of surface on which multiple fantasies were projected. Foreign journalists were one group: they routinely visited and joined the *labuhan* between 2007 and 2009, framing Maridjan's performance in terms of mystical ancient Javanese traditions that stood in stark contrast to the modernity of volcano science. Maridjan represented the survival of premodern traditions threatened by the modern world and a quickly developing Indonesia. In Kinaredjo, the busloads of Indonesians seeking to meet the traditional gatekeeper were projecting their fantasies about Central Javanese traditions and nostalgic ideas about "local wisdom" (*kearifan lokal*), as if they were not informed by and in conversation with cosmopolitan sources. These same tourists also brought an influx of cash that supported a booming local tourist trade in volcano Jeep tours, shops, and products. But Inandiak lamented that the burning of incense, like that burned for the spirit soldiers in Maridjan's childhood dream, was allegedly banned in the village because it was an affront to more orthodox visions of Islam. Most devastating, in Inandiak's reading, was not simply the commercialization but what made it possible, the severing of the north-south relationship that the *labuhan* was designed to maintain. That connection was perhaps her own fantasy of Maridjan: the brute force of his new fame, the journalists and guests and the money all served to disrupt Maridjan from his simple but vital task of tending to the axis; it was as if Maridjan were the true "Nail of the Cosmos," as if he were the last one holding together a spiritual-political-material geography.

Surprisingly, Maridjan's fame meant that stories of the axis and the pantheon of gods in the volcano spread beyond the obscure ethnographies of anthropologists and appeared in journalists' stories, locally and internationally, and came to represent a well-known tale of the clash of the mystical and modern, ritual and science, rocks and spirits, and the commodification of the sacred. It is perhaps that the defection of Maridjan from the sultan, and his subsequent return as media star, set the conditions for Maridjan to act as a cipher to work out these much larger and more troubling conditions of modernization, not only in Indonesia but also with a much wider resonance. It is with this in view that we return to plate tectonics, following an episode in 2010, nearly sixty years after the *Lusiad* and *Monsoon* took their samples from Nyai Ratu Kidul's domain. Once again, the spiritual geography of Java finally came to be intercalated with plate tectonics through the work of a volcano scientist named Surono. The system that Maridjan represented, surprisingly, became a model not of ancient "local wisdom" but for modern volcano science. Though Maridjan was a tragic victim of commercialization and corruption, he was soon after transformed into a model for responsible volcanology.

SURONO · Surono completed his undergraduate thesis at the Institute of Technology Bandung (Institut Teknologi Bandung; ITB), the same institute that had been founded in the final decades of Dutch colonialism and at which Theodor Klompe created the Department of Geology and taught introductory geology courses to John Katili. Surono wrote his undergraduate thesis in seismology, learning the techniques of Japanese masters, who in turn had learned from the gravity measurements of Felix Vening Meinesz. ITB was also the institute at which Katili received the first awarded doctorate in geology and later became professor in 1961. While Katili was working as Director General of Mining near ITB (and after having requested that Warren Hamilton redescribe the tectonic structure of the archipelago), Surono graduated in 1982; he had learned to identify the origins of earthquakes and whether they were generated from magma moving underground toward a caldera or from tectonic movements created at a distance.[49] Studying such differences was crucial for volcanologists because the differences were used to indicate whether an eruption or earthquake was oncoming or if the ground was simply moving due to different tectonic stresses. Surono continued his work at the Université Savoie Mont Blanc with Michel Halbwachs, a volcanologist and seismologist who would also supervise the work of Jean Philippe Metaxian (we will encounter Metaxian in more detail in chapter 6). Surono wrote his PhD dissertation about the effects of magmatic intrusions—the movement of magma inside volcanoes—a part of which was the application of seismology to identifying the subterranean movement of magma. His test cases were the eruptions of Mount Kelud in East Java and in the Long Valley in California in 1990. By the time he completed his dissertation in 1992 and became the Head of Volcano Physics for the Badan Geologi (Geological Agency) in 1993 (Katili's former position), his homecoming was to a world in which the language of plate tectonics was the orthodox discourse for Indonesian volcanism and which he would apply to the volcanic crises that would make him one of the country's most famous scientists.

Like Katili, Surono also became a public figure. In 2006, he was appointed as head of the Pusat Vulkanologi dan Mitigasi Bencana Geologi (Volcanological Survey of Indonesia, formally the Center for Volcanology and Geological Hazard Mitigation). Such a position was public-facing if the director chose it to be. The office in Bandung was the central head-quarters for monitoring all Indonesia's volcanoes, and each provincial outpost on every rumbling slope eventually sent its records there for analysis. With this oversight and so many eruptive events, the head of volcanology was often consulting with the media, explaining what was happening with the earth and what people should do about it. Surono was drawn to this public work, perhaps more than Katili who was quickly shuffled into powerful political and diplomatic positions. Surono even became a media celebrity, intervening in and shaping discourses about the earth. The following section describes what happened in his confrontation with Maridjan in 2010 and how the intercalation of the plate tectonic narrative with the north-south axis occurred.

THE ERUPTION OF 2010 · In July 2010, for the first time in recent memory, the *labuhan* ceremony departed from Kinaredjo without the gate-keeper. Maridjan was either too ill or ashamed, perhaps, from the disgrace of the energy drink bribery, to attend. Inandiak describes a photo of Maridjan standing in his yard, alone, watching the departure of the procession without him.[50] Soon after, Merapi began to act up again, and by September 2010, the observatory was recording that the volcano was inflating. The number of earthquakes registering on the seismographs was increasing. The observatory raised the alert level to number II, with the expectation that a repeat of the events of 2006 was on the way. In October, however, the activity levels surpassed scientists' expectations and increased exponentially.

Earthquake swarms set off landslides along Merapi's southern slope. Residents reported that the ground was vibrating, not shaking or rolling like a wave, but buzzing.[51] Inandiak, who lived ten kilometers away, said that it sounded like the volcano was "banging from inside."[52] On October 20, 2010, the observatory raised the level to "On Guard"—meaning be ready to evacuate. By late October, the observatory recorded 500 volcanic earthquakes over a single weekend. Surono arrived in Yogyakarta from Bandung around this time to take over the monitoring. At this stage, his explanation was that the volcano was "recharging" from below, along the axis between the South Sea and the volcano. In other words, magma was on the move from Ratu Kidul's abode to the palace of Sapu Jagad. He said the following: "The magma has been pushed upwards due to the escalating seismic energy, and it's about a kilometer below the crater."[53] The observatory ordered evacuations from Maridjan's village and its surroundings. Recalling 2006, Maridjan refused to leave. Fearing that his refusal would legitimate others to stay put, the president, Susilo Bambang Yudhoyono, once again called Maridjan to ask him to leave. Yudhoyono even suggested that back in 2006 it had been Maridjan's refusal to leave that may have caused the earthquake in the south.[54] Journalists and friends disobeyed evacuation orders to visit Maridjan, interview him, ask for advice, or bring him supplies. In these interviews he was humble, repeating that he was "foolish," just a member of the "little people" (wong cilik). People should trust the scientists, he said—"they have the seismographs."[55] Yet, he would stay; it was his home. Surono became belligerent. It once again became a conflict of science versus magic, mysticism versus modernity. Surono told a journalist from PBS, "Merapi['s] logic is more sure than superstition. I believe the [logic] of Merapi, not voodoo."[56] On the night of October 25, a massive pyroclastic flow billowed out of the crater and spilled down the sides. Maridjan was in his house with reporters and close friends, praying, as the ash cloud moved through the forest above them at twenty kilometers an hour; it lit trees on fire like matches and then descended onto his house, desiccating the bodies of Maridjan and thirty-four others as he lay in sujud, prayer position. The image of his prostrating body went viral as people mourned his passing, and news outlets reprinted it in Indonesia and abroad. The BBC ran a headline that read, "Spiritual Guardian of Indonesian Volcano Dies."[57]

In the following weeks, the eruption intensified, reaching a level of destruction not seen since 1930. Nearly 350,000 people were evacuated to temporary refugee shelters. More than the equivalent volume of one Empire State Building was ejected from the crater in a single month. The eruption lasted longer than three months. Surono remained in Jogja through most of it, updating the media throughout the crisis, becoming its figurehead, and making pronouncements about the crisis operations. Newspapers were fascinated by his personal history, the fact that he was a father of two and willing to give up his time with his family to spend months in Jogja during the crisis. Immediately after Maridjan's death, Surono was called upon by the public and by journalists to replace the gatekeeper; he was given the honorific used for Maridjan, mBah, a Javanese sign of respect for elders. Newspapers reported that his accurate forecast was proof that he had taken the place of Maridjan. Seismographs and tilt meters had won in the competition between modernity and tradition, science versus voodoo. As the eruption in 2006 had done for Maridjan, so the 2010 eruption made Surono famous. He became the gatekeeper protecting the interconnection between the realm of Ratu Kidul and Sapu Jagad.

THE SPIRITUALITY OF PLATE TECTONICS · The modernist narrative of science versus voodoo, technology versus superstition, did not last long. In two scientific papers analyzing the eruption, Surono began to develop a plate tectonic narrative that intercalated with the narrative of the north-south axis of the *labuhan*. Surono, with his colleagues, argued that the origin of the eruption of 2010 was in the South Sea, through the Opak Fault that ran from the Indian Ocean, roughly beneath the Opak River, to the base of the volcano. That fault axis corresponded with the axis along which the *Lusiad* and the *Monsoon* had taken their samples in the 1960s. It was also that same axis along which Hamilton had argued that the Indian Ocean trench was intercalating with the magmatic arc and feeding Merapi with lava. Surono called the Opak Fault the "plumbing system" that carried magma from the zone of subduction under the ocean in Ratu Kidul's realm. That plumbing system lay below the same river system that was said to carry Nyai Ratu Kidul's vehicles back and forth to visit Kyai Sapu Jagad. As the poet G. J. Resink put it in 1997, referring to the river Code, a tributary of the Opak River, "Whoever as a child heard the sound of the kentongan (slit-drums) along the river Code as the drums accompanied R[atu] Kidul on her journeys high above the water to the volcano Merapi learned early on to associate the R[atu] with fresh as well as with salt water."[58]

The plate tectonic understanding converged with the spiritual geography: they both maintained that the oceanic and volcanic were connected by the Opak. What also happened in the years following the death of Maridjan was a transformation in Surono's attitude toward the political circumstances in Indonesia. His change was made apparent in an interview in *Tempo* in 2015 titled "Penuhi Hak Gunung Berapi" (Respecting the rights of volcanoes).[59] Photographed in a casual sarong at his house in Jakarta, he argued that scientists had become arrogant, too fixated on instruments, and technocratic. Technology made it appear as if volcanoes could be mastered, as if the earth could be made predictable. The reporter asked him about his position vis-à-vis traditional knowledge and spiritual geography, and how they might fit into a modern scientific framework. He responded:

> Local knowledge is not mystical; it is about a respect for nature applied to everyday life. When I was little, in my village, there was a ritual called *sedekah bumi* [ritual offerings for the earth]. It is a form of local knowledge that expresses gratitude for earth's abundance during harvest season. There is nothing like that today because it can be considered idolatrous, even though the aim is good, you know. If I don't communicate with the mountain, how can I read its signals? I salute local knowledge on Merapi.[60]

Surono's reference to the banning of the *sedekah bumi*, or the giving of offerings to the earth, was a comment on broader political transformations in Indonesia. Around the same time, statues of *wayang* characters had been razed in West Java by hardline Islamic groups. Concern was emerging—perhaps accurately, perhaps not—that the northern provinces of Indonesia were harboring ISIS cells. The new president of Indonesia, Joko Widodo, had been the subject of a conspiracy theory, promulgated by his opponent during the presidential election of 2014, according to which he was posing as a Muslim but was in fact a Christian. It was widely understood that a non-Muslim would never be elected; Widodo promptly joined the Hajj pilgrimage to prove otherwise. Moreover, Surono was a Javanese Christian, and when I interviewed him in 2016, he explained that he had long navigated anti-Christian discrimination within the civil service. His shift to lamenting local knowledge, including that which Maridjan stood for, was amid what he understood to be a rising conservative Islam that threatened those traditions. Volcano science, the kind rooted in reliance on modern instruments, the very kind that he was trained in and had championed during the eruption in 2010, he came to believe, went hand in hand with conservative Islam; technocracy and strict monotheism, as he saw it, buttressed each other.

Nearly one year after Surono's interview, the *labuhan* was held in Kinaredjo (figure 3.3). The position of *juru kunci* had been taken up not by Surono but instead by Maridjan's son, Asih. On the morning of May 8, 2016, the procession left from the *kraton* in Jogja for the South Sea, where a crowd of local and foreign tourists followed the noisy parade to the spot where Senopati was said to have meditated and met Nyai Ratu Kidul. The *abdi dalem* hoisted the offerings to her on large bamboo rafts and set them adrift on the waves until they disappeared in ways remarkably similar to

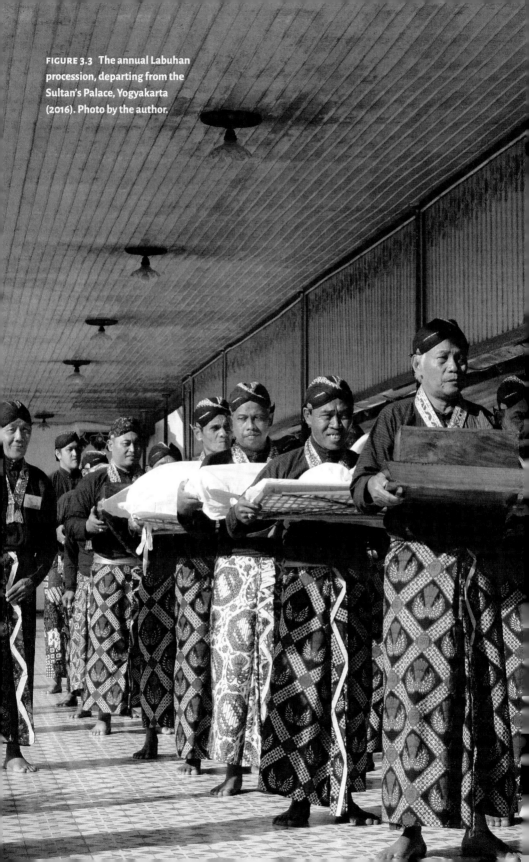

FIGURE 3.3 The annual Labuhan procession, departing from the Sultan's Palace, Yogyakarta (2016). Photo by the author.

those depicted in Tirtakoesoema's description from 1921. Later that night, in Kinaredjo, a *wayang* performance was held for the *labuhan*. Surono arrived before the performance began and was quickly greeted by fans and local dignitaries looking for selfies and handshakes. Journalists from *Tempo* and local newspapers pumped him for eruption predictions. As the performance was about to begin, he was ushered to one of the finest seats in the house, beside Maridjan's concrete grave and a large portrait of Maridjan wearing his signature aviator-style glasses; rose petals were scattered on the ground and across the grave. Surono, when asked for predictions, relied on the model of the plate tectonic plumbing system running from south to north and said that it was still a long time before the magma would sufficiently fill the volcano. He said that Merapi was still empty from the eruption in 2010. Much of that material was currently being mined or eroded down the river systems, back to the ocean, the domain of Nyai Ratu Kidul. Moreover, "What I know," he said, "is that with the Merapi *labuhan*, the community is trying to live in harmony [with the volcano]. The community is gathering to give thanks for the blessings of Merapi."[61]

CONCLUSION · During the *labuhan*, when the *abdi dalem* released their offerings to the queen of the Indian Ocean on bamboo rafts, they were releasing them to the very spot from which the *Lusiad* and *Monsoon* had taken their samples. Offerings, as we have seen, had been released there since at least the early eighteenth century, and probably much earlier, too. They were given to the ocean because, in part, there was an understanding that oceanic processes were causally connected to volcanic processes, which were in turn connected to political processes. The wealth and diversity of stories about the queen traveling back and forth along the rivers to the peak of the volcano was a way to acknowledge that the Indian Ocean and the volcano coproduced each other; their relationship was tectonic and constitutional. The stories that Dutch ethnologists and Javanese aristocrats were interested in in the 1920s and 1930s also acknowledged that the two geographies constituted each other in and through the foundation of the polities of the sultanate. Tectonics *was* politics, or as Kathryn Yusoff and Nigel Clark have put it, tectonics was geosocial.[62] This was what Surono indirectly came to realize and why he returned to the *labuhan*: to leverage the political significance of the spiritual geography of Merapi. A longer view of scientists' engagements with these spiritual geographies reminds us that they are not new, nor have they ever been as radically distinct as some scientists would have liked to think. The spiritual geographies of Ratu Kidul and Sapu Jagad prefigured the insights of plate tectonics, and in some instances, the very same ritual pathways hosted scientists while they undertook their work and came to see the connections between volcano and ocean. The theory of plate tectonics, it must be acknowledged, emerged in part *from* these ritual pathways. To refuse to acknowledge this is to hold to an overly narrow conception of what influence is. The very same paths that nineteenth-century pilgrims used to access the spirit world that connected the ocean and volcano were those that enabled scientists to begin to understand that the volcanoes and the ocean were fundamentally connected. The significance of this is not two separate but analogous insights happening in the same place but of seeing that, in an expanded sense, the plate tectonic insights of European geologists were *enabled* by and subsequently reproduced the core insight of Javanese spiritual geographies.

Yet, even if the genesis of the theory of plate tectonics is in the spiritual geography of Java, the modern geological sciences have been dismal at thinking geology politically. Javanese spiritual geographies, by contrast, explicitly and ritualistically acknowledged that the polity emerged in and through the relationship between the volcanoes and the ocean. The reason that intercalation helps think through these issues is because it enables us to see how earth knowledges and politics, local and global, have consistently, explicitly, and unrepentantly come together. The spiritual geographies of Java insist on the coproduction of geology and politics; the theory of plate tectonics was then added to these terms and became mixed up with spiritual politics, which in turn were locally significant in negotiating religious politics, all the while being utterly modern, global, and celebrating "local knowledge." Intercalation is not only another word for syncretism; it aims at something different, at how earth knowledges came into contact, transformed each other, and were bound together. It is a way to foreground processes of interlocking, dismantling, and reassembling the social and political effects of claims to newness, and how older knowledges enable new forms of knowing.

_____

CHAPTER FOUR

AD 1006

GEODETERMINISM

Cultures of Catastrophe and the Story of a Date

_____

What we are witnessing is the collapse of the world.

EDUARD SUESS, 1885

A SILENT MYSTICISM: VOLCANOLOGY IN THE TWILIGHT OF THE COLONY · At the turn of the twentieth century, the longevity of the Netherlands' colony in Indonesia seemed increasingly uncertain. The popular novelist Louis Couperus, seen by some of his contemporaries as one of the best, captured the late colonial fault lines in his 1900 novel, _The Hidden Force_:

> Beneath all this show the hidden force lurks, slumbering now and unwilling to fight. Beneath all this appearance of tangible things the essence of that silent mysticism threatens, like a smouldering fire underground, like hatred and mystery in the heart. Beneath all this peace of grandeur the danger threatens and the future mutters like the subterranean thunder in the volcanoes, inaudible to human ears.[1]

Couperus captured the pervasive sense of alienation Europeans felt between themselves and Native Javanese. While they lived side by side

and, often enough, together (many Javanese were domestic laborers living in Dutch colonial houses if they were not laborers on the plantations),
their relations were frequently marked by a sense of cultural incompati-
bility. At the time the novel was published, 35 million colonial subjects in
the colony were governed by a mere 250 Europeans; between them were
15,000 indigenous civil servants and the formidable Netherlands army.
The social worlds of colonist and colonized were thus asymmetrical and
inextricable. Couperus saw here unease and tectonic friction; the mysticism of the Javanese, meant, for him, that the belief in the power of the
invisible world was "alien in race and mind."[2]

Cultural difference, though, was not always conceived of as an alienated relation. The Ethical Policy, introduced in 1901, only a year after *The
Hidden Force* was published, was the result of a liberal turn in governing
the colony that sought to mend frayed relations between colonists and
Natives by addressing nearly a century of forced labor, extreme poverty,
famine, and economic insecurity through the institution of liberal economic regulations. The policy created new foreign-controlled companies
in the archipelago such as Royal Dutch Shell, which had been founded in
1907 between British and Dutch companies. The British Billiton Mining
company and the US Standard Oil further established their operations
in Sumatra at this time.[3] New exports of tea, oil, rubber, and tobacco
became major sources of revenue for the colony, and economic liberalization was linked to ambitious expansions of railways and the modernization of cities.[4] The Ethical Policy was cultural, too. It was the result
of a transition to thinking that colonialism ought to be a benevolent,
civilizing force; it would promote Native culture, increase the standards
of Native living, and raise education levels. As a result, during the first
decades of the twentieth century, the first government archaeological offices were founded, and between 1907 and 1911, the temple at Borobudur
was restored. Native language studies and access to education were expanded, and some of the first exhaustive ethnological studies of Javanese
folk cultures were initiated as well. An unprecedented obsession with
Javanese culture emerged. Theosophy lodges began to spring up across
Indonesia and served to foment new interest among colonial elites in the
occult and "sacred records of the east." The new interest in local culture
fed Couperus's and others' fascination with epistemological difference
and alterity. The tension that Couperus saw between Native and colonial
European worlds emerged also from anxieties about the future of the
colonial project itself; how could colonialism improve its subjects if they

were fundamentally, existentially, internally different? Perhaps the colonial project had met its limit in the "hidden force"?

Volcanologists were not immune to these questions. In some cases, their science was integral to negotiating these colonial tensions as volcanoes were understood as keys to the Native mind. Volcanology became a way to link the cultural politics of colonialism to the earth. The science of the earth's formative processes became a space for testing out ideas around what constituted an environmental catastrophe, whether culture suffered from such catastrophes, and what the direction of history was (cycles of destruction and rebuilding or a single direction of progress). All these questions set the stage for new ways of doing science that persist to this day in global volcano science. Reinout van Bemmelen, beginning in the 1920s, sought to incorporate geological history with Javanese history. Forgotten early modern Javanese stone inscriptions—he came to understand them by way of a prominent Javanese Theosophist—contained novel records of how Javanese culture was the product of volcanism. He thus developed a novel theory of geodeterminism in which Javanese culture and history were the result of geological forces. He was also, at the same time, participating in broader colonial discussions about the causes of Javanese cultural decline. Like many other European intellectuals, van Bemmelen thought the Javanese were living in the ruins of great Hindu and Buddhist civilizations and that the progressive era of the 1901 Ethical Policy meant coming to terms with that lost time. Discussions of cultural decline and ruination, however, also reflected the colonial Europeans' own anxieties about the colonial project: as they considered how and why early modern Java was ruined, they also imagined their own colony as a future ruin. Java's antiquities helped the colonizers think through their own impermanence. Another layer to this endeavor was that, for colonial European intellectuals, understanding how Javanese culture perished went hand in hand with reviving those lost cultures in the present *for* the Javanese. Historical revivalism connected the present to the past, but it was also an extension of the educative dimension of the Dutch colonial "debt of honor" to the Natives; it would teach the Natives about their own forgotten culture.[5]

Like all revivalisms, this project was revisionist; one of its aims was to undermine Javanese Islam. Colonial intellectuals were fascinated with the decline of the early modern Hindu and Buddhist period because it represented a Javanese world before the arrival of Islam, a world that was more congruent with orientalist and colonial visions of world history. That world, the colonial Europeans thought, could still be witnessed in the survival of customs and the Javanese language in the present; these were seen as the essence of the Javanese, while Islam was viewed as merely a superficial layer. Revivalism—although steeped in the circles of the educated colonial elite, Theosophist lodges, and publications—also found sympathetic proponents among the Native Javanese elites, who fomented anticolonial nationalisms. They sought to bolster the authority of their highly stratified, rigidly hierarchical Islamic monarchies while also being critical of the colonial apparatus. The Hindu and Buddhist past revealed for them histories and traditions of life before European colonization that could be put into the service of critiquing that colonialism. The revival of the pre-Islamic past by volcanologists, including its alleged "silent mysticism," brought these disparate and often conflicting energies and ambitions together.

This chapter investigates the way that volcano science negotiated these late-colonial anxieties by following the development of the theory that a massive eruption destroyed early modern Javanese culture in AD 1006. It was argued that the eruption caused the decline of Hindu-Buddhist Java (the use of AD in dating the possible eruption here reflects the colonial scientists' implicit application of a Christian temporal framework to their understanding of geological history). The narrative of the destruction of Javanese culture by way of volcanic cataclysm naturalized ideas about cultural decline while simultaneously expressing colonial concerns over the possibility of volcanic hazards and the "subterranean thunder" that Couperus described. This colonial story, however, radically changed with the nationalist revolution and as the history of local Islamic kingdoms gained precedence. Narratives of the Hindu and Buddhist past became pressing in different sorts of ways; what was considered a crucial, geodetermined cultural identity suddenly lost much of its significance as new, postcolonial, and future-oriented imaginaries emerged. The story of the significance of AD 1006 as a catastrophic event continues to circulate in popular and scientific narratives in Indonesia, however, cultivated by the appeal of stories about one-off, massive, environmentally and culturally catastrophic events. It is an apocalyptic narrative through which we can explain the history of both nature and culture. Couperus's conception of a "hidden force" as "subterranean thunder" remains with us, then, in the form of anxieties about the inhuman powers of the earth, its radical indifference to human striving, and its capacity to transform and destroy at a moment's notice; and yet, some people seem much more competent than others at reading its signs and making a home with it.

THE CALCUTTA STONE · In October 1920, Dirk van Hinloopen Labberton delivered an address to a small assembly at the Royal Academy of Sciences in Batavia; the title was straightforward: "Oud-Javaansche Gegevens omtrent de Vulkanologie van Java" (Old Javanese sources on volcanology from Java).[6] Hinloopen Labberton, a philologist and ethnologist by training, was for the first time presenting to the Royal Academy on volcanological matters. Usually, he spent his time teaching Javanese to colonial officers and studying Sanskrit or Kawi; he was also a member of the burgeoning international Theosophy movement. His detractors nicknamed him "the astral rabbit" for his spiritualist sermonizing; he was also, according to some estimates, "irritating."[7] Like other Theosophists, Hinloopen Labberton was, by and large, supportive of the rising tide of Javanese nationalism. He had, for instance, delivered sympathetic speeches to Boedi Oetomo, a group of Javanese aristocrats interested in restoring Javanese heritage and resisting Dutch rule. Hinloopen Labberton was also fascinated by early modern Javanese culture and assisted the Bataviaasch Genootschap van Kunsten en Wetenschappen (Batavian Society for the Arts and Sciences) in reprinting sixteenth-century Javanese texts.[8] In 1912, he published a pamphlet, *Wayang, or Shadow Play as Given in Java*, in which he argued that the shadow play traditions of the early modern period could be used as sources for contemporary Javanese "national ideals"— meaning the nationalist, anticolonial struggle.[9] Javanese nationalism, he suggested, was an expression of much older, pre-Islamic, ancient Saivite and Buddhist Javanese culture from the Indian subcontinent. In the Netherlands East Indies, that culture had been superseded or syncretized with Islam by the fifteenth century and, as he put it, ancient Saivite and Buddhist cultures were "clad in Mohammadean garb."[10] By accessing the ancient Hindu and Buddhist past, he thought, the nationalists could better articulate their aims of expressing an authentically indigenous perspective.[11]

When Hinloopen Labberton presented to the Royal Academy, he argued that geologists, too, could learn from Hindu-Buddhist Java. He suggested they consider recently published translations of an intriguing piece of evidence from the Calcutta Stone, an inscribed tablet the height of a person and weighing over two tons. The stone had been purloined from East Java during the British interregnum, between 1811 and 1815, by Stamford Raffles, who ruled the island during that brief period before colonizing Singapore. At the time, Raffles had written to his Scottish patron Lord Minto that he would like to send the "Javan rock" to him so that "it may tell eastern tales of us, long after our heads are under smoother stones."[12] Raffles stole the stone and sent it to Minto in Calcutta.[13] Three-quarters of a century later, Johan Kern, the formidable Dutch philologist and historian of Hinduism and Buddhism in the Indies, was one of the earliest to publish transcriptions and interpretations of the Sanskrit, based on rubbings made from the stone.[14] Kern explained that the inscription was the history of the early modern king Airlangga's escape from a "great flood of disasters" in Java when it was plunged into a period of war and social turbulence.[15] Hinloopen Labberton, however, disagreed with Kern and thought that Kern's translation of the Hindu concepts of *pralaya* and *mahapralaya*, on which the notion of the great flood of disasters was based, were flawed. Hinloopen Labberton argued that the inscription "everything return[ed] to chaos before a new mist emerge[d]," when applied to a state or polity, meant a literal and "profound transformation of nature," in other words, a natural disaster, not war and social crises as "disasters."[16] Moreover, Hinloopen Labberton explained that the inscription conveyed that the events transpired in the year 928–29 of the Indic Saka calendar. Hinloopen Labberton converted the dates to the year AD 1006, a difference of seventy-eight years from the Gregorian calendar, and implicitly reframed the events within a Christian temporal horizon.[17] Hinloopen Labberton then went on to explain that with this evidence and the generous assistance of his geologist friends, they could perhaps help to solve a riddle of profound importance for late colonial culture: Why medieval Javanese culture declined, became a ruin, and in Hinloopen Labberton's words, "went silent"?[18]

Hinloopen Labberton asked the question for the following reasons. Early modern Javanese culture had produced some of the world's most ambitious monuments. The Borobudur temple, for instance, made of black volcanic andesite at the foot of Merapi, was the largest Buddhist monument known anywhere. Colonial visitors to the temple in the 1920s drew enthusiastic comparisons with the pyramids at Giza.[19] Shortly after its completion, however, it seemed as though it was suddenly abandoned. A dozen kilometers to the east, and also at the foot of Merapi, was the massive Saivite Prambanan temple, equally impressive; but it had also been abandoned. In his *History of Java* from 1817, Raffles included an illustration of the overgrown ruins of Prambanan with a smoking Merapi caldera in the background because he, too, was fascinated by them (figure 4.1). When he toured the island in 1812, he recorded that the nearby Dieng plateau contained nearly 400 temples, all of them similarly abandoned.[20] The whole of Central Java, he wrote, "abounds with ruins of temples, dilapidated images, and traces of Hinduism."[21] In fact, the Hindu and Buddhist cultures that made them seemed to have come to a sudden halt as no new temples were built for centuries, and then only did they emerge in the east of Java and Bali. It was not until the emergence of Muslim kingdoms in the fifteenth century that new monuments were built in Central Java. Many colonial intellectuals thought there was no transition between them; it was, instead, a period of collapse, followed by silence.

Hinloopen Labberton's presentation mattered because he suggested for the first time to his geologist friends that a volcano may have caused the rupture of medieval Javanese society: that volcanic cataclysm was what was recorded on the Calcutta Stone, and that it had happened in the year AD 1006. The date immediately captured the imagination of scientists, and it became a lure to thinking about how geology shaped Javanese culture and how Native Javanese culture bore the inscriptions of geological events. Volcanologists soon began to imagine that they lived among a culture ruined by volcanic action; yet that culture still retained

FIGURE 4.1 "The Large Temple at Brambanan," with Mount Merapi in the background. Stamford Raffles, *The History of Java* (London: Black, Parbury and Allen, 1817), 20.

discernible fragments, flickering through the cracks of a superficial Islamic outer shell. For volcanologists such as Reinout van Bemmelen, it was an impetus to rethink history and how cultures were brought into being and taken apart by volcanic forces.

THEOSOPHY AND THE ORIGIN OF THE JAVANESE · When Hinloopen Labberton gave his presentation in Batavia, he was registered as the general secretary of the Dutch East Indies section of the Theosophical Society.[22] The Theosophical Society was, at the time, an impressive international institution with "lodges" in thirty countries; in 1928, there were 45,000 members worldwide.[23] The Theosophical project was vast and heterogeneous in its commitments and profound in its impact. It contributed to heterodox religious and spiritual practices in Europe by appropriating philosophical traditions from India, Africa, and East Asia (often from those regions colonized or occupied by European states).[24] Theosophists created the idea of the occult as a coherent doctrinal system containing philosophical, spiritual, and scientific insights developed in the ancient Asian world. European colonization and the forced imposition of Western science and technology, they maintained, drove those insights underground. Theosophy promised not only to nourish the "brotherhood of mankind" and push against the alienating forces of modernization but also to develop a "spiritual science" that resurrected forgotten histories of Asian knowledge. This "occultism" would help to resolve existing modern tensions between religion and modern science because ancient occult wisdom was seen as unaffected by the modern distinction between science and religion, reason and intuition. Occultists imagined that Asian thought would resolve the disenchantment and alienation of modern Western scientific thought. As Alfred Percy Sinnett, an early British Theosophist, put it in his 1884 introduction to occultism, *The Occult World*, "Secluded Orientals may understand more about electricity than Faraday, more about physics than Tyndall."[25] Colonized cultures of the East were seen as providing the key to understanding the failures of the West, and in doing so, Theosophists fabricated the East as a "tradition." At the same time, occultism also provided a mechanism of legitimation through which colonists could critique their own colonial conditions, and this came to play an important role in the development of the postcolonial movement in Indonesia. As Sumathi Ramaswamy has shown, Theosophy was a project of reenchanting modern science that did not come from outside of science but rather from inside its very own ranks; it was the scientists who were the Theosophists, scientists who were in the lodges undergoing séances and then returning to their offices and fieldwork.[26]

The Theosophists' publishing operation produced hundreds of titles, including the periodical *The Theosophist: A Magazine of Brotherhood, Oriental Philosophy, Art, Literature and Occultism*, published at its headquarters in Adyar, Chennai, where it had moved in 1882 from its original headquarters in New York City. The organization was presided over at first by Helena P. Blavatsky, a Ukrainian aristocrat who had fled Russia as a teenager and became a celebrity in New York by conducting public rituals and séances. Her later replacement as leader of the Theosophists in Chennai was Annie Besant, a British socialist organizer with the Fabian Society and the Social Democratic Federation. In the East Indies, Theosophists' were interested in the history of Javanese culture and its Hindu and Buddhist influences; many Theosophists wanted to use Javanese culture's "occult wisdom" to make sense of the radical scientific transformations of the time, such as the deepening of geological time, the age of the earth, and evolutionary time.[27] By linking Javanese culture with "ancient wisdom" and connections to the deep past, colonial scientists could consider themselves not at the periphery but at a kind of center linked to the ancient cultures and scientific wisdom of India. Their project was, in this regard, self-redemptive, as they understood that their role as colonizers was to expose the wisdom of Javanese culture *to* the Javanese who had forgotten, or been alienated from, their own cultural identity by the twin forces of Islamization and European colonization. Europeans thus became the arbiters and authorities of Native knowledge at the same time as they saw themselves as its inheritors. In 1925, in the Netherlands East Indies, official Theosophist membership was 1,735 (though it was by no means made up only of Europeans). It also included a contingent of powerful Native Javanese drawn directly from the aristocracy and central sultanates. These important Javanese members often represented the syncretized Hindu-Buddhist-Islamic dynasties with histories reaching to the earliest times of Dutch colonial presence in the fifteenth century (described in the previous chapter). There were also Theosophist members from the Dutch ruling class, including plantation owners, mining engineers, industrialists, and scholars such as Hinloopen Labberton.[28] The lodges held libraries stocked with international editions, Theosophist publications, of course, and volumes on anticolonialism, internationalist socialism, and communism. Lodges were impressively international in their distribution, located in and connecting through publications and travel with India, South America, Australia, New Zealand, Europe, Africa, Japan, Hong Kong, China, the Caribbean, Eastern Europe, and the United States. They were spaces where members practiced occult sciences, mysticism, séances, and rituals; and there were, no doubt, overlapping social functions and a plurality of intentions among Javanese elites, capitalists, and scientists, each disillusioned in their own ways with life in the colony.

The Theosophist gave space to Javanese nationalism in its May 1920 issue, which included a report by Hinloopen Labberton on a speech by Prince Aryo Kusumodiningrat, the brother of the sultan of Surakarta, dedicated to Theosophists and "Javanese brothers."[29] Kusumodiningrat was also a general in the Royal Netherlands Indies Army, and Hinloopen Labberton was his tutor. In his speech, Kusumodiningrat interpreted a story from the *wayang*, arguing that it could speak to the "ill-proportioned state of social conditions, the economic disorder, political envy, antiquated systems of education, etc.," in society.[30] For Kusumodiningrat, investigation into ancient Hindu and Buddhist culture was a way to critique Dutch colonialism through a nostalgic recalling of the very traditions to which his own monarchy was tied.

Theosophists also helped foment the revolutionary, anticolonial Indonesian nationalist movement in more material ways. The young Sukarno read books in the Theosophist library in Surabaya, where his father was a Muslim member of the lodge. His fellow revolutionary and future first vice president, Mohammad Hatta, was offered a scholarship from an individual who was a Theosophist to study in the Netherlands, though he rejected it. Theosophist publications provided Javanese anticolonial nationalists access to socialist and communist publications that called for internationalist brotherhood and decolonization. Yet, some aristocratic European and Javanese Theosophists celebrated the caste system *as* Native culture.[31] Therefore, a complex relationship emerged in the lodges between ideas about colonialism and tradition, internationalism, socialism, and Javanese revivalism as a solution to Western materialism and science. The ruined Hindu-Buddhist past, they thought, belonged to the oldest flourishing civilizations and was equal, if not superior, to the great achievements of Western history; thus, medieval Java deserved to be studied with the sophistication of the European Enlightenment. To understand how these ideas came to make sense of the relationship between

Javanese volcanism and Javanese culture and the conflation of volcanology with anthropology, it is necessary to consider more carefully some of the foundational ideas of Theosophy.

The Theosophical movement's matriarch, Helena P. Blavatsky, published the six-volume *The Secret Doctrine* in 1888 to elucidate the doctrine of the occult. The occult was a systematic body of thought and based, she wrote, on mystical revelation. Occultism was also an ambitious, labyrinthine comparative religious reading of Hindu, Buddhist, Jewish, Egyptian, and Christian religious texts as historical, scientific truth, from which she created the cosmologic and cosmogenic scaffolding for the Theosophical movement. In volume 1, *Cosmogenesis*, she told the story of the origin of the universe as it was supposedly written on an unnamed "archaic manuscript," "a collection of palm leaves made impermeable to water, fire, and air, by some specific unknown process."[32] The palm leaves contained two images: the first was a white disk; in the second, the disk had a center. She explained that these images were of the cosmos before differentiation and after the emission of "primordial energy." She then drew on the same Hindu concept Hinloopen Labberton had drawn upon when interpreting the cosmology of the Calcutta Stone, the *pralaya*, and argued that it inaugurated the onset of cosmic differentiation: "It is the point in the Mundane Egg," from which everything emerged.[33] After differentiation set the universe in motion, the luminous disk permeated all matter, remaining co-present throughout the universe's evolution and material permutations. The primordial dualism between essence and reality allowed Blavatsky and other Theosophists to posit a realm buried behind the material world that did not succumb to conventional modernist conceptions of natural law. In some instances, this realm was called the *astral plane*, and Theosophical speculation was, according to some authors, derived from practices of revelation that tapped into that spiritual world.[34] Blavatsky explained that even her own retelling of cosmic evolution was in part derived from revelation.

Her vision of anthropogenesis was an outright attack on her near contemporaries Charles Darwin and Thomas H. Huxley. Against them, Blavatsky argued that the creation of man preceded the creation of animals. The evidence, she wrote, was scattered across the religious and sacred texts of the world's religions. Reading across Hinduism, Judaism, ancient Greek philosophy, and Buddhism—with the Islamic and Arabic tradition notably absent—she found evidence that humankind did not evolve from animal forms and neither did it descend from a single human form or place (as in the Edenic traditions) but was instead polygenetic. In fact, there were "seven Adams," or "seven races."[35] "Seven human groups on seven different portions of the globe," with the first appearing 18 million years ago (which was ancient but not unheard of among some of her geologist contemporaries).[36] Blavatsky's anthropology, in this regard, deftly incorporated geological time and reversed Huxleyan and Darwinian evolution. Her anthropology pointed in new and unusual ways to the "missing links" to lost worlds, such as the Javanese.

Anthropogenesis, the second volume of *The Secret Doctrine*, was a meandering genealogy and history of the seven races as they appeared in various guises in mythological, allegorical, and "secret" source material. Blavatsky argued that modern science was ignorant of this history, but she also selectively drew on scientific conclusions for authority when they buttressed her claims. Her evolutionary story began with the first race who were made of shadows; the second "budded" in a kind of autogestation from the first; the four later races began to resemble modern humans. One of those later races populated the lost continent of Atlantis and were the ancestors of the people of Southeast Asia who, she explained, were "brown and yellow giant Races" and the "first *completely human species*, however much larger in size."[37] Blavatsky was not precise about their geography, but she tells us that they occupied a continent after Lemuria in the Indian Ocean was flooded and sunk by earthquakes and volcanoes.[38] The continent was "toward the Southern Pole," which she adds, is "the *pit*, cosmically and terrestrially—whence breathe the hot passions blown into hurricanes by the cosmic Elementals, whose abode it is."[39] Atlantis rose and sank into the ocean several times, forming land bridges that connected and disconnected from other continents and enabled early races to migrate.

Through the rising and sinking of Atlantis, Blavatsky explained, its residents built stone megacities that then perished by the force of volcanic disasters. The ruins could be seen in the monuments on Easter Island, but also in Sri Lanka, portions of Africa, and perhaps Australia, too. But it could not be doubted that their descendants were modern Malays, the Javanese, and indigenous Austronesians.[40] Beginning in the earliest Tertiary, she explained, the race of giants was subjected by the forces of the earth to a protracted annihilation and diminution in size: "It changed the face of the globe, and no memory of [their] flourishing continents and isles, of its civilizations and sciences, remained in the annals of history, save in the Sacred records of the East."[41]

And thus, in Blavatsky's new narrative of the origin of Southeast Asians, the ruins of Borobudur and Prambanan that colonial Theosophists were trying to understand suddenly pointed to the very origins of humanity and its lost first races. Blavatsky expanded the horizon on the antiquity of Southeast Asia beyond what was even visible on the Calcutta Stone. In her rendering, the Javanese were connected to the primordial races. She was, of course, not alone in this speculation, nor was she unique in looking for primordial human ancestors in Asia or India. But her interpretation mattered because European colonial Theosophists came to see themselves as contacting ancient people, and ancientness carried authority in the new, liberal colonial atmosphere.

Blavatsky influenced Charles W. Leadbeater, an Anglican priest, who became a prominent Theosophist and second in command to Annie Besant, first in Adyar and then in Australia. Between 1909 and his death in 1934, Leadbeater was one of the most powerful Theosophists in the organization. He visited Java in 1914 and stayed with Hinloopen Labberton several times; he then returned in 1929 and wrote the articles that would become *The Occult History of Java*.[42] He developed Blavatsky's narratives and incorporated Hinloopen Labberton's reflections on the massive eruption of AD 1006. In *The Occult History of Java*, Leadbeater argued that through clairvoyance and access to the *astral plane*, he understood that Java had once been part of the Atlantean colony. (The idea was from Blavatsky, whom he surely read, so one should wonder why Leadbeater had to travel to the astral plane to find it.) Nevertheless, he argued that Java had become a separate state during the destruction of Atlantis by volcanic action. Modern Java was given its current shape when ancient evil Atlantean rulers endeavored to control its volcanoes. The rulers were so fearful of eruptions that they demanded sacrifices from the Javanese to satisfy the volcanoes. The evil rulers were so conniving that they created a magical force that "magnetized" the volcanoes so they would forever require sacrifices. Thus, Javanese culture was thereafter governed by the fear of volcanoes and oppressed by the brutality of nature.

The oppressors then gave way to a Hindu named Sakaji (or Aji Saka, after whom the Saka calendar was named), who responded to the curse by implanting offerings permanently into the ground to counteract the forces of the Atlantean rulers. One of these offerings was the hill on which Borobudur was later erected, beneath which was the nail; and Borobudur was, therefore, in Leadbeater's history, a monument built to commemorate the implanting of the nail to subdue the volcanoes. It was a permanent offering that freed the Javanese from the oppressive forces of nature—a familiar narrative of culture emerging from and through the control of nature—in this case, volcanic nature.

Leadbeater thus drew a line from Atlantis to the construction of Borobudur in the eighth century. He also borrowed from Hinloopen Labberton and Kern to invoke the story on the Calcutta Stone: "Merapi threw out an incredible amount of sand and ashes, destroying almost the whole of Erlanggha's Mid-Java kingdom, and entirely burying . . . Borobudur. . . . Some centuries passed before it was possible to re-occupy Mid-Java."[43] The offerings, it seemed, failed, though we do not learn why from Leadbeater's account, only that the Javanese are descended from these earliest people and that their greatest monuments were erected to free themselves from the tyranny of volcanic nature—in the end only to perish by the very same volcanic forces they had tamed. For Leadbeater, Theosophy was, in part, a project of revealing these hidden and ruined histories to connect contemporary Javanese culture to its primordial past and ancient genealogy. Such a project dismissed Islamic influence in Java; cultural renewal, so he thought, occurred through a resurrection of the pre-Islamic past and in this way, then, the Theosophists saw themselves as also giving back to the colonized their culture. To Javanese Muslims (which nearly all were), they would reveal and restore the memories of their own forgotten achievements—they would remind the Javanese of the Hindu beneath the "Mohammadean garb."

Leadbeater's nostalgia for the Hindu past may have been associated with his yearning for a hierarchical caste system in Javanese society. In 1929, he was in Java for the fifth time when he defended Dutch colonialism because of the "pedagogical work" it could do for Natives. He praised the hierarchy of the Hindu caste system and asked that Native Indonesians bow to him in Theosophical meetings. In the same year, he was also beset with issues in the Theosophical organization; the child Messiah that he and Besant claimed to have discovered wandering on a beach in Adyar in 1909, Jiddu Krishnamurti, had defected from the organization and denounced them. Theosophy was by that point world famous but on shaky ground. While back in Java, Hinloopen Labberton was arguing strongly against decolonization and rising postcolonial nationalism. For both Hinloopen Labberton and Leadbeater, narratives of the cataclysmic destruction of Java were ways to undermine the influence of Islam and to celebrate the rigid hierarchies of the Hindu-Buddhist caste system at the very same moment that Dutch colonial hierarchies seemed to be in their twilight years.

AD 1006: THE CATASTROPHE · Hinloopen Labberton's interpretation of the Calcutta Stone found support in scientific evidence only in 1941, twenty-one years after it had been presented it to the Royal Academy. Reinout van Bemmelen, after visiting Merapi, wrote:

> MERAPI—State during 1941—In outward appearance, the Merapi was quiet. . . . In January and July many local tremors were registered (respectively 48 and 52). Avalanches of the lava dome and of the upper slopes of the cone occurred only sporadically. The present active Merapi cone rises above the ruins of the one that was destroyed [in] 1006 A.D.[44]

Van Bemmelen likely knew of Hinloopen Labberton's interpretation of the Calcutta Stone from his presentation in Batavia or its republication in *Natuurkundig Tijdschrift voor Nederlandsch-Indië*. His interpretation provided the first physical evidence from the landscape that linked the ruins of Central Java and the decline of Javanese culture to a single cataclysmic volcanic event. Van Bemmelen found the evidence when he was on Merapi to monitor an increase in volcanic activity. His work led him to map the volcano, and in doing so he saw for the first time the remains of the ancient eruption. To better understand his reasoning, we need to first examine the conditions under which van Bemmelen was on Merapi in 1941 and the theory that allowed him to connect it to AD 1006.

The "outward appearance of quiet," he described, began in 1939, when he witnessed thick, tough lava rising through the conduit and appearing at the summit. When the lava hit cold air, it solidified into a plug, trapping the molten, viscous lava below. Bursts of it continued to rise through cracks, oozing through the plug, and van Bemmelen foresaw that in a "very quiet way," the lava was spilling into the crater until it reached a breach in the western wall and rolled down the slope. As it flowed, the outer surface of the lava cooled and hardened into a thin stone skin while the interior remained liquid. The rocky dermis weighed on the liquid below until it cracked, and then ignited; the lava then grew another new layer of stone skin, only to crack again.

Van Bemmelen thought these were the symptoms of the end of an eruption cycle. The eruption cycle began with the extrusion of lava, followed by large explosions.[45] As lava protruded through the conduit, it shattered and incinerated the plug, creating earthquakes, rock falls, and avalanches. The plug fell into itself, igniting a furnace of hot clouds that shot to the upper edges of the troposphere. As the volume diminished over months, perhaps years, so too did the severity of the explosions. Eventually they were followed by the strengthening and rigidifying of the plug, which, according to van Bemmelen, lasted approximately one year. At the end of it all, the cycle would begin again: new lava injected from the inside, extrusion, explosions, diminution, and quiet.

Van Bemmelen considered the process cyclical, in part because he thought that *all* orogeny was cyclical. Since the early 1930s he drew on and significantly developed his theory of *undation*, according to which, as Erich Haarmann argued, the earth's crust was bulging from a "yet unknown cosmic force."[46] These bulges would crack and fall under the weight of gravity, forming ripples and folds across earth's surface like waves in a pond. These processes, he understood, were defined by cycles.

Van Bemmelen was convinced that undation provided a synthesis of current geological theories. Unlike his Dutch colonial contemporaries, who were exploring ideas of continental drift that imagined continents plowing through a liquid substratum, undation posited vertical uplift and bulging followed by lateral displacement as the primordial force driving the horizontal movement of continents. It was not that van Bemmelen was a staunch fixist, like many US and European geologists were at the time; it was rather that his understanding of the mechanism of drift substantially departed from Vening Meinesz's, Umbgrove's, and Wegener's. Like many of his geologist contemporaries, Van Bemmelen understood that the earth's outer layers were defined by a primordial differentiation between two substances, *sima* and *sial*: the upper and lower layers of the crust and mantle. "The real foundation of the Undation theory is," his colleague Molengraaff wrote about van Bemmelen, "this tendency to differentiation of the outmost 100 km of the original silicate mantle as a consequence of its cooling."[47] In other words, during the earth's early stages, an explosive, hot, liquid material separated from a hard, cold, exterior skin. The material that formed the earth underwent a primal process of differentiation that separated interior from exterior, solid from liquid, and this original differentiation set in motion all the other differentiations that followed. Here van Bemmelen was in the company of Blavatsky, who had written about the primal differentiation of the universe, and supported a broader theme common to both geology and theology: how the earth and cosmos proceeded from wholeness to differentiation, from one to many; undation was, in this way, also a cosmology undertaken with modern scientific methods.

For van Bemmelen, volcanoes were "necks"—or, perhaps again echoing Blavatsky's schema, the "point in the Mundane Egg"—through which this primordial differentiation between surface and subsurface, solid and liquid, could be witnessed. Van Bemmelen often described undations as giant waves, and volcanism was the mechanism that transferred the interior to the exterior, where it then weighed down and compressed the surface back into the earth. Undations were the mechanism through which the earth's surface reproduced itself. This rising and falling would, van Bemmelen thought, have a rhythm to it—not a mechanical beat like a machine, but a loose, irregular rhythm.

Measuring the rhythm required identifying its geography, including the shape and dimensions of undations. Where did they begin and end? How big were they, and how much did they weigh? He first had to map them to identify their cycles and shed light on the relationship between individual volcanoes and the system, or the undation, they belonged to. This was why he ordered the first detailed geological map of Merapi. Understanding its undation could shed light on its eruption cycles and—crucially—help determine whether it was about to erupt.

Throughout 1941, fieldwork was undertaken to compose the map. Van Bemmelen drew his own schematic version based on the results at a scale of 1:50,000, which for the first time explained the distinction between two separate Merapis, one ancient and one modern (figure 4.2). He determined that the caldera was in fact inside a much larger and more ancient one. This allowed him to understand that the explosive, eruptive activity witnessed throughout the year was the result of the "young Merapi." This also suggested that eruption cycles were perhaps more varied than previously supposed, operating on modern and ancient time scales at the same time.

He pointed to the protruding hills, each 300 or 400 meters tall, on the flanks, sometimes forested or cultivated with tobacco and vegetables at Gunung Toergo, Gunung Plawangan, and Gunung Kendil;[48] and he argued that they were "parasitic," protruding from the old cone, like pipes into the subterranean magma system.[49] The "young Merapi," he saw, was filling the void of the old. Then he turned to Hinloopen Labberton: "A Sanskrit and Old-Javanese stone-inscription relates the story of a flood

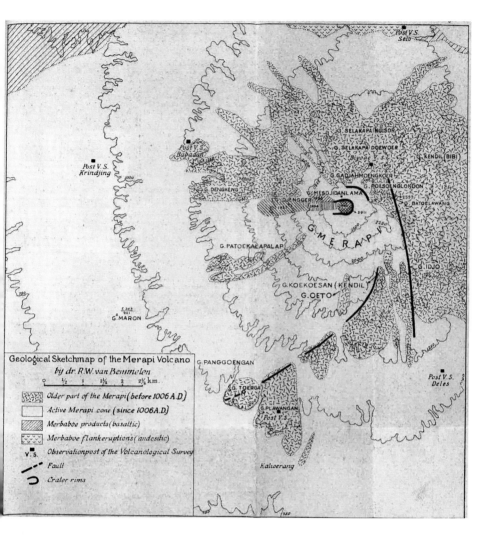

FIGURE 4.2 Mount Merapi with its pre-1006 eruptive material marked with dark hatch. Reinout W. van Bemmelen, "Geological Sketchmap of the Merapi Volcano," *Kogyo Jimusho, Bulletin of the East Indian Volcanological Survey for the Year 1941*, nos. 95–98 (1943/1949): figure 17.

of calamities, having occurred in 928 Sjaaka (AD 1006). . . . The stone inscription speaks of the Maha Pralaya of Java, which means the end of an epoch of the country by a natural calamity. . . . Since then Central Java was suddenly silenced for centuries. The Hindu-Javanese Culture shifted to East Java."[50] Van Bemmelen thus found the evidence of the stone inscription in the landscape by attempting to determine the cyclical nature of volcanic history. He came to see Merapi as a ruin, surrounded by the ruins of Javanese culture on its flanks. His insight was similar in key respects to Verbeek and Fennema's, from their 1896 *Description géologique de Java et Madoura*; they also understood Java's volcanoes to be the ruins of once great mountains. What was different in van Bemmelen's interpretation was his sense of futurity. His understanding of the cyclical nature of volcanological time was related to his own anxieties that Merapi was about to explode. He had witnessed a massive eruption of Merapi in 1930, merely a decade earlier, and he believed it could potentially erupt again in a massive, cataclysmic, and culture-annihilating moment. Van Bemmelen's map gave expression to the anxiety that the colonial world of the Netherlands East Indies could be on the verge of becoming another ruined civilization on the slopes of Merapi.

As Couperus wrote, "Beneath all this peace of grandeur the danger threatens and the future mutters like subterranean thunder in the volcanoes, inaudible to human ears."

IN A JAPANESE JAIL · It should not be surprising that van Bemmelen was coming to terms with the impermanence of the colony given the surge in anticolonial struggles and the onset of the Second World War. The decline of Javanese Hindu-Buddhist culture was being thought together with the rhythms of volcanic catastrophe at the very moment that the permanence of the colony seemed in doubt. Only a few months after van Bemmelen discovered the physical causes of AD 1006, the colony crossed a threshold. On March 7, 1942, government offices in Bandung were bombed; the Japanese army then threatened to attack Batavia, and the following day the Dutch government signed an unconditional surrender.[51] Colonial government services, including the geological and volcanological departments were dissolved, and 7,000 civilians from Bandung were sent to internment camps.[52] Scientists were forced to mine for metals and coal for the war effort. Van Bemmelen, his wife, Lucie, and son, Nout, were sent to internment camps; Lucie's mother later starved to death in a camp in Ambarawa.[53]

Van Bemmelen was imprisoned with six other geologist colleagues until Merapi began to erupt; he was then put in charge of the volcanological service, renamed Kosan Kakari.[54] Some have questioned why van Bemmelen was asked (or volunteered) when his other colleagues remained imprisoned, and it has been suggested that he was a traitor for cooperating with the Japanese.[55] What is certain is that he traveled to Merapi with Colonel Wada because the authorities were concerned with evacuating the population, and Wada ordered him to continue his studies. Van Bemmelen's reports were addressed to the ruling authorities in Nippon and adopted the imperial Japanese calendar, beginning with the founding of the Japanese kingdom in 660 BCE. The year 1942 became 2602.[56] The cycle of outflow had lasted nine months during 1939–40, van Bemmelen maintained, and the current cycle was already eight months along and looked similar. He concluded, "We may predict that the present cycle will end in the near future."[57]

Shortly thereafter, he was returned to an internment camp where he stayed until the end of the war. A bitter struggle for Indonesian independence against the reestablishment of the Netherlands colony ensued, and the retreating Japanese military either willingly transferred their weapons or they were seized by Indonesian nationalists, some of whom, including Sukarno, were associated with the same Theosophist lodges that had fomented the Hindu-Buddhist revival.[58] The German director of the volcanological service, Charles Stehn, died in prison in British India in 1945, and van Bemmelen wrote his obituary.[59] The Chinese Indonesian scientist Tan Sin Hok, who was a colleague of Johannes Umbgrove's, was killed in Bandung, perhaps for being Chinese and a high-ranking colonial collaborator, "by a horde of extremist Indonesians," as his obituary put it. His house was burned down as his wife and children fled.[60] The Netherlands reestablished a government and vied for control by reopening agencies. It resulted in standoffs between postcolonial Republican and Dutch colonial offices. The Dienst van de Mijnbouw (Department of Mines), for instance, reopened in Bandung, but its rival, the independent Indonesian republican office opened in Magelang and then moved to Yogyakarta. This duel between competing governments lasted into the 1950s.

Released from the camps amid a hostile postcolonial environment and without a job to return to, van Bemmelen repatriated to Holland and rewrote his manuscript for *The Geology of Indonesia*. He continued to develop his theory of undation against the grain of popular geological theories, and his work became more explicitly cosmic and theological: "The earth's rhythm," he wrote in 1972, "is composed of a great variety of periodicities" that accumulate into a great cosmic polyphony. "All geodynamic processes develop harmoniously," according to the imminent laws of matter and "propelled by the primeval energy of our cosmic system. . . . This is the 'dynamic harmony' of our cosmic evolution."[61] It became an aesthetic cosmology

inspired by the beauty of the geological-cosmic system, written by someone in exile after the end of the colony. He continued to believe in the
cyclical nature of geological processes and that they represented cosmic
forces of harmony and destruction. Mountain building and thus volcanism were the expression of this dualism. This also formed his conception of human life and culture; as he put it in 1954, "Mountain building
provides the very basis of our existence on earth."[62] One could not, therefore, distinguish volcanology and anthropology.

He thought that the purpose of human life and civilization was to understand the dynamism of the cosmic order so as to live in accord with it.

In the internment camp, he wrote:

I believe in beauty
From God the Creator of Nature
I believe in the Sacred
From the fire full of passion

'42–'45
In a Japanese jail
R.W. VAN BEMMELEN[63]

A NATIONALIST VOLCANO · The year AD 1006 had a different fate in postcolonial Indonesia. The Hindu and Buddhist past was eclipsed in the new
Republic of Indonesia by the novel significance of the Central Javanese
sultanates of Yogyakarta and Surakarta. This final section examines the
pivot away from Hindu-Buddhist revivalism in the aftermath of decolonization to a nationalist history centered on Islam. This transition transformed how the agency of Merapi was understood to have shaped Javanese history and culture.

Publications by the volcanological service ceased in 1941, and observatory outposts had been ransacked during the tumult of the revolution. George A. de Neve wrote that "at the transfer of Sovereignty [to
the Indonesian Republic], the Volcanological Survey could be satisfied
with fifteen maximum thermometers and a Rolleiflex-camera!"[64] Observatories were rebuilt wherever possible, but by 1950 there were only six
personnel in the Dinas Gunung Berapi (Volcanological Survey, formerly
Vulkanologisch Onderzoek) to monitor more than sixty volcanoes.[65] Air
reconnaissance of Merapi was undertaken in November 1950 and again
at the beginning of 1953 to survey great distances with few personnel

FIGURE 4.3 Mount Merapi as seen from the air. *Berita Gunung Berapi* 1, nos. 1–2 (September–December 1952): 44.

(figure 4.3). Flying also allowed scientists to bypass political conflicts on the ground.[66] Darul Islam had proclaimed an Islamic state, seceded from the republic and controlled a volcanic region in West and Central Java that spanned the peaks of Galunggung, Telaga Bodas, and Guntur.[67] Cornelis van Dijk explained that "into these so-called '*de facto* territories of the Islamic State of Indonesia' no Republican Army soldier dared venture."[68] Republican volcano scientists would not have fared any better.

The first volcano-related publication of the new republic appeared in December 1952 under the title *Berita Gunung Berapi* (Volcano news) (figure 4.4). It was a popular magazine directed at bringing volcano science to a broad republican, nationalist readership. It contained poetry and was written in Indonesian, English, French, and Javanese. There was an obituary for Suwarnaatmadja, a scientist killed by a volcanic eruption on Kelud in 1951, set among surveys of the activity of the archipelago's volcanoes. The editorial explained how its editors imagined the magazine playing

a role in such a "heavy" national moment: "The form is still simple—like ancient humans—but our hopes are grand: with the publication of this magazine, we hope the people will pick it up with cheer and use it as a tool in our national development."[69]

During 1946 and 1947, according to the magazine, "nothing of importance occurred" on Merapi.[70] The cycle of ejecting lava, hardening, then stabilizing, which van Bemmelen had witnessed during the war, had subsided. This quiescence lasted for almost a year until September 29, 1948, when the lava that had risen and hardened under van Bemmelen's watch, now had new lava injected into it. Republican scientists undertook an expedition to the summit and witnessed blocks and boulders shedding from the new lava dome plug, and rock falls were counted twenty-five times a day.[71]

Nothing major occurred until 1953, when observers noticed that Merapi was again increasing in activity. Blue smoke was appearing, and the dome was expanding. It pushed against the crater wall, and in March a piece fell off and became a landslide. Ash was soon dusting leaves on the western slope. The following month, scientists noticed that a new lava plug had formed on the northwestern part of the caldera. They were like eyes, "clearly seen at night as two glowing points,"[72] out of which avalanches and hot clouds emerged. Observers understood that the source of the lava was moving inside the dome and that the conduit was shifting its path. In May, there were more than two thousand avalanches from a new source, all of them flowing down the western slope into the Apu River.[73] The observers sought to catalog the new developments, but their instruments were unreliable. For five months, the seismographs at Babadan were either broken or their components malfunctioned, and the recordings on paper were unclear or incomplete. With unreliable equipment, observer accounts contained gaps that would continue to plague the organization for years.

Later that year, in December 1953, more than nine hundred avalanches were recorded.[74] In the middle of that month, on December 20, President Sukarno inaugurated the Shiva temple at Prambanan in front of more than a thousand spectators and a sea of red and white Indonesian flags.[75] The event was part of the new republican nationalist strategy to create "unity in diversity." Sukarno said he would not pray to Siva, but that local Hindus were welcome to do so. The Theosophist concern with the Hindu past and the golden age of Javanese civilization was eclipsed by a future-oriented Indonesian nationalism.

Borobudur and Prambanan had been restored by Dutch colonial archaeologists captivated by the Javanese early modern golden age, and their work continued haphazardly in the new and unsteady period. The Dinas Purbakala Republik Indonesia (Archeological Service of the Republic of Indonesia) and its archaeologists had been trained by the Dutch, and in the postrevolutionary period they continued their work within the framework of a postcolonial nationalist future. Maintaining ethnic and cultural diversity without exacerbating factional conflicts was one of Sukarno's primary geopolitical concerns, and the heritage projects of Borobudur and Prambanan were part of his strategy of articulating the unity of a state with thousands of languages, cultures, and identities; the temples were also crucial to asserting the central significance of Java as the historical center of Indonesian civilization and culture, which dovetailed with the importance of Java as the site of governance and the capital city in Jakarta. But recapturing the lost glory days of early modern Java was no longer on the horizon nor pursued with the same energy and significance as during the late colonial period.

Instead of being epicenters for the revival of the Hindu-Buddhist past, the sultanates of Yogyakarta and Surakarta acquired a new significance as the symbolic foci of a new postcolonial mystical-technical republicanism. Sultan Hamengkubuwono IX, who had appointed Maridjan as gatekeeper of Merapi, had refused to cooperate with the Dutch authorities when they sought to reclaim the city after the departure of the Japanese army. With the permission of the sultan, Sukarno and Hatta established the first independent government of the republic in Yogyakarta while the country was still officially under the rule of the Dutch. In return for the support, Sukarno allowed the sultanate to be recognized in the constitution and the sultan to remain the hereditary governor of the realm within the republic. No other sultanate was granted the same privileges. When Sukarno inaugurated the Shiva temple, it was within the Republic of Indonesia but also the realm of Hamengkubuwono IX. In the 1950s, Sukarno was reported to have adopted the much older practices of the sultans by sleeping with Nyai Ratu Kidul in a hotel close to the Indian Ocean. His consorting with her signaled the republican alignment between the presidency and the history of the sultanate, with the president as the continuation of the sultanate line; or at least it was a continuation of the tradition of powerful rulers requiring marriage with the goddess to maintain their power. The axis between Merapi and the South Sea, along with the *labuhan* to deities in the volcanoes and the ocean, persisted in the postcolonial ruling Javanese conception of Islamic Indonesian political power; and volcano science was brought into alignment, too.

In 1953, the first central observatory was established in Yogyakarta to coordinate the activities of the seven observatories and watchtowers on Merapi's flanks.[76] It would organize and execute evacuations of three major regions: the sultanates of Surakarta and Yogyakarta, and the Kedu plain.[77] The stations were connected through radio and telephone;[78] they consolidated the management of Merapi to Yogyakarta, away from its previous sites in Magelang and Muntilan to the west, and brought Merapi's management within the realm of the sultan (figures 4.5 and 4.6). The result was to unify the history of the sultanate and its deep political geological relationship with Merapi with republican optimism for modern science. In 1954, Sukarno and Hatta visited the Merapi observatory at Babadan, a few kilometers from the caldera. It is telling that they conducted their tour flanked by Sultan Hamengkubuwono IX and George A. de Neve, the director of the republican Volcanological Service and one of the authors of *Berita Gunung Berapi*.[79] The four men represented the new republican synthesis of volcanology that brought together the legacy of Mataram, science, and the postcolony. They toured villages near the observatory and comforted survivors of recent eruptions, but they were also there to inaugurate the opening of the renovated observatory and to inspect the most recent evacuation and monitoring strategies. Sukarno was photographed waving outside the observatory (figure 4.7), while Hatta was photographed using the radio that would connect the observatories

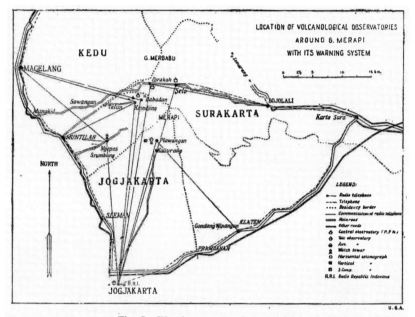

Fig. 5. Warning system of G. Merapi.

Main duties of P.P.M. :
1. Compiling all reports from Merapi observatories.
2. Executing the warning instructions in case of danger.
3. Renewing Merapi's guarding system, adapted to present conditions (condition of the volcano itself and of the slopes).
4. To carry out summit investigations (particularly from the air).

Activity in 1953.

FIGURE 4.5 This map shows the new warning system for Mount Merapi, centered in Yogyakarta. It reflects the new nationalist technological networks and imaginaries superimposed on the spiritual coordinates of the sultanate. Surjo, "Volcanic Activities in Indonesia during the 1950–1957 Period," *Berita Berkala Volkanologi*, no. 100 (July 18, 1961): 35.

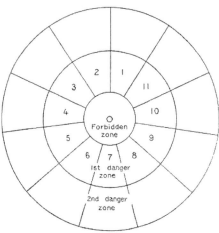

The division of the Merapi
in
3 concentric zones and 11 sectors.

FIGURE 4.6 The new division of Mount Merapi into concentric danger zones. Surjo, "The Merapi Guarding System," *Chigaku Zasshi* (Journal of geography) 67, no. 4 (1958): 34.

FIGURE 4.7 President Sukarno at Babadan, Djajawinangun (1954). Courtesy Balai Penyelidikan dan Pengembangan Teknologi Kebencanaan Geologi archive.

on the peak with the headquarters in Yogyakarta. They were accompanied by a film crew that documented their visit, and they gave speeches to crowds in front of the observatory. The new communications network plugged the observatories into the sultanate and the republic. The old conception of the sultanate governing and being governed by the volcano and the sea was thus folded into the new radio and telephonic nationalist infrastructure.

THE LEGACY OF THEOSOPHY IN JAVANESE MYSTICISM · Theosophists largely left Java during the revolution. Hinloopen Labberton, after a period spent in Japan as the president of the Theosophy Lodge, retired to Ojai, north of Los Angeles, where he lived in a community founded by Krishnamurti, the Messiah who had defected. Charles Leadbeater moved to Australia, where there was a growing Theosophy movement. He wanted to be its guiding light, and he founded a new group of saints, "The Seven Virgins of Java," composed of seven young women from prominent European Netherlands East Indies families (some of whom were also Masons) who emigrated with him. They were somehow related to his ideas about the "World Mother," a powerful female deity governing the world.[80] In Java, Theosophist lodges had lost their significance during the republican struggle, and the movement fizzled. Some of its energies and core preoccupations, though, found expression in other movements such as Subud and later Kejawen, or Javanism.

Subud was founded in 1933 by Muhammad Subuh Sumohadiwidjojo, an accountant for Sultan Hamengkubuwono IX, who apparently experienced a star falling on his head every night for several months. He conceived of this and other signs as indications that he was meant to lead a new spiritual movement. He then began organizing a group called Susila Budhi Dharma—its portmanteau became Subud—in Yogyakarta and then Jakarta. Subuh identified as a Muslim, but the movement was nonsectarian. Instead, it was focused around the *latihan*—Indonesian for "practice"—a form of group silent meditation in which members would make direct contact with spiritual forces in ways that sometimes resembled possession and ecstasy. The group expanded its international network in 1957, when Subuh met John G. Bennett at his estate in Coombes Springs, Kingston-on-Thames, southwest of London (figures 4.8 and 4.9). Bennett became an advocate for Subud to his British and US followers, some of whom were celebrities and film stars, including Eva Bartok.[81] Before meeting Subuh,

Bennett had been a key go-between between Islamic mysticism and sympathetic British audiences in the post-Theosophy world, introducing and advocating for George Gurdjieff and Pyotr Ouspensky, publishing several books about them, and translating their work. Bennett's work also operated at the intersection of spirituality and geology: between 1938 and 1944, he was the first director general of the British Coal Utilization Research Association, which was funded by coal mine owners and the UK labor government. The association was focused on the scientific development of coal and energy usage for industrial development, and Bennet's coal mining in Turkey and Greece coincided with his introduction to Theosophy and his growing relationships with Ouspensky and Gurdjieff in Constantinople. Energy, unsurprising given his work with coal, was a key motif in Bennett's thinking, and like Theosophists, he envisioned his project as the unification of "Asiatic" spiritual traditions with modern science. When he later became an advocate for Subud, it was because he understood that Subud was the most recent incarnation of a spiritual movement that could save humankind from alienation. By way of Bennett's and others' work as go-betweens, Subud expanded its international network and in 1971 held its fourth World Congress at the sprawling Subud compound in Jakarta. Nearly two thousand members arrived from eighty countries, and Suharto spoke at the opening ceremony, blessing the movement for its ambition to "better mankind" and emphasizing, awkwardly, that it was not a cult.[82] In the same year, the organization founded a bank, the Subud World Bank, which later became Bank Susila Bakti, one of the largest banks in Indonesia.[83] The group established an engineering and architecture consultancy, International Design Consultants, in 1966, and by 1968 they had built factories and schools in Jakarta.[84] In 1972, they built a utopian mining village for the Canadian mining company International Nickel (PT INCO) in Sulawesi, on the shores of Lake Matano. The town included six hundred houses as well as schools, a hospital, a supermarket, and a growth plan for a projected population of eight thousand over ten years. In the early 1980s, Subud also led a large-scale redevelopment plan for central Sydney's Darling Harbour, where they intended to include a large building for the latihan. The building was axed by the New South Wales government, but the master plan remained largely intact.

Subud was a modern capitalist-mystical organization, merging regimented latihan group practices wherein spiritual forces directly possessed its followers with an expansive drive for business and an overt insistence on development, progress, and the moral perfectibility of mankind. The

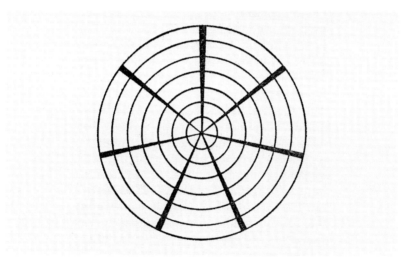

FIGURE 4.8 J. G. Bennett and Muhammad Subuh at Coombe Springs, UK.

FIGURE 4.9 The Subud emblem, "The Seven Soul Powers." For J. G. Bennett, the symbol represented modernity: "The circle has always been regarded as the symbol of endlessness, for it has no stopping point. The circle as a symbol means that belief in the possibility of unlimited development, endless progress of the human soul." J. G. Bennett, *Concerning Subud* (London: Hodder and Stoughton, 1959), 112–13.

Australian engineer Raymond van Sommers, who met Subuh through Bennett at Coombe Springs, became one of the organization's core members and dedicated disciples. He described the spiritual dimension of completing the master plan for the mining town in Sulawesi after grueling hours of work: "The surprising result was that I passed through the fatigue and—*feeling totally at one with my own nature*—I was able to complete the extensive report and documentation on time. This was such a powerful spiritual experience that when it was complete I felt that I should present a copy to [Subuh]. I knew that he would understand."[85]

As Theosophy did for colonial industrialists and plantation owners in Java, Subud promised a new spirit of capitalism, a spiritual practice for engineers, factory owners, financiers, and others disillusioned with Christianity or Islam but unsatisfied with secularism. It promised unalienated labor and a re-enchantment with work, progress, and world development. But when Subuh died in 1987, the organization no longer had a charismatic leader, and it fizzled and largely disappeared, forgotten by all except a few scattered practitioners.

AD 1006 TODAY · The appeal of the date AD 1006 as a marker of Javanese cultural cataclysm continued to simmer away in archaeologists' and geologists' circles and in the popular press. The Indonesian archaeologist Boechari in 1976 revisited van Bemmelen's evidence of the ancient eruption but pushed the date later, claiming that the *prahlaya* was in 1016, and argued that Kern had misunderstood the date on the Calcutta Stone.[86] The French filmmaker and volcanologist duo Katia and Maurice Krafft (whom we will meet again in chapter 6) were also drawn in to the narrative, and in 1976 they wrote: "The summit of Merapi was pulverized . . . and covered the center of Java in a thick layer of ash."[87] In 1979, Barry Newman, a journalist for the *Wall Street Journal*, was in Krindjing, on the flank of Merapi, writing a story when he too reported that in 1006 Central Java had been destroyed.[88]

But the notion that one giant eruption destroyed medieval Java started to lose its purchase throughout the 1970s and 1980s as archaeological evidence began to reveal that eruptions may have occurred multiple times throughout the ninth, tenth, and eleventh centuries.[89] Some argued that it may not have been a huge eruption at all and that Hinloopen Labberton may have been mistaken in his interpretation of the meaning of *pralaya*. Perhaps Kern had been correct, and it had been a war waged between rival states that caused the collapse of early modern Javanese civilization. Others argued that disease had decimated the population, or perhaps the laborers who built Borobudur and Prambanan were so tired of end-less work and enslavement to despots that they gave up on their rulers in an act of mass exodus.[90]

In the early 1980s, volcano scientists from the United States Geological Survey began collaborating with Indonesian scientists to settle the con-troversy. They undertook sediment analysis to recalibrate van Bemmel-en's hypothesis and argued that there was no evidence of a single massive eruption but rather that over time, many small eruptions intersected with social and political forces to compel the Javanese to move eastward. "Ex-plosive eruptions occurred before, during and after construction of the major temples of Central Java," they wrote. "We cannot prove that erup-tions caused the decentralization of civilization in Central Java, but we can say that these early eruptions would have been very disruptive."[91] They imagined food shortages, perhaps famines, and the undoing of irrigation networks and agricultural systems that could have exacerbated already existing social and political fault lines. The collapse of classical Java was thus not a single event but a more gradual multidimensional weakening of social and natural systems. They ended their reflections in a way not dissimilar to van Bemmelen's, speculating that because Merapi had in the past erupted with greater force and devastation than in recent history, it might therefore do so again in the future. They de-emphasized the power of the date AD 1006, even if they still thought that preparations should be made for a future massive eruption. The shift in attitude was decisive, though, and historians and archaeologists were no longer tantalized by the idea of a single date and single event, nor was the enterprise synced up with a colonial attempt to push against Islam and reveal to the Java-nese their true natures as Hindus and Buddhists.

THE LURE OF GEODETERMINISM · Salam village is a few kilometers east of Borobudur. In early 2004, a farmer there was digging an irrigation ditch to expand his small palm plantation when his spade hit the stone roof of a buried Hindu Temple. Over the next few years, the local university ar-chaeology department and government agencies excavated four temples, the largest of which was four and a half meters tall. The tops had long vanished, but some intricate ornamentation was still legible: above the opening to the *Lingaa*, the carved phallic volcanic stone on which milk, honey, and flowers would have been poured, was a smiling fanged dragon watching over worshippers. A relief of Mahakala, one of Siva's avatars and guardian of the underworld, was on another wall. Lokapala, guardian of the cardinal directions, protruded from another rough stone surface.

On a hot August afternoon in 2019, I drove down the main road through Salam to visit the temples. The village was freshly painted in anticipation of Independence Day celebrations, and large portraits of national heroes, including Sukarno and Hatta, hung from lampposts while red and white national flags fluttered in the light wind. We pulled up to a rusty fence and were signaled by a guard to enter. Losari, excavated and on display to tourists, was protected from the elements under a corrugated roof. It is likely that the temples had been buried by hundreds, if not thousands, of years of silt overflowing from Merapi. The elderly guardian of the site, Wiranto, explained that only a few months earlier another temple had been discovered a few hundred meters away in a rice field; it was from the same period, the glory days of the Hindu-Buddhist kingdoms—which, he explained, had been "destroyed by a massive eruption in 1006."

It is perhaps no surprise that anxieties over the end of the world and cultural extinction come and go. Nor is it a surprise that they are ways of thinking through and digesting the pressures of a moment. For colonial scientists and their interlocutors, the disappearance of medieval Java was important to think about as the Netherlands East Indies were waning and, indeed, as European colonialism was on increasingly shaky foundations around the world. Thinking about cultural decline by way of volcanic cataclysm was simultaneously a way to consider the fragility of the colonial project, progress, and the achievements of civilization. It was also a way for colonial scientists and ethnologists to participate in cultural revivalism. Volcanoes became figures of the untamable, a nature beyond control, in the late colonial imaginary, and thinking about their volatile unpredictability went hand in hand with reflection on the political systems that caused or intersected with them. Javanese nationalism was the "subterranean thunder" that Couperus had in mind, and decolonization was a kind of energy ready to burst to the surface. And when it did, it was no surprise that it was forward-looking and less concerned with natural calamities in the past. The postcolonial moment was too fresh and fragile to worry too much about its own passing; as Rudolf Mrázek described the new republic, it was weightless.[92]

Tracing the shifting meaning of AD 1006 reminds us of the malleable and contingent ways in which volcanological forces are understood to be part of society. For Theosophists and colonial volcanologists, thinking with volatile geology was never distinct from engaging with speculative, theological, and mythical narratives of the earth and cosmos. In other words, volcanology was theology by other means; narratives of cultural collapse were made sense of through this mixture of Christian, Hindu, and Buddhist stories of how the earth enabled cultures to thrive or brought them to their ends. Volcano science became a way to sink theological narratives into the physicality of the ground, to give them a secularized framework by making them measurable and observable. The year AD 1006 was geotheology.

CHAPTER FIVE

GEOPOETICS

Johannes Umbgrove's Cosmic
and Aesthetic Science

Standing next to it, on it, in the middle of it . . .
JOHANNES UMBGROVE, 1928

THE ORIGINS OF GEOPOETICS IN JAVA · Johannes Umbgrove was perhaps the first Western geologist to describe his method as geopoetics. He developed the idea in two influential works, *The Pulse of the Earth*, from 1942, and *The Symphony of the Earth*, from 1950. They were widely read at the time by European and US geologists and influenced their thinking, but they have since been neglected outside of specialist circles. These impressively synthetic and synoptic texts sought to bring together the history of the galaxy, the earth, the lithosphere, species, and consciousness. Linking all of this, as the core mechanism, was volcanism. Umbgrove was, like his predecessor and inspiration Eduard Suess, a synthetic geologist who wanted to theorize the fundamental structures of the earth, all living things, and the universe. Indeed, one of the goals of geopoetics was to connect across vast spatial and temporal scales and not, as it has subsequently come to mean, poetry about geology. For Umbgrove, geopoetics was poetic because it was speculative; it worked at the limit of what was known by science to connect diverse strands of knowledge. Crucially, geopoetics was also scalar: it meant connecting across scales; it did the work of showing how the smallest dimensional entities connected with the largest, and the nearest with the most distant. In this sense, it was ecological; it insisted on thinking relationality as ontologically primary, as the basis of being. Umbgrove also called it *complementarity*, a science of connectivity and cosmic cohabitation.

What was also remarkable about Umbgrove's geopoetics was that it was created in Java and influenced by his encounters with Javanese volcanoes, Islam, and Hinduism. Geopoetics was another product of the Javanese spiritual tradition that went on to shape the modern science of earth systems. Rather than geopoetics being counter to the tradition of the modern sciences, it was central to their very development: scientists saw themselves as practicing *geopoetry* in their reconstruction of the history of the earth; and geopoetics allowed for the development of new earth narratives in an early and mid-twentieth-century context of geological theory that often shunned big, speculative ideas. Umbgrove's conception of geopoetics also enabled geologists to think through the relationship between catastrophic events in the history of the earth and the increasingly long durations of time that were coming to be known. But above all, the really underappreciated significance of geopoetics was that it was a dandy science, unashamedly excessive, speculative, and fascinated by beauty; it was science that saw that the cosmos, earth, and humankind must be profusely, gorgeously, unexpectedly connected. We are lithic, planetary, and cosmic in all our excessive differentiation. The geopoet-dandy-scientist's work was to trace the powers of difference-making that pulsed through the earth and cosmos; it was a celebration. A history of geopoetics is a history of the underground and overlooked story of dandy geology, a history forged on the slopes of Javanese volcanoes and in conversation with the spiritual traditions of that island that enabled Western geologists to rethink everything.

The concept of geopoetics developed by Umbgrove in Java does not resemble the typical contemporary usage of the term. Recently, geopoetics has become significant in literary theory and nature writing linked with the French-Scottish writer and scholar Kenneth White. White used the term to explain how literary and narrative traditions shaped geographical space and how geography has transformed the literary imagination. Geopoetics has also been theorized from another direction by geographers. Angela Last has deployed it as a mode of decolonial geophysics by drawing on the Guadeloupian author Daniel Maximin. Last argues that geopoetics is a form of critical thought that exposes how conceptions of nature are linked with and enabled by the geopolitical histories of European empire and colonialism. In Last's reading, Maximin's critical geopoetics leverages the Caribbean as a privileged site through which to read the intersections of empire, science, and conceptions of nature.[1] Geopoetics, by Last's account, is rooted in Caribbean postcolonial thought spanning *négritude*, Fanon, and Glissant. Glissant has been especially fluent at refusing the distinction between the geophysical and cultural or the conception of nature as a stage on which geopolitics unfolds. Instead, Caribbean geopoetics asks "what a geopolitics might look like that proceeds from a 'geo' of permanent material imbalance."[2] The significance of Pelée, the storied stratovolcano on Martinique and the subject of much postcolonial theoretical reflection, cannot be understated in this imaginary of geopolitics. Geopoetics has likewise provided a frame for critical postcolonial geological thought from the outside, as practiced by Kathryn Yusoff, who also was inspired by Caribbean writers.[3] Yet, geopoetics has an earlier history rooted in Java and in dandy science. For Umbgrove, geopoetics did not begin from imbalance, ideas of chaos, or discord but from ideas of linking, cycles, and rhythms. It was a polyphonic vision of a primal force of differentiation that traveled from the deepest regions of the earth's center out to the galaxy. Umbgrove was interested in a vast cosmic connectivity bound together through polyphonic differences, differences that multiplied complexity. Volcanoes were not violent; they were expressions of complex rhythms. Features that Last attributes to colonial geology and geophysics—its desire for control and management of people and nature, the transformation of nature into a resource, the false separation of nature from culture—were also criticized by Umbgrove's geopoetics. He was a geologist with classical geological training, and at the same time, he was a colonial scientist with a deep suspicion of Javanese Islam. His notion of geopoetics was later taken up by Harry Hess, a former soldier who helped articulate the theory that the ocean floor was not immobile but instead spread over time. Geopoetics, then, was both at the center of standard twentieth-century geoscience and at its margins. Umbgrove complicates the picture of the geosciences for us; he was no simple foot soldier of European empire bent on controlling and ordering nature. Instead, as a theorist of a dandy geology, he was inside and out at the same time, in a cosmos of self-differentiation created in Java.

· Geopoetics was Umbgrove's understanding of what it meant to do geology. In contrast to his technically oriented Dutch contemporaries who were often trained as mining engineers, Umbgrove's geological science was based in an overwhelming aesthetic experience. It meant being drawn into the strange and unfamiliar and its capacity to overtake the scientist from the outside in. Landscapes confounded him and beset him with riddles. Geopoetics was not economic geology; he thought that looking for oil was "mind-numbing" and that a company geologist was "exploited as an automaton."[4] "Only if I ever fall into utter poverty and misery, will I have anything to do with BPM," he wrote after visiting the Batavian Oil Company, a subsidiary of Royal Dutch Shell, at one of its extraction sites in Borneo in 1928. "My aversion to such outgrowths of money making has increased in no small measure," he continued.[5] Geopoetics was the antithesis of, even an escape from, economic geology.

His conceptions of a joyful and expansive science had its foundations in Umbgrove's time in Java between 1926 and1929, where he arrived as a twenty-seven-year-old to work in the colonial geology division in Bandung. He came to know and travel with Reinout van Bemmelen and worked under the tutelage of Charles E. Stehn. The world of geology he entered was not defined by strict distinctions between spiritual and scientific pursuits. Their boss, A. C. de Jongh, a mining engineer and director of the Geologische Opsporingsdienst (Geological Survey), was also member of the local Theosophist lodge and had recently published "On the Valency of the Chemical Atoms in Connection with Theosophical Conceptions Concerning Their Exterior Form" in the Occultism section of the 1914 *Theosophist* magazine (figure 5.1). In his article, de Jongh attempted to give a chemical explanation for Charles Leadbeater and Annie Besant's "occult chemistry" experiments from Chennai, in 1908, which formed the basis of their *Occult Chemistry: Clairvoyant Observations on the Chemical Elements*, published in 1914 (figures 5.2, 5.3, and 5.4).[6] In their work, Besant and Leadbeater described that through clairvoyant powers they could "actually *see* a molecule of physical matter." They then used the method of clairvoyance to map and describe the invisible molecular world.[7] De Jongh's article was an attempt to lend scientific credibility to Bessant and Leadbeater's work by combining it with the mainstream understanding of the structure of atoms. Umbgrove, however, was not impressed by the Theosophists or by de Jongh in particular: "Theosophy may in principle have some good in it, but in practice it is quite a delirious movement. Here in the Indies, especially in Bandung, it is flourishing, and their 'lodge' has many members, including our boss [de Jongh] (who is better informed about it than he is about geology)."[8]

The purpose of Umbgrove's professional post was to study coral reef evolution and structure in the Bay of Batavia, so he made frequent visits from Bandung to Batavia and to the islands north of the city by boat. When he was in Bandung, he socialized not in the Theosophist lodge but in the upper-class colonial hotels; he played tennis and violin, and danced (and, in his nearly two hundred letters to his mother during that time, showed little interest in courtship). He read popular histories of the Indies and on weekends, or as frequently as he could, visited calderas around Bandung and Central Java, staying with plantation owners or in colonial hotels. He spent a mobile three years circulating by car or by train between calderas and coral reefs. These routes between volcano and sea influenced his work of the 1930s and 1940s, publishing as he did on coral reef formation, caldera origins, and the structural history of the East Indies and then on the rhythms that govern the earth and cosmos.[9]

Like Van Bemmelen, Umbgrove was fascinated by cyclical time; he tried to reconcile the traditions of geological catastrophism that posited the significance of earthquakes and floods and other unexpected events in geological history with the Lyellian steady-state conception of earth history. For Umbgrove, geological time seemed to be made of both catastrophic events like volcanic eruptions and reliably repetitive events like the rotations of the earth and galaxy. He struggled to understand how novelty emerged in a cosmos of repetitions and to link those repetitions to the production of biological and geological difference. Java's volcanoes compelled him to try and resolve that puzzle.

Umbgrove's thinking was also shaped by the social relations of the colony and its racialized hierarchies. He was able to visit calderas only because of the Javanese drivers who brought him there, the porters who carried his scientific instruments, and, to use his term, his "houseboy" Amir, a native Sundanese, who cooked and cleaned and woke him up in the morning. It was also because of Javanese labor that he toured the Javanese and Sundanese ruins of Central and West Java, which put him in contact with the antiquity of Hinduism and Buddhism that influenced his conception of geopoetics. The staff of the Geological Survey between 1923 and 1933 included thirty-seven trained geologists, the majority of whom were Europeans, and more than one hundred Indonesian staffers.[10] Umbgrove's relationship to these conditions was not unique: he praised the

ON THE VALENCY OF THE CHEMICAL ATOMS

IN CONNECTION WITH THEOSOPHICAL CONCEPTIONS CONCERNING THEIR EXTERIOR FORM

By A. C. de JONGH
Mining Engineer

TRANSLATORS' NOTE:

In fairness to the Author it should be stated that the MS. of the above article was written in Dutch and was translated without the Author's assistance. The translators, a non-chemical Dutchman and an English chemist, ignorant of Dutch, co-operated in the manner of the blind and lame men to the best of their ability. Seeing however the extremely technical nature of the paper—bristling not only with chemical technical

FIGURE 5.1 A. C. de Jongh, a mining engineer, attempted to give scientific credibility to "occult chemistry" in his article "On the Valency of the Chemical Atoms in Connection with Theosophical Conceptions Concerning Their Exterior Form," *Theosophist* 35, no. 10 (July 1914).

I

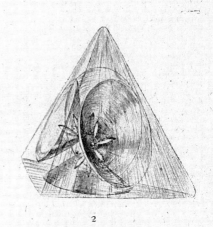

2

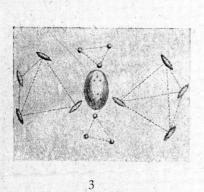

3

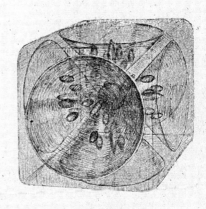

4

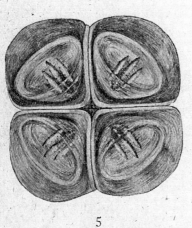

5

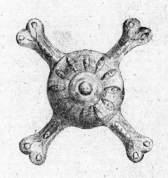

6

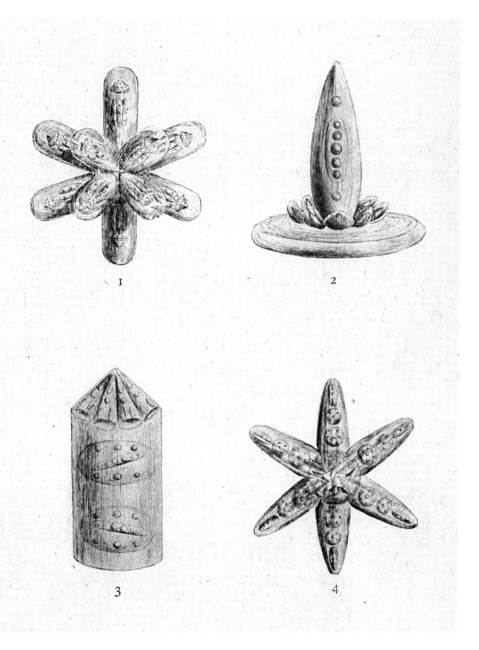

FIGURES 5.2 AND 5.3 Occult visions of molecular structures, according to Annie Besant and Charles Leadbeater. They argued that molecular structures conformed to the Platonic solids. Annie Besant and Charles W. Leadbeater, *Occult Chemistry: Clairvoyant Observations on the Chemical Elements* (London: Theosophical Publishing House, 1919), plates III and IV.

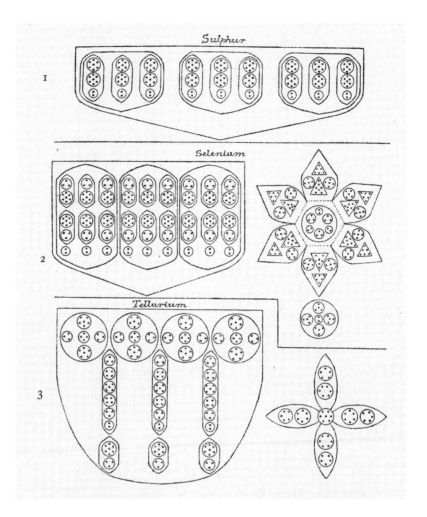

FIGURE 5.4 The occult structure of sulfur, selenium, and tellurium in plan view. Annie Besant and Charles W. Leadbeater, *Occult Chemistry: Clairvoyant Observations on the Chemical Elements* (London: Theosophical Publishing House, 1919), 42.

beauty of the colony and thought it an exemplar of Dutch colonialism and its efforts to modernize the Indies. He thought Dutch colonialism brought progress to the distant colonial outpost, raised the standards of Native life, and brought a superior European culture to a region in decline since the arrival of Islam. His colonialism was, in his mind, and in the minds of many others, benevolent. He was empathetic toward the Sundanese, an ethnicity of West Java, and commented in his letters to his mother on their kindness, gentleness, and meticulousness. He thought that his Sundanese laborers at the geological offices were precise and careful workers. Yet, he also trafficked in familiar stereotypes: he complained that Natives were prone to thievery, unreliable, untrustworthy, and adulterous. Islam was a "scourge," and like his Theosophist and Sanskritist contemporary Dirk van Hinloopen Labberton, he considered it a cloak lying on top of a grander more respectable Hindu and Buddhist tradition.

His views of colonial social structure and his easy adoption of racialized social hierarchies as the narrative of colonial progress reveal foundational tensions in the geopoetic project. For Umbgrove, it was a method of connecting scales from the "remotest distances of the universe to the inmost depths of ourselves"; it was a way of seeing, of illuminating the interlocking scales of space and time, yet it was also by nature a method of erasure.[11] Geopoetics opened the space of the universe in the minutest detail, but in the same movement, it made the very infrastructural, technological, and social hierarchies that facilitated that visibility imperceptible. The new conception of the earth that geopoetics helped to shape, and that would later frame the plate tectonic revolution, was a naturalized version of this story, a story of earth's evolution that erased the Indonesian labor and culture that made it possible. The rest of this chapter tries to change that.

DIENG: THE AESTHETICS OF GEOLOGIZING · Like many new arrivals in the colonial East Indies, Umbgrove was struck by its beauty. He referred to its "fairy-tale like" qualities.[12] The landscape reminded him of stories he had read as a child. The bright colors and the heat, the banyan trees with their weeping arms, the volcanic peaks puffing smoke, the deafening cicada cries in the forest, all found a place in the regular letters he wrote to his mother during his stay. The experience of beauty and the desire for travel were linked in his conception of doing geological fieldwork. As soon as he arrived in Bandung, he began to take trips to the local volcano, Tangkubahn Perahu, and then farther afield. On one of his early voyages in October 1926, he visited Ciremai, a stratovolcano east of Bandung and near Lake Patengan, to which he drove two and a half hours with his colleagues Dittloff Tjassens, Visman, and van Merkestijn. The volcano was surrounded by a volcanic complex. He described going there:

Climb up again to the [elevation of] tree ferns and other plants, which only grow above 1200 meters, then appears a stretch of beautiful forest with tremendous, tall trees, and then the great lake suddenly shines through the thickets. It is an old crater lake with an island in the middle. We left the car by itself and went for a swim, and then baked in the sun. Wonderful, wonderful.[13]

Returning nearly a month later, he wrote in more detail about the same route and the human and nonhuman infrastructure, and he stressed the rhythm of the revealing and concealing of the landscape. He frequently emphasized the way that the landscape seen from volcanic craters was defined by the changing conditions of visibility, alternating between enclosure behind clouds and then suddenly clearing into long, unobstructed views from above. His unnamed porters played a role in this: they appeared with his luggage and equipment to enable the journeys and just as quickly disappeared behind Umbgrove's enchantment with the landscape.

> The winding road took us to the tea plantation Rantja-Bolang and then the threatening sky broke loose: a tremendous pouring shower as early as 7:30 in the morning. . . . It soon cleared up a bit, so that we picked up a coolie a little further down at the tea company and then drove on for another fifteen minutes. . . . We had started at an altitude of 2000 meters, so wonderfully fresh (almost European temperature), the coolie was warm with all the raincoats that he was carrying (besides many sandwiches and a camera). We arrived at the Kawah Poetih which means "white crater," very understandable because the entire expanse is white-yellow from sulfur mud. We left the boy with our luggage there, and as the weather seemed to be getting better, we hurried on; a steep climb after 45 minutes brought us to the top of the Patoeha at the edge of the old crater; along the rim it was a pretty sight in the steep, deep cauldron through which clouds chased. We were very lucky, however, because when we were at the highest point the cloud cover broke shortly afterwards and we enjoyed one of the most beautiful views I have ever seen. Low bushes grow above so that the view is unobstructed; to the northeast the Bandung plain with all its mountains, the other side from Pengalongan with its row of volcanoes. Far below us [is] Telaga Patengan with surrounding tea plantations and behind the southern mountains the Indian Ocean.[14]

Umbgrove frequently returned to similar scenes and invoked how overwhelming the experiences were—"the most beautiful," "delightful," "unbelievable." Later, when he joined Charles Stehn for a reconnaissance to Krakatoa when it was beginning to erupt, they circled the volcano in a small ship, trying to photograph the eruption. Umbgrove recalled how they were both so enthralled with the beauty of the eruption that they nearly forgot to take photos at regular intervals for later scientific analysis.[15] The regimented, disciplined work of scientific observation (which would later be published by Stehn[16]) was interrupted by the pleasure of unmediated witnessing. This was part of the aesthetic dimension of Umbgrove's fieldwork: negotiating the desire for overwhelming experiences and for submersion in new landscapes and the desire to narrate a new natural history of the hidden forces that made them.

The relationship between his scientific work—"geologizing," as he called it—and his aesthetic approach to Javanese landscapes, was made explicit in a visit in 1927 and 1928 to the Dieng plateau in Central Java and a subsequent paper he published in 1930. Dieng is a few kilometers northwest of Merapi and Borobudur; it is where Raffles had visited and recorded dilapidated temples. Umbgrove arrived in November 1927 and described it as "the plain with the temple ruins, the epitome of abandoned and dilapidated greatness." It was no surprise that he was interested in the ruins; as we know from previous chapters, geologists were fascinated by lost cultures from the pre-Islamic, Hindu and Buddhist past. Umbgrove had recently read Willemine Fruin-Mees's popular two-volume history of the pre-Islamic kingdoms and the arrival of Islam to Java.[17] Fruin-Mees's account was also published in Malay to popularize the pre-Islamic history of Java for Malay speakers. Dieng and Borobudur were discussed in Fruin-Mees's texts largely in terms of the genealogies of their kingdoms. She wrote that Dieng was founded in the ninth century and included an aerial photo of the ruined Candi Bima, a sacred Hindu structure, at the center of the plateau, surrounded by volcanic slopes (figure 5.5). The photograph shows the plateau without people, seen with the aloofness of air travel, likely from a military reconnaissance flight, a view that was becoming increasingly common in tourist representations of Java.[18]

During his visit to Dieng, Umbgrove also visited Borobudur, where he described the scene as—once again—"fairy-tale like." Sitting on top of the monument, alone, surrounded by Merapi and Merbabu volcanoes, he described the scene as "full of indescribable splendor."[19] He then reflected, "It is a pity that this high culture and high religion has now completely disappeared here and has left us only a few lifeless monuments."[20] Like Hinloopen Labberton and Leadbeater, he invoked how that ruined culture persisted: "For even now that nauseous Mohammedanism is no

FIGURE 5.5 Aerial view of Candi Bima on the Dieng Plateau, Java. The Hindu
temple was built between the seventh and ninth centuries. Willemine
Fruin-Meese, *Sedjarah Tanah Djawa: Zaman Hindoe Ditanah Djawa, Djilid I*
(Weltevreden: Balai Poestaka, 1921), plate 3.

more than an external and thin shell, and much of the old lives on in the
countless histories of the gamelan-long nights. Ardjoeno is still respected
today and in some places, flower offerings are still made [to] the old Bud-
dha images."[21] Hinduism and Buddhism persisted, in this sense, also as
ruins, buried or partly visible, underneath "the thin shell" of Islam. The
monuments of Borobudur and Dieng and, by extension, the Javanese,
were relics; they were the antiquities of lost greatness, spectacular in, if
not because of, their ruination.[22] Umbgrove also invoked a conception of
Java as ruin that Verbeek and Fennema had articulated in their *Description
géologique de Java et Madoura* (Geology of Java and Madoura) in 1896, when
they showed that volcanoes were ruins of once great mountains—an idea
of the landscape, including its cultures, as ruins. Geological matter was
the materialization of past events laid to waste; once living creatures and
cultures had become fossils, and mountains crumbled into the sea. Natural history, as Umbgrove later put it in *The Pulse of the Earth*, sees the past
as a scattering and piling of ruins atop each other; it was not only human
events on a stationary backdrop but also their transformation and inte-
gration with the landscape itself. Umbgrove, no doubt, was negotiating
contrasting concepts of ruination as a form of cultural and natural de-

cline with colonial notions of progress. At Borobudur, he stood in wonderment, looking at the beauty of the ruins from the perspective of the new roads, railways, and cars that had brought him there, all made possible by the colonial Ethical Policy that had promised to improve the Indies and the archaeological service that had excavated and restored the site between 1907 and 1911. Doing geology could connect the Javanese to their ruins, and connecting to their past could modernize them. Colonial geology, in this way, collapsed natural and social history; it was modernization, but it was also leverage against the influence of Islam.

Umbgrove returned to Dieng in January 1928 with Reinout van Bemmelen and a cache of new maps and aerial photographs taken by the colonial air force. Van Bemmelen left after the first day, while Umbgrove remained another day and half. "It is so delightfully beautiful here," Umbgrove wrote to his mother, "nature so overwhelmingly grand and varied, the days are a pure enjoyment."[23] He described the landscape as "a few dozen craters of different sizes and forms, enormous old lava flows, beautiful deep green lakes, wild valleys and flowing streams."[24] He remained to narrate a new history of the plateau as a linked history of nature and culture and wrote, "You hardly know what a joy it is to investigate a country like this, find problems, including ones that can keep you on the line for two and a half days while standing next to it, on it, and in the middle of it . . . 'la joie de connaitre.'"[25] This problem, he explained in "Het ontstaan van het Diengplateau" (The origin of the Dieng Plateau) (1929), was whether or not the plateau was the ruin of a once massive volcano and why the city that was built in it was abandoned. When the colonial geologists first arrived, they believed in Verbeek and Fennema's interpretation from the *Description géologique de Java et Madoura*, which had been influenced by Franz Junghuhn's interpretations from the 1850s.[26] For Verbeek, Fennema, and Junghuhn, the ruined city complex, of which the Candi Bima temple was a remnant, had been built inside an ancient crater. As Verbeek understood them, Javanese volcanoes were once larger and had decayed over time, and he applied the same interpretation to the plateau. When a Hindu culture emerged there in the early modern period, he argued, the crater was already extinct, and early engineers built drainage works inside of it to remove water from the plateau (the city was, after all, situated at the bottom of a natural bowl). Junghuhn and Verbeek thought that the engineers must have used a faulty design that led, instead, to flooding themselves in. Moreover, they also thought (arrogantly so) that the engineers had not been able to fix their predicament, so they simply gave up and left the city to ruin.[27]

Umbgrove, with good reason, was unconvinced, but not because Verbeek's argument assumed the incompetence of the engineers. Rather, Umbgrove found that recent records showed that earthquakes were emanating from different parts of the ring of hills around the plateau, and aerial photos and maps showed clusters of distinct calderas. This suggested to him that the plateau was not at the center of one single, massive, ancient volcano but was instead surrounded by numerous volcanoes of different ages. It was not one volcano, but many. After hiking up and down the slopes and traversing the plateau, he found no evidence that the engineering works of the ancient city had caused flooding. Rather, he argued that massive eruptions or earthquakes from nearby volcanoes caused the abandonment of the city. Umbgrove included in his publication a photo of Candi Bima (figure 5.6), indicating a "small explosion crater," filled with water. It is difficult not to see a reference to Fruin-Mees's photo—an aestheticized, picturesque, silhouetted temple on the hill, unpeopled, empty, and ruined. In this case the photograph was taken from the ground, from the plateau and in the abandoned space of the ancient town. Umbgrove developed a history that again connected volcanism to the Hindu and Buddhist past and explained that past as defined by natural catastrophe; it naturalized ruin and cultural decline, a geodeterminism that he would later connect to much more vast, cosmic cycles of recurrence and repetition in what he would call "the pulse of the earth."

What began with aesthetic wonder at ruins transformed into a new history of the earth. Indeed, that was "geologizing": being overtaken by an experience of the landscape, informed by a picturesque framing of it absent any people. Doing so required being there, traversing it, "standing next to it, on it, in the middle of it."[28] In other words, fieldwork. But it was not the conventional surveying practices common to the Geological Survey; instead, it brought science and tourism together. It was also tied to a desire to explain how geological processes were cultural; geological history was, in this instance, social history, and doing geology was, according to this early experiment in geopoetics, layering the social in the geological.

The Fourth Pacific Science Congress was held the following year, in May 1929, to showcase science and modernization in the Netherlands East Indies for 142 foreign scientists from Pacific countries. The botanical and ecological work of the Buitenzorg Botanical Gardens played a major role, as it was a crucial center of scientific research in the Indies, providing expertise related to the plantation economy. By 1930, it employed 700 scientists, many in applied fields. But the Congress also showcased the

FIGURE 5.6 Candi Bima, with a view of an explosion crater filled with water in the foreground. Johannes Umbgrove, "Het ontstaan van het Diengplateau," *Leidsche Geologische Mededelingen* 3, no. 1 (1928), figure 14.

development of new radio technologies, veterinary sciences, archaeology, and volcanology. Fieldtrips were taken to plantation field stations but also to Krakatoa, Borobudur, and Prambanan, highlighting for foreign scientists the links between volcanism and Hindu-Buddhist antiquities. Umbgrove was tasked with leading a delegation to the Bay of Batavia, where he met American scientists whom he would later call upon for employment during the difficult economic times of the interwar period. As Andrew Goss has noted, the Congress marked a transition in the international appreciation of Dutch colonial science, especially botanical science, as it was increasingly seen as competitive with other Western standards and as Dutch scientists were beginning to take on positions at foreign universities.[29] At the end of 1929, Umbgrove was offered a position as assistant to Charles Stehn in Rotterdam; thereafter, he finally advanced to a post and professorship in Delft. It was in Delft that he theorized his aesthetic method, building on his work on the Indies' volcanoes.

GEOPOETICS: FROM THE REMOTEST DISTANCES OF THE UNIVERSE TO THE INNERMOST DEPTHS OF OURSELVES · Many Dutch universities closed during the Second World War, and thus Umbgrove was released from his administrative and teaching duties, which enabled him to write. As

Japanese forces moved into Southeast Asia and expelled the Dutch from Indonesia, Umbgrove was developing geopoetics into an expansive, cosmic narrative linking the history of the galaxy, mountains, and species, with volcanism at its center.

The opening pages of *The Pulse of the Earth*, published in 1942, indicated that the book would not be a narrowly specialized geological book. He drew on Eduard Suess, the Viennese engineer and geologist who had transformed theories of the earth in the previous century by synthesizing vast amounts of geological research into an encompassing portrait of planetary tectonics. Umbgrove thus aligned his work with his predecessor's planetary-scale tectonic endeavor. What was striking about Umbgrove's reference to Suess was that it was done not only to enlist Suess as an authority but to link him directly to Umbgrove's own encounters with the Hindu cultural history of Java. This was accomplished, specifically, by quoting Suess quoting the *Ramayana*: "As Rama looks out upon the Ocean, its limits mingling and uniting with heaven on the horizon, and as he ponders whether a path might not be built into the Immeasurable, so we look over the Ocean of time, but nowhere do we see signs of a shore."[30] Umbgrove drew on Suess drawing on the *Ramayana*, one of the key texts of the Hindu philosophical tradition and a central story of the Javanese *wayang*, to describe deep geological time. Umbgrove was, in other words, acknowledging that Western conceptions of geological deep time were prefigured by the Hindu cosmology. He was also acknowledging that that tradition was at the center of the scientific geological canon through Suess's very reliance upon it. Western geological modernity was, in this sense, the return of Hindu cosmology, collapsing the new into the old, Suess the Viennese into Javanese culture.

These first pages stated that *The Pulse of the Earth* would guide the reader through the Immeasurable. The geologist, Umbgrove stated, used geological reasoning to explain the relationship between horizontal temporal scales (deep time) with vertical spatial scales (the micro with the macro), a process, Umbgrove explained, that was "geopoetical."[31] What he meant by "poetry" was not the traditional genre of writing but the speculative dimension of geology that operated at the limits of what was known by the modern sciences—in so far as that data was available to the geologist. Geopoetics operated at the space between the knowledge of the modern sciences to understand how those edges connected and related to each other. Its first principle was connectivity, and connectivity was the basis, the fabric, as it were, of the Immeasurable, of deep time. As the Immeasurable (obviously) could not be measured, the purpose of geopoetics was striking: it was to connect the largest to the smallest, the ancient to the new, the interior of the human body to the cosmos. The connective tissue, for Umbgrove, was pattern and rhythm.

The Immeasurable was musical. Night transitioned to day, tides advanced and retreated, seasons came and went. He saw periodicity as the structure of deep space and time: sea levels rose and fell, mountains were built and depleted, carbon concentrations rose and fell, the galaxy rotated. Repetition indicated pervasive patterns, and the geopoetical project was to trace how these periods related, affected, or conditioned each other across their scales. Periods of recurrence could not unfold independently of each other, Umbgrove reasoned, so they must connect. He called their interactions *polyphonic* after the Baroque musical style that centered on voices in ever-increasing, complex harmonies. Nature was not defined by simple repetitions but by interrelated *periodicities*, cycles producing increasing complexity and diversification.

His interest in periodicity was not idiosyncratic; it was a central preoccupation for many geologists at the turn of the twentieth century. Understanding the cyclicity of tidal motion was crucial for setting time standards and shipping tables, and for determining mean sea level, which in turn became data for determining geographical information such as altitude.[32] In the early twentieth century, geologists that Umbgrove read wondered if the cycles of the earth's rotation had an effect on the shape of its relatively liquid crust and mantle.[33] The theory of eustasy, for instance, sought to understand these liquid dynamics, and a number of geologists took seriously how the periodicity of the earth's rotating mass could contribute to shaping its surface.[34] Periodicity was also of interest to some geologists concerned with developing ways to measure geological time: they considered what could define a geological age when many temporal systems such as years were derived from lunar and solar cycles and the rotation of the earth. The US geomorphologist G. K. Gilbert was skeptical of the Lyellian principal that the present was the key to the past and wondered if it could be presumed that ancient earth, solar, and lunar cycles were the same then as they were in the present. Could geological ages be derived from present earth cycles when the ancient earth may not have functioned, as uniformitarian principles suggested, according to the same cycles as the earth did in the present?[35] Even if the calendrical system of years were only a standard of temporal measure, it contained a bias toward steady-state earthly cycles on an earth that may have operated very differently. The question of cycles and their rates of return, therefore, was a significant issue not only for establishing the age of the earth but also for developing the standards of measure upon which to base geological time.

If cyclical time was a significant theoretical concern for some geologists and a practical problem for others, it was rare for geologists to accord it the significance that Umbgrove did in his cosmological system. This significance was due in part to his studies of volcanism and mountain building. By studying the formation of mountain chains through volcanism and its associated events of lifting, slumping, and folding, Umbgrove came to understand that volcanoes were defined by cycles in geological time he called *transgressions*. He placed transgressions at the center of his system and tried to connect them vertically, to cosmic forces above and to processes below in the earth's core, and finally, horizontally, to the geography of biological evolution. His attention to orogenic cycles prompted him to see, too, that they were connected to the rotation of the galaxy, cooling and warming climates, and bursts of species diversification and extinction.

In 1939, Umbgrove published an article titled "On Rhythms in the History of the Earth" that set out some of the principles he would develop in *The Pulse of the Earth*. He argued against Amadeus William Grabau, a prominent paleontologist based at Peking National University (following his dismissal from Columbia University in 1919 for his pro-German sympathies).[36] Grabau developed a theory of "pulsation systems" that attempted to redefine the cycles of global sea-level rise and fall throughout the earth's history.[37] While it was long understood that sea levels had risen and fallen in the past, Grabau's new categorization of "transgressive-regressive" systems described periods in which seas rose and fell and "transgressed" on the continents while the continents remained fixed in place. He proposed to reorder the conventional geological stratigraphic divisions and introduced several new ones, showing that the "transgressive-regressive" system shaped the geography and evolution of biological life and continental geology.[38] Umbgrove did not, in principle, disagree with Grabau's idea of cycles of oceanic pulsations but argued instead that Grabau did not go far enough because he did not include mountain building in his system. One had to consider, Umbgrove argued, deeper structures in the earth's interior and complementary periodicities throughout the body of the earth, such as the rise and fall of mountains.[39] "Can these different phenomena be connected, and thus give an insight into the certain rhythmical processes in the deeper parts of the earth?" Umbgrove asked. "I, personally, am convinced that we must answer this question in the affirmative."[40] He argued that the next step in a Grabauean analysis was to posit counterpoint rhythms rather than beginning from a single oceanic source for the planetary rhythm of transgression-regression. Umbgrove came to understand that earth and cosmic history were defined, instead, by multiplying rhythms and their intersections.

In the early pages of *The Pulse of the Earth*, Umbgrove noted that the galaxy rotated roughly every 250 million years. This, he realized, correlated with the "epochs of compression" of the earth's crust during which great mountain chains were built: the Cambrian and the end of the Paleozoic.[41] Each epoch of compression, he cautiously suggested, was also defined by increases in the complexity of geological and biological systems. Compression caused not only mountain building and increased volcanism but also the lowering of the ocean floors, complementary movements that catalyzed the warming of environments and that sped up biological differentiation and diversification. These rhythms, even if they corresponded with galactic rotation, also pointed to a "common deep-seated" cause in the interior of the earth that remained, he thought, mysterious. They might be thermal cycles, as Vening Meinesz (and others) had been thinking, and with whom Umbgrove had been corresponding and publishing with for nearly a decade by that point. He had been familiar with and sympathetic to theories of continental drift since the 1930s and contributed an overview of continental drift theories as they applied to the Netherlands East Indies in Vening Meinesz's *Gravity Expeditions at Sea*. He was also familiar with ideas that linked drifting continents and mobile sea beds with deeper thermal cycles.[42] He was not, however, convinced either way whether thermal cycles were responsible for the buckled crusts, intense volcanism, and seismicity of the East Indies; but unlike the geological establishment in Europe and the United States at the time, he and his colleagues were sympathetic to the explanatory power of the theory. In *The Pulse of the Earth*, he proposed instead that convection currents should be thought of in an even more expansive context; they were ultimately counterpoints to galactic rotations and therefore caused by, or somehow related to, yet unknown cosmic processes. He was honest about the ambition of his project and its potential unverifiability, yet, in the final chapter of his work, he wrote:

These vague descriptions designate the paramount source of all sub-crustal energy, which manifests itself with a periodicity observed in a whole series of phenomena in the earth's crust and on its surface, viz. the alternating decrease and increase of compression of the earth's crust and the closely related epochs of folding, the process of mountain-building and submersion of borderlands, the periodic formation of basins and dome-shaped elevations, the magmatic cycles and rhythmic cadence of world-wide transgressions and regressions, the pulsation of the climate, and—lastly—the pulse of Life.[43]

The Pulse of the Earth was a determinedly orogenic-centric vision of the cosmos and life. He accused Grabau of not looking deeply enough at planetary counter rhythms, while he also placed the rise and fall of mountains, which he witnessed on Java's volcanoes, at the center of earth's story. By extension, he was fascinated with linking biological history to mountain building and the history of humans to the history of mountains. Pushing this even further, he asked, "Can it be mere chance that the Psychozoic—which received its name from the fact that Man, his supremacy over the world at that time—coincides with an exceptionally intensive phase of mountain-building and glaciation?"[44] Planetary differentiation through physiographic differentiation was inseparable from biological differentiation; it was a planetary and cosmic determinism. He was departing from familiar forms of national or biological forms of geographic determinism by way of the interior of the earth, its mobile surface, and the galaxy. Volcano science, in this iteration, was a theory of cultural formation and consciousness. The *Psychozoic* was a term that Umbgrove likely adopted from the US geologist and physician Joseph Le Conte's use of it in the late nineteenth century, though it was also often used by Umbgrove's contemporaries. Le Conte defined the Psychozoic in a way that clearly anticipated contemporary attempts to define the Anthropocene: "The geological importance of the appearance of man is not due only or chiefly to his transcendent dignity, but to his importance as an agent which has already very greatly, and must hereafter still more profoundly, modify the whole fauna and flora of the earth."[45] Umbgrove elaborated it thus: the Psychozoic "received its name from the fact that Man, the specialist of spiritual and intellectual differentiation, appeared on the stage and began to extend his supremacy over the world."[46] In Umbgrove's schema, "spiritual and intellectual differentiation" was an extension of planetary differentiation; differentiation was counterpoint, a deepening of complex interrelations, and the capacity for the planet to transform itself from within.

This was the geopoetic method: tracking down the connections between rhythms that linked the galaxy to species modification. Doing so obviously resisted simplified schemas, and Umbgrove's aesthetic system was antireductionist. What made the cosmos beautiful, according to him, was the very abundance of relations among its parts and that their interconnecting rhythms generated ever-more complexity. The principle of Baroque counterpoint expressed exactly this, as it had for van Bemmelen: the relationships among parts make more parts, which in turn make more relationships, and then more parts, in a cascade of interrelationship. The geopoet, then, is on an ever-expansive, if not impossible, search to map the rhythms of relationships in a cosmos of compounding relationships. In other words, the Immeasurable. As he put it, "the characteristic of a living organism," though he could have been speaking about a rock or any other thing, "must be sought in unknown 'linkings.'"[47]

COMPLEMENTARITY, GERMAN IDEALISM, AND THE *UPANISHADS* · *The Symphony of the Earth* introduced a new term to describe Umbgrove's system, *complementarity*. He wrote, "Remarkably enough, however, [complementarity] remind[s] one of certain aspects of the Brahmanese *Upanishads*."[48] In *Life and Matter*, a collection of essays from 1943 that formed the basis for *Symphony of the Earth*, he explained that the *Upanishads* prefigured his ideas of complementarity and, thus, his attempt to bring together deep geological time and cyclical time.[49] "An analogous conclusion can already be found in the old *Upanishads* where the problem of the life of man was called 'Atman,' and the inexplicable in the whole of nature, 'Brahman.' The utmost wisdom to which that ancient high culture has come can be formulated as Brahman equals Atman."[50]

Umbgrove came to the *Upanishads* by way of Paul Deussen, a German orientalist, disciple of Schopenhauer's, and friend of Nietzsche's. Deussen introduced Nietzsche to Hindu and Buddhist thought; he also introduced Hindu philosophy to German Idealism through works including *The Philosophy of the Upanishads* (1906), in which he argued that the *Upanishads* were the founding moment of world philosophy.[51] That moment was then repeated in ancient Athens, and then again with Kantian idealism, and finally with Schopenhauer.[52] Each moment, though historically and temporally disparate, was based on the same insight: the universe and human consciousness are illusions.[53] Knowledge of the world was entirely dependent upon the categories of time, space, and causality, which as Kant had shown, were faculties of the mind and therefore distortions placed upon the universe, not the universe in itself. Nature in itself was unknowable except through the distortions of consciousness. As Deussen put it:

> The whole of religion and philosophy has its root in the thought that (to adopt the language of Kant) the universe is only appearance and not reality (*Ding an sich*); that is to say, the entire external universe . . . always and only tells us how things are constituted for us, and for our intellectual capacities, not how they are in themselves and apart from intelligences such as ours.[54]

This, Deussen thought, was the core of the *Upanishads*. Rather than Kant's language of *an sich*, the "in-itself," the *Upanishads* used the term *Atman*, which was reality beyond illusion; it was thus also what mind was, though consciousness was unable to comprehend it in itself.[55] The purpose of human life was to undergo progressive steps to approach *Atman* and release itself from illusion. For Deussen, this was the radical idealist Kantian project.

How did the geopoet see himself in this? The final chapter of *The Symphony of the Earth* was the emphatic yet unresolved answer; it was about the problem of the relationship between life and matter, living and nonliving systems. Umbgrove was led to this from the spatial problems of the relationship between cosmic forces and the earth. The arc of the book was broadly from the cosmic scale to the micro, from the structure of the cosmos and earth to the distinction between living and nonliving. In the book's final chapter, "Life and Its Evolution," Umbgrove acknowledged that the modern sciences had been fundamentally defined by the very problem of explaining the distinction between life and nonlife, *bios* and *geos*.[56] He explained that evolutionary biology, vitalism, materialism, holism, thermodynamics, and quantum mechanics had each sought and failed to define the border between *bios* and *geos*. They were founded on the difference yet could not adequately define it. It was here that his theory of complementarity stepped in. Complementarity named not the location of the division between organic and inorganic, or between life and matter, but the copresence and codependence between them. It sought not to demarcate the boundaries between the two but to acknowledge a gradient of "livingness" in all systems including rocks and rivers, animals and humans. Yet this livingness was not a vitalism. It was misguided, he thought, to define the line that divides the living and nonliving; rather, one should ask how all kinds of things are complementary. This, he argued, resisted modern scientific preferences for simplicity, dualism, order, and linearity. Instead, it celebrated the cosmos as things bound up with each other. Drawing inspiration from Alfred North Whitehead, he refused the separation between thought and world. *Brahman* equals *Atman*.

> Whitehead's conclusion is therefore that in the Kosmos there is no absolute independent reality, but that all things are closely bound up with one another, and that Homo Sapiens is a part and a link in the whole development of the Kosmos: "The universe is always one, since there is no surveying it except from an actual entity which unifies it."[57]

This was the insight that made the theory of complementarity an extension of the *Upanishads* (according to Deussen's rendering of it). Umbgrove went on, "The whole universe is not governed by a reality, conceived as lying outside it; it is in all things permeated by the reality which is the universe itself in its entirety."[58] The universe itself in its entirety is *Atman*, which was all thought and representation. Deussen argued that the cosmos was consciousness, and all consciousness was the expression, even if flawed, of *Atman*, the universe in itself. For Deussen, one of the achievements of the *Upanishads* was to render cosmos and consciousness noncontradictory.

Invoking the *Upanishads* concluded the geopoetic enterprise, and Umbgrove acknowledged again that modern science reached insights prefigured by those of early modern Hinduism. Rather than a story of linear, progressive, self-correcting science, it was a repetition of old insights—of the West coming to understand what the East had already accomplished in the past. As much as Umbgrove disliked the Theosophists, invoking the significance of the *Upanishads* mirrored the very same occultist idea that discovering the "ancient records of the east" anticipated modern scientific discoveries. It was also true that his time in Java, reading histories of the Hindu and Buddhist early modern period, and renarrating the geological histories of its ruins on volcanoes, set the conditions for him to see his own system as an extension of it.

GEOPOETICS AND PLATE TECTONICS · The destiny of Umbgrove's geopoetics as outlined in *The Pulse of the Earth* and *The Symphony of the Earth* was to help the formulation of another new earth history, the theory of plate tectonics. Geologists rarely referred directly to Umbgrove, perhaps out of a hesitancy to theorize in terms of aesthetics or beauty in a post–World War II geoscientific culture that eschewed dandyism. Also, the ever-accumulating empirical evidence quickly dated his work, but the influence of geopoetics on geophysics was nevertheless profound.

Umbgrove's work on the tectonic history of the Netherlands East Indies and his collaborations with Vening Meinesz put Umbgrove in contact with American oceanographers at the Lamont Geological Observatory at Columbia University. While US geologists and engineers were trying to develop new models for understanding the formation of the ocean floor and continents, Vening Meinesz taught them how to use gravity meters and find new underwater trenches. In September 1950, Vening Meinesz, Umbgrove, and their Leiden colleagues B. G. Escher and J. M Bergers participated in the colloquium On Plastic Flow and Deformation within the Earth, in Hershey, Pennsylvania.[59] It was a small event of twenty-four US and European scientists and the United States Geological Survey, the Carnegie Institution of Washington, and commercial interests represented by Westinghouse Electric. The purpose was to discuss prevailing theories of the center of the earth, including the controversial idea of convection currents. Umbgrove made a case for working more closely with chemists to understand the processes deep inside the earth and their effects.[60]

Harry Hess from Princeton University was also present to discuss theoretical problems associated with the discovery of the ocean trench systems he had been taught to find years earlier by Vening Meinesz. He brought these issues to bear on the problem of mantle convection: "At present it is not possible to prove that convection currents exist in the mantle, nor is it possible to show that they cannot exist. The difficulty of explaining persistence of the root in island arcs without appealing to such currents leads the writer to be strongly disposed to favor them."[61] US scientists were becoming increasingly convinced, in part based on the work of Vening Meinesz and Umbgrove in Indonesia, of the possibility that convection currents were influencing continental drift.

Nearly a decade later, in 1962, eight years after Umbgrove died, Hess published his "History of Ocean Basins," in which he set out his new theory of the mechanism of ocean-floor spreading. In the opening paragraphs he stated that "like Umbgrove, I shall consider this paper an essay in geopoetry."[62] Hess described The Pulse of the Earth as a "brilliant summary" yet maintained that new evidence had made it out of date. But

Hess misunderstood Umbgrove's geopoetics; he thought it meant fabulation, fiction, and flights of fancy. In other words, the opposite of (his own conception of) modern science. As Martin Rudwick put it, Hess invoked geopoetics "as if to excuse an otherwise unacceptable piece of speculative theorizing."[63] Calling his theory geopoetry was also a way to hedge his argument among a community of US geologists vociferously opposed to continental drift. Geopoetics allowed Hess to make a pathbreaking argument, but he also did a disservice to Umbgrove's project.

Hess's geopoetic story went thus: In a mythical mode he recounted that the earth first formed from solar particles 4.5 billion years ago. Once those particles transformed into a solid earth and its shape roughly resembled the modern earth, there occurred the *great catastrophe* (Hess's emphasis), which very closely resembled Vening Meinesz's origin story of the originary "convective overturn." For Hess, this catastrophe was the moment when convection currents began to loop between the earth's center and the crust, which amplified the differentiation between surface and center and formed the nickel-iron core with a "primordial single continent" above the current (again reminiscent of Vening Meinesz). He speculated that 50 percent of continental material was created by the great catastrophe. The ocean basins and continents have since rested on top of a viscous underbelly. The great catastrophe allowed him to postulate the origin of a dual convection cell system in which heat rose, spread through, and under, the surface of the earth, then descended back toward the center. This rising and falling was the mechanism of ocean basin evolution. He focused on the mid-ocean ridges in the Atlantic and Pacific, where there was recent evidence that the volcanoes there had moved away from the ridges over time; and he proposed that the legacy of the great catastrophe could be seen in the expansion of the ocean floor away from the center, traveling between 3,000 and 6,000 kilometers before crashing into the continents and diving back toward the center of the earth.[64]

This proposal, drawn directly from the tutelage of Vening Meinesz and Umbgrove and their work in Java, contributed to American geophysicists accepting the model of mantle convection as the mechanism of the earth's evolutionary history. Soon after, it became the orthodox model for almost all Western geophysicists. The framework was Umbgrove's; the origin story was Vening Meinesz's. It is not meaningless that Hess invoked the great catastrophe either, a story of ruin and ruination: the very form of the modern earth was depicted, once again, as a compromise between catastrophism and Lyellian conceptions of consistent deep-time processes. Hess brought together ruination with creation: creative destruction defined earthly evolution.

The Pulse of the Earth also influenced Hess's colleague at the Lamont Geological Observatory, Bruce Heezen, who collaborated with Maurice Ewing on a decades-long project mapping the ocean floor with vessels funded in part by the Pentagon that carried "golden calf" (four-pendulum) gravity meters, made seismic refractions, took photographs and samples, and measured magnetism throughout the Atlantic and the Pacific during the 1940s, '50s, and '60s.[65] They mapped the mid-ocean ridges that Hess would later place at the center of earth's evolution. They also took measurements off the coast of Java (that Warren Hamilton used in his plate tectonic description of Indonesia) at the same sites where the *Lusiad* and *Monsoon* descended into the realm of Nyai Ratu Kidul, the goddess of the South Sea. Heezen read *The Pulse of the Earth* as a graduate student and underlined sections in the chapter on the structure of the ocean floor, the same chapter in which Umbgrove engaged the ideas of Grabau's pulsation theory.[66] According to historical geographers Ronald E. Doel, Tanya J. Levin, and Mason K. Marker, Heezen was captivated by Umbgrove's observation that structures on continents mirrored those in the ocean floor. They maintain that this influenced Heezen to use contemporary geophysical techniques in the ocean to answer big questions about the evolution of the earth that led US scientists to believe in the theory of plate tectonics.[67]

CONCLUSION · Umbgrove's work has largely been forgotten, and his role in developing geopoetics as a geological method has been sidelined by recent postcolonial and literary theoretical developments of geopoetics. For some, geopoetics has come to mean little more than a style of writing lyrically about geology. For others, it is a countermovement to the geological tradition, opening discourses of geology to ways of thinking by people who are often considered to have been excluded by science. Geopoetics has, for some, become a way to redeem or re-enchant the earth sciences. As Kathryn Yusoff invokes it, it offers a way to think geologically that undermines the division between *bios* and *geos*, life and matter, which, following Elizabeth Povinelli, is a foundational division that structures late liberal capitalist societies.[68] The distinction between the living and the dead underlies a frequently hierarchical distinction between what can be a commodity and what cannot, or what can be exploited and what should be protected. Geopoetics promises, for some theorists, a refusal of this distinction. Yet, what Umbgrove reminds us of is not only that geopoetics has played a crucial role in modern earth theory but also that the fundamental problem of the relationship between *geos* and *bios* has been an ongoing, deeply troubling, and unresolved preoccupation. Umbgrove's geopoetics was not in opposition to modern geophysics; in fact, it shaped it in crucial ways from below, as its dandy geoscience undercurrent, its unapologetic, unusual, aesthete science. The very orthodox conception of earth's evolution as a process of plate tectonics emerged from and was enabled by Umbgrove's geopoetic enterprise, and geopoetics resulted from a complex dialogue with the Hindu philosophical tradition as it was read in the colonial landscape of the East Indies and intersected with the European geological tradition via Suess and Deussen. What a strange and surprising cosmopolitan trajectory it was, an undercurrent of geological thought that rejected the desire for order and control of nature in favor of celebrating an aesthetic earth defined by its interconnected scales and endless creative ability to differentiate from the innermost depths of ourselves to the outer reaches of the cosmos.

CHAPTER SIX

VOLCANO
OBSERVATORIES

Proximity and Distance in Science and Mysticism

ARCHITECTURES OF CONTACT · Pulses, beeps, scratches, a cosmos of tuning in, connecting, touching: repetitions coursing on the scale of the earth and on the scale of the heart. What is the nature of distance between ourselves and the interior of the earth? How far does it go? Can it become utter immediacy? Crossing scales takes work. The immediate is sometimes a dream of intimacy. Volcano scientists and mystics sometimes shared this fantasy: overcoming the matter of the world, the relentless, grating distance it creates in all things; the dream was to become better than matter, collapse the interior of the body with the interior of the earth, the one contained in the other, the macrocosm folded into the micro, the thresholds between them crossed by planetary pulses and waves emanating through a vibrantly communicating, raucous earth, an earth that was never silent, always on the side of the too much to contain, even grasp. Waves could overcome distance; they could create immediacy; lithic intimacy was the dream. Architecture was, surprisingly, the first port of call: built on the edges of volcanoes, observatories became vehicles with which to experiment with ideas about what a human body was and how it could be connected to the earth. Watching meant feeling,

feeling meant collapsing distance, bringing the volcano near while protecting the fragile all-too-human flesh and organs of the person watching; it was science as mediation and mystical transference, lithic communion. And the science spread. From the architecture of the observatories there issued tools and techniques—seeing machines, hearing machines, drawing machines, measuring machines, communicating machines, networking machines. The machines conjured volcanic interiors, tremors, smells, sounds as bells, bleeps, waves, and pulses. A chattering earth, speaking, drawing, sometimes screaming. Observatories spread across the hills, and their machines flowed through the villages where they were picked up and remade and rethought into new visions of what it meant to live alongside volcanoes, to be a human body on a volcano. We inherit these visions in all their twists and turns.

In Indonesia of the 1930s, volcano observatories were first built on volcanoes to protect the plantations and wealthy colonial villas on the upper slopes.[1] Scientists carefully considered where to build observatories so that they were near enough to the crater to observer it yet also far enough to remain safe, creating a more difficult problem than it seemed at first. How close was too close? Where was it safe during an eruption? One solution devised on Merapi was to build in remote terrain at the tops of hills with clear views of the crater. The structures were bamboo huts with thatched roofs and were connected via telegraph wires to other huts and offices in the lowlands. One of the observatories situated on a hill at Maron proved to be a good idea in terms of the view, but when the volcano erupted in 1930, so much sand, ash, and rock was shot out of the volcano that the rivers burst their banks and even the hut was washed away; the seismograph inside was destroyed. The devastation caused by the 1930 eruption resulted in a sequence of scientific experiments with the tension between distance and observation; the experiments also engaged, surprisingly, with questions about what a human body and the earth were each made of.

Ideas about distance, the meaning of matter, and the material makeup of the human body and earth then spread from volcano observatories across the slopes to the communities for the simple reason that the areas where observatories were built were busy. Observatories were near villages, farm fields, miners, and plantation workers. Being there meant that scientists lived among these communities and entered into exchanges with them. Locals helped build the observatories; some locals even worked their instruments; others became monitors. Observatories changed the villages because they were the first buildings at those elevations to become electrified and to include telephones, seismographs, radios, and telegraphs; they were, in other words, the technological vanguards that imported lowland technologies to rural frontiers, connecting mountain villages to the lowlands by sending telegraph and radio signals across great distances at unprecedented speeds, collapsing the distance between craters and urban centers. Volcanism became newly legible with seismograph scratches on paper, glass tubes and bottles for chemical analysis, thermometers, telescopes, and photographs: a new world of volcanic communication opened at the site of the observatories, transforming ideas about how the earth could communicate.

But observatories also fit in. They were ubiquitous and camouflaged. Their architectures were made to look much the same as rural village houses with walls of bamboo and roofs of clay tile. In later years, they were built to resemble Dutch middle-class holiday bungalows (figure 6.1). Scientists slept and ate there with their families and took photographs of themselves relaxing (figure 6.2). Washing was hung out to dry on ad hoc clotheslines strung across the porch (figure 6.3). In a sense, they were the invisible architectures of social choreography, ubiquitous yet creating new forms of spatial and temporal proximity between volcanoes and the people who lived with them, collapsing distance and compressing time.

Communities on the slopes of the volcanoes had, of course, long developed local forms of volcano monitoring. Ancestral graves, sacred hills, ritual pathways, and sacred stones were all linked to understanding, predicting, and monitoring volcanic activity. Plawangan observatory on Merapi, for instance, was built beside Turgo, a hill where many deities lived. The plateau at Pasar Bubar was a spirit market that deities visited at night. The lookout post for the Jrakah observatory was on the way to the graveyard of ancestral deities. Hills and promontories that were transformed into scientific stations had long been sites for local deities connected to volcanic activity. Volcanic activity could also be forecasted through dreams and trances. Local traditions of monitoring were in conversation with the political events in the Yogyakarta and Surakarta courts in the lowlands. Divination was, therefore, thick with local, political, and mythical history that could not but encounter and, in some cases, transform and be transformed by the new ways of monitoring that emerged in observatories in the 1930s. In the rich, storied world of Javanese spiritual geographies, scientists negotiated different conceptions of what exactly it was that they were monitoring. Was a volcano the edge of the earth

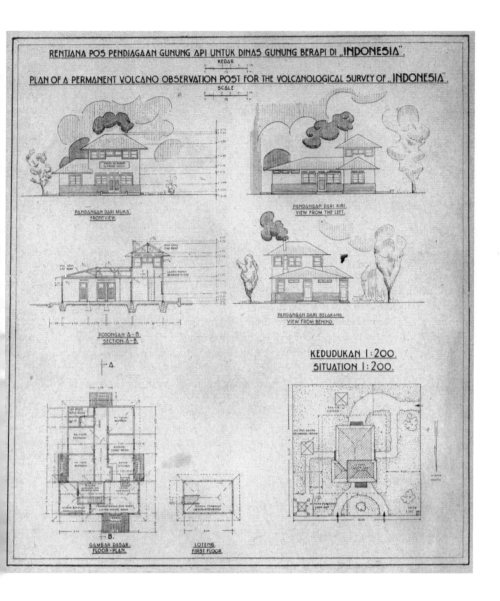

FIGURE 6.1 A 1952 proposal for volcano observatories rendered in the style of middle-class colonial bungalows. George A. de Neve, "Rentjana Pos Pendjagaan Gunung Api untuk Dinas Gunung Berapi di 'Indonesia,' / Plan of a Permanent Volcano Observation Post for the Volcanological Survey of 'Indonesia,'" *Berita Gunung Berapi* 1, nos. 1–2 (1952): 82.

FIGURE 6.2 Neumann van Padang posing in front of the emergency bunker at Babadan, 1931. *Dr. M. Neumann van Padang ingan vd vluchttunnel Babadan*, photographic album, Balai Penyelidikan dan Pengembangan Teknologi Kebencanaan Geologi archive.

FIGURE 6.3 The observatory at Babadan in its first iteration, 1931. *Dr. M. Neumann van Padang ingan vd vluchttunnel Babadan*, photographic album, Balai Penyelidikan dan Pengembangan Teknologi Kebencanaan Geologi archive.

connected to the deepest of planetary and cosmic processes? Or was it made of seismic waves and pulses that very much resembled the electrical pulses of the human heart? Or, perhaps, they were made of Javanese spirits and deities? This chapter explores how volcano observatories became sites through which these different conceptions of matter, meaning, the body, and cosmos came together.

EPISODE 1: EINTHOVEN'S HEARTBEATS · Willem Einthoven Sr. was born in 1860 in Semarang, a busy port city on the north coast of Java, where his father was a physician.[2] Like many Europeans in the colony, Willem returned to the Netherlands to study, and he completed high school and medical studies in Utrecht.[3] In 1886, when he was only twenty-five, he was appointed chair of Physiology at the University of Leiden.

Nineteen years later, working in his cavernous, instrument-strewn laboratory, he was trying to solve a problem with his technicians.[4] They had successfully designed and built an electrocardiograph that amplified and recorded with unparalleled precision the electrical pulses emitted by a patient's heart. For the first time, the heartbeats of healthy and ill patients could be accurately compared. Wholly new diagnostic opportunities emerged; arrhythmia, the condition of irregular heartbeats, could be exactly identified and then precisely linked to physiological causes. But the problem was that the instrument required five people to operate it; it filled two rooms and was powered by a giant electromagnet.[5] If the purpose was to study sick, often immobilized patients, how could they be expected to travel to his machine? He needed to reverse the arrangement and bring the machine to them. Einthoven wondered: "Since electric currents daily bring us information by telegraph from all parts of the world, why should not the currents originating in the heart be conducted from the hospital to the laboratory?"[6] He wanted to fold heart beats into the telegraph system.

The first telephone cables had been recently installed in Leiden, and in 1906, Einthoven connected his electrocardiograph to the university hospital a mile away through the buried cable.[7] After troubleshooting for interference—because voices in the phone network could interrupt the heart signal[8]—a chair was set up for a patient from which they could rest their hands and feet in buckets of salt water (figure 6.4). Electrical pulses that caused the heart to contract (systole) passed through the telephone cable to the lab and to Einthoven's other impressive invention, the string galvanometer: a thin, metal-coated string suspended within a massive, twirling, electromagnet.[9] When the heartbeats reached the string, they interfered with the string's natural oscillations, like a finger plucking a harp. The machine then projected shadows of the string's movement onto a photographic plate that was mechanically replaced at a regular interval like a motion-picture camera. Einthoven called the results a telecardiogram, as heartbeats became signals passing through communications infrastructure like a telegram.[10] He imagined connecting the chair to hospitals in The Hague and even Amsterdam and beyond, from which patients could send their heartbeats from across the country back to his lab for analysis.[11]

By 1912, in association with private instrument makers, the device was made small and light enough that it became practicable to transport it directly to hospitals.[12] In the meantime, Einthoven imagined other possible uses for the uniquely precise string galvanometer beyond the study of heart rhythms. Elsewhere, string galvanometers of Einthoven's design had been set up in England, Russia, Japan, and continental Europe, including in Guglielmo Marconi's radio laboratory, where they were being used as receivers for telegraph signals. The geopolitics of war then intervened and opened a new path for Einthoven's invention.[13]

Einthoven's son, Willem Frederik Einthoven Jr., studied electrical engineering at the Polytechnic College at Delft while assisting his father in the laboratory. He proposed that they design a version of the galvanometer for wireless communication with the Netherlands East Indies.[14] Wired communication within the Indies had been first established in 1856, and by 1900 there were over two thousand telephone subscribers in Java's larger cities.[15] As Rudolf Mrázek has identified, wired communication played a crucial role in facilitating ideas of the modernization of the colony.[16] Yet, wireless communication would not be successful until 1918, and even then, communicating across such vast distances was beset by interference from weather and from competing wireless signals. For Einthoven Sr. and Jr., the unmatched sensitivity of the string galvanometer could help by offering a more precise receiver able to connect to the Indies. This was also strategically significant because during the First World War, telegraph connections with the Indies had become politically complicated as the cable networks required base stations for transmission in the British territory of Singapore.[17] Because the Netherlands remained neutral in the conflict, the threat was that they could no longer rely on the cable network, effectively severing communication between the East

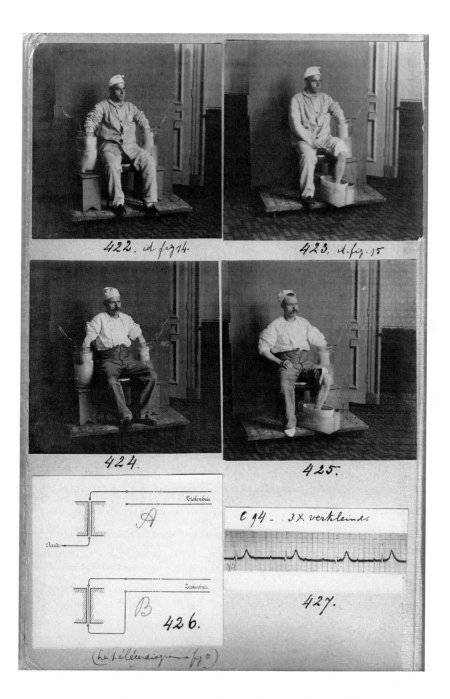

FIGURE 6.4 Patients connected to Willem Einthoven Sr.'s electrocardiograph machine through buckets of salt water and telegraph cables. "Pagina in fotoalbum 'diapositieven II' van physiologisch lab." Leiden. Object number P11636-30. Courtesy Rijksmuseum Boerhaave.

Indies and the Netherlands.[18] The Einthovens offered to develop their improved wireless device to bypass the geopolitics of the British base stations, and the technical solution Einthoven Jr. suggested was that they enclose the galvanometer in a vacuum to further increase its sensitivity to aerial signals.

The Einthovens' project was secret, and lab work progressed behind locked doors.[19] After "a few years of hard work," in 1917, Einthoven Jr. boarded a ship for Java with the string galvanometer in a vacuum. Not long after his arrival, the Einthovens tested it and were able to communicate through a six-millimeter receiver string in Leiden.[20] Einthoven Sr. explained that by "accurately tuning it" to the "ether oscillations" sent from a transmitting station, a series of dots and dashes were successfully projected onto a moving strip of paper.[21] The Einthovens had potentially overcome the burdens of geography and had re-established reliable connectivity between colony and metropole. They were using the same technology that they used for visualizing the human heartbeat for visualizing the sound of a voice at a great distance. The human body and the geopolitics of the Netherlands' relationship to the Indies became uniquely tied up in the string galvanometer.

It is worth pausing on the Einthovens' terminology here, too. For Einthoven Sr., the use of the word *tuning* had a technical meaning: It meant removing interference and increasing the sensitivity of the string of the galvanometer. It meant choreographing the frequencies between the oscillations of the incoming wave and the oscillations of the string on the galvanometer, like a receiver tuning into a radio station. Tuning required finding the rate at which the string could *receive* the oscillations of the pulse from overseas. Shortening the string to a mere six millimeters in length increased the natural rate of its oscillations to 40,000 per second. In contrast, the incoming signal from Bandung, 12,000 kilometers away, was a wave 7.5 kilometers long; the long wave frequency intercepted with the shorter, faster oscillations of the string to create the pattern of long and short dashes of Morse code (figure 6.5).[22] Einthoven Sr.'s meaning of tuning implicitly suggested something very important: the compression of time and space by operating with the geography of a six-millimeter string in a vacuum. Tuning promised to maneuver around geopolitical forces. Technically, this also meant managing the properties of the string of the galvanometer and the precision to stretch the string to the exact length without breaking it or loosing grip, so that it could oscillate at exactly the right rate to register a signal. By manipulating the awkward

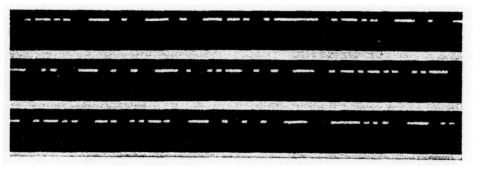

FIGURE 6.5 "String-galvanometer recording made in Leiden of wireless signals from Bandoeng." Willem Einthoven Sr., "The String Galvanometer and the Measurement of the Action Currents of the Heart," in *Nobel Lectures, Physiology or Medecine 1922–1941* (Amsterdam: Elsevier, 1965), 99.

scale and weight of the instrument in the lab, the Einthovens brought Java closer; that was the other implicit meaning of tuning: re-establishing proximity, bringing the colony close.

EINTHOVEN IN A BUNKER · The Einthovens' string galvanometer also created a new way of thinking about volcanoes that helped to resolve one of the central challenges for volcano monitoring: how to know from a distance what was happening inside the crater. Eruptions often created flows of massive clouds that obscured visibility. Fieldwork to study calderas during quiet periods involved long, arduous, and sometimes dangerous hikes, while camping was challenging on difficult terrain and nearly impossible during eruptions. Fieldwork also did not allow for continuous in situ observation. One solution was to build observatories in a crescent shape around the crater from south, west, and north; most of them were no closer than three or four kilometers from the summit, and each observatory was kitted out with a seismograph. Seismographs, it was hoped, could overcome the distance between the observatory and the crater. In addition to this, the observatories were networked to each other and to the urban center of Muntilan in the lowlands via telephone and radio receivers. The Babadan observatory, built in response to the washed away ruins of the Maron observatory, on July 4, 1931, in the northwest, was linked to an alarm that dinged during eruptions. Scientists also deployed military and engineering techniques for surveillance. At Ngepos, they built a prison-like steel lookout tower that allowed them to peer above the tree line. Vladimir A. Petrushevsky even built foxholes from which to watch eruptions, a technique he learned as a White Army officer during the Russian Revolution.[23] At Babadan, scientists created a bunker that, as Newman van Padang explained, contained oxygen tanks that were based on standards from submarines and that would allow three observers to survive for eleven hours without oxygen. The tunnel to the bunker was sealed at both ends with heat-resistant reinforced glass, a metal door, and industrial hinges. It also included, according to van Padang, "benches, food, drinking water, asbestos overalls, spades and other tools to be used in case the terrain should be covered with hot eruptive material on the men leaving the tunnel."[24] It was in this bunker that scientists sought to combine the innovation of the string galvanometer with the seismograph.[25]

In 1943, Reinout van Bemmelen was pulled from a Japanese internment camp to investigate a potential eruption of Merapi. He told the colonels that they were on the verge of a massive eruption (this was at the same time that he drew the first map that indicated the cataclysmic eruption of AD 1006 that supposedly annihilated ancient Hindu-Buddhist Java). Van Bemmelen saw that the lava at the summit was glowing red, illuminating the night sky, and that it was dangerously on the verge of exploding.[26] There were already two million cubic meters of stone and lava lying on top of more recent, weaker material from the eruption in 1930 and that threatened to give way and slide down the western flank toward Babadan.[27] He imagined massive clouds of super-heated pyroclastic avalanches, hot sand, and boulders flowing into the rivers from the summit. If it came to pass, he wrote, it would "cause death and destruction if they reach the densely populated and cultivated area of the west foot."[28]

Scientists had already installed a Weichert seismograph (from Germany) in the bunker at Babadan. It was the most common model in the world at the time, but it was flawed. Like Einthoven Sr.'s first electrocardiograph, it was massive and difficult to move. The metal and wood box contained two hundred kilograms of weight and a large, inverted pendulum that terminated in a phonograph-like, fragile stylus.[29] The weight was fixed to the ground while the pendulum hovered independently; the idea was that the stylus remained stationary as the bulk registered and amplified movements through the ground first to the pendulum and then, through an intricate system of pulleys and hinges, to the stylus, where its needle scratched them on a paper roll blackened with candle soot.

The Weichert was prone to mechanical failure, though. Van Bemmelen wrote that it was unable to "hear"; it was not sensitive enough to register small distant shakes and shudders from landslides or slumping, nor could it register breaking rocks that could collide with villages on the slopes. The Weichert was better at registering larger tremors such as volcanic and tectonic earthquakes. The lack of sensitivity of the machine, in effect, kept observers blind and at a distance from the crater. Van Bemmelen reasoned that the amplifiers and transmitters created by the Einthovens might enhance the Weichert's sensitivity. As he saw it, the string galvanometer was a better "ear," and "in this way, the omen of an approaching catastrophe might be recorded."[30] Increasing sensitivity meant, again, overcoming distance, and overcoming distance meant collapsing the delay between the present and the future, the crater and the slopes. If the instrument could be tuned in just the right way, observers in the dark tunnel could see and hear again and continue to choreograph the population with events in the distant crater.

Einthoven Jr. worked under the authority of the occupying Japanese military and received permission from Mr. Maseh, the newly installed director of mines, to collaborate with van Bemmelen.[31] They set to work on combining the electromagnet developed for the string galvanometer with a suspended moving coil that amplified minor movements in the ground and then triggered a bell and red light. Telephone calls could then also be made to Muntilan and sirens along the slopes sounded.[32] Van Bemmelen wrote that the "rumbling of escaping gasses, the clinking of rockslides, the roar of avalanches, the resonance tones of the lava dome, varying with its mass," could all be witnessed for the first time on seismograph paper; a new resolution appeared from what was once invisible in the distance.[33] Observation no longer required seeing or hearing the volcano in situ. Scientists were brought to the caldera from the darkness of the bunker through the scratching on the seismograph paper, just as Java had been brought to Leiden through pulses in the air. The seismograph was an extended ear stretching through space and into the future. Via the relay of warning signals, it would also bring the events in the caldera to the slopes five kilometers away and before the event materialized. Einthoven Jr.'s short-wave seismograph tuned them in.

By the time van Bemmelen and Einthoven Jr. installed the seismograph in the bunker at Babadan in May 1943, the activities on Merapi had petered out, and the eruption that van Bemmelen had predicted never came to pass. Einthoven Jr.'s seismograph disappeared and was never put to another recorded use or developed further; the geopolitics of war intervened again, this time to interrupt Einthoven Jr.'s fantasies of proximity; he was interned and died in a prisoner of war camp in 1945.[34] The dysfunctional and bulky Weichert remained in the bunker for decades.

HEARTBEATS IN AN OIL FIELD · The string galvanometer had another, even more peculiar, afterlife in oil and gas prospecting. It was frequently used to convert shock waves created by hundreds of pounds of exploding dynamite into ink scratches on paper. Prospectors read the seismograms for salt domes, a cap that often trapped petroleum deposits beneath them. The Texas-based Petty Geophysical Engineering Company was at the forefront of using string galvanometers for this purpose and developed their own versions of the technology in 1918.[35] In 1954, the Robert H. Ray Company, which resulted from a merger with Petty Geophysical and became one of the largest geophysical prospecting companies in the world, ran an advertisement in an oil and gas prospecting trade journal with a photo of Einthoven Sr., an image of a heartbeat wave, and a silhouette of a heart. In large letters, it read, "The earth has *heartbeats*, too!" This was followed by explanatory text:

> Dr. Einthoven was the father of the modern electrocardiograph, which has been of great benefit to mankind. The seismograph, which records accurate graphs of the earth's heartbeats, has also been beneficial to mankind in its contribution to the development of the oil industry.
>
> We, at Robert H. Ray Company, have been recording the earth's heartbeats or seismic reflection for 20 years now and believe that this vast experience makes us able diagnosticians.[36]

The Robert H. Ray Company understood not only their debt to medical diagnostics but also that the technology made the earth and the human body similarly legible. This could be understood as a poetic metaphor or, more cynically, as the co-option of a respected Nobel prize–winning diagnostician by the oil industry. But acknowledging the significance of Einthoven Sr. was more than this; they were also acknowledging that the seismograph represented the human body and the earth through the same signals. They collapsed the difference between the interior of the body and the earth; it was an invocation of much older ideas of the macrocosm contained in the microcosm of the body, articulated no less by a fossil fuel prospecting company.

EPISODE 2: KEJAWEN · The magazine *Mawas Diri* (Self-Improvement) was published in Jakarta between the 1970s and 1990s (figure 6.6). It mixed spiritual with philosophical and nationalist issues and brought together Java-centric history and studies of Hinduism and Buddhism with political history and personal growth. Damardjati Supadjar, a philosopher, consultant to the sultan of Jogja, and lecturer at the University of Gadjah Mada, was a frequent contributor. He was also a thinker of Kejawen, or Javanism, an ethno-nationalist philosophy with roots in the Theosophy movement and the nationalist revolution of the early twentieth century. Javanism flourished in the Suharto period, especially in the 1970s and 1980s, when it was given official endorsement as an *aliran kepercayaan* (belief system), by the government. Suharto even personally supported the movement and many of his own beliefs were aligned with it.[37] In 1970, nearly fifteen thousand people in Surakarta reported membership in one of the city's thirteen *kebatinan*—or belief-system groups, which included many Kejawen groups.[38] An account by Jan Bakker from 1973 lists nearly 280 *kebatinan* groups across Indonesia, many of the largest being versions of mystical Islam connected with Kejawen.[39] At the core of the movement was the elaboration of a syncretic Islam and ideas of traditional Javanese identity; it also resisted the most popular forms of modernist, more orthodox Islam as embodied in organizations such as Muhammadiyah. But Kejawen, it was emphasized, was not a religion, it was a belief *system*, and therefore did not compete for membership with the major religious organizations. As such, practices such as ancestor worship, ritual processions, trance dances, and offerings to local deities—practices strictly frowned upon in more orthodox Islamic circles—were framed as "tradition," not as religion, and thus carved out a space for themselves where they could be practiced without competing against religious doctrine. Framing practices as such also aligned with Kejawen's ethno-nationalist character by associating rituals and deities with the central Javanese sultanates and notions of ethnic identity. This appealed to Suharto and his regime, which was overwhelmingly made up of Javanese military generals who were interested in asserting Javanese cultural identity as the basis for Indonesian national identity. Kejawen cut across class, bringing working-class farmers together with the ruling generals around shared ideas of Javanese ethnic superiority and romanticized notions of Javanese history.

A 1990 article by K. Kartosutedjo, titled "Rooster Call as an Indicator of the Presence of a Hotline" and published in *Mawas Diri*, dealt with the themes of proximity, distance, technology, and the body from a Kejawen

FIGURE 6.6 The magazine *Mawas Diri* (Self-Improvement) brought together nationalist themes with ideas of spiritual development. This cover depicts characters from *wayang* theater. Cover, *Mawas Diri* 9, no. 19 (September 30, 1990).

perspective.[40] In his folksy, funny essay, Kartosutedjo made the case that rooster calls—ubiquitous in Indonesian urban and village life—were lines of mystical communion with God. A hotline, he wrote, was a "means of spiritual communication between heaven and earth."[41] Angels such as Jibrail (Gabriel) also used hotlines; the ladder used on Lailat'ul Qodar (Qadr night) to communicate with heaven was a hotline, and so, too, was the date on which the Christian Holy Spirit descended. Kartosutedjo went on to relay how in Indonesian traditions, rooster calls suggested spiritual well-being or the presence of supernatural forces. A church in Bandung, for instance, was even in the shape of a chicken because the sect believed that the crowing rooster was a "messenger of the descent of the Holy Spirit."[42] The Bugis kept roosters on their boats to warn of the presence of evil and ghosts; the Sundanese said that if a rooster crowed at night, there would be a pregnant virgin in the morning. Kartosutedjo wrote that a friend had recommended to him that the best time to meditate was in the morning when the rooster crows harmonize and the hotline emerged between this world and the "real world," the world of God. "The rooster crow," he related, "is a miracle for getting rid of the influence of demonic forces, ghosts, demons and magic of all sorts."[43] It was a literal, telephonic, connection between the material and immaterial world, the sacred and profane.

One might think that the invocation of the telephone was merely a convenient metaphor; but it was more than that. The hotline was a model for conceiving of spiritual life as a technology, and it was a way to understand modern technology spiritually. Doing so made rooster calls and telephones playfully legible as extraordinary mystical devices. To dismiss them as metaphors would miss the work that they actually did in making both modern technology and the material world uniquely meaningful. Kartosutedjo did not simply apply the logic of the telephone to nontelephonic things, he leveraged the meaning of rooster calls with modern communication technologies until they cracked open, revealing unforeseen capacities to make sense and meaning, to create and connect worlds. What is more, the rooster-call-as-telephone was not wholly new but adapted folk and religious narratives of rooster calls to the modern telephonic world; he was pulling folk beliefs—many of which were in danger of becoming redundant through technological progress—out of the dustbin of history by suggesting they had always been at the vanguard of technological progress. The rooster, in other words, anticipated the telephone.

Kartosutedjo's story reminds us that Kejawen mystical narratives were often also technological narratives. Not only did they wrestle head-on with the meaning and epistemological capacity of new technologies; they were also often about communication. He used modern technology to connect realities often lived as separate or discrete: the given world and the world of God, the profane and the sacred, the present and past, the living and the dead. These realities were therefore geographical too, referencing technologies that brought discrete places together and built bridges. We can begin to see, then, how Kartosutedjo's rooster circles us back to volcano observatories, seismographs, and string galvanometers. For many volcano scientists, their technologies were also wrapped up with similar stories about crossing borders, bringing the distant near, electrical pulses that emanated from either Merapi's crater or the human heart. All of it was concerned with collapsing distance, bringing bodies and the earth closer together, mediation to create intimacy, closeness as a technology. In mystical stories of Kejawen, many of the same technologies (telephones, radios, and seismographs) were also used as the basis for mystical experiences. Kejawen mysticism, however, was not actually about unmediated experiences of the divine; instead, it was thoroughly preoccupied with how technological mediation facilitated spirituality. On volcanoes, Kejawen mystics even used the same technologies introduced by volcano scientists in observatories as the very mechanisms for their own mystical communication.

PULSES IN KENINGAR · Keningar is at the end of a paved road, one thousand meters above the Indian Ocean and four kilometers from the observatory at Babadan. The village predates the erection of the observatory in 1931 and is one of the villages that the observatory was built to protect.[44] I was there in 2016–17, and then frequently afterward. Above Keningar was forest, and then the summit of Merapi, roughly four kilometers away. Riverine chasms of volcanic debris bordered the village to the north and south, and nearly seventy families lived in a cluster of houses clad with dark gray volcanic stone. Narrow alleys connected the village to the fields of rice, tobacco, chilies, and hardy vegetables. Some residents worked in artisanal mines extracting volcanic stones, sand, and ash from the river valleys. During daylight hours, a stream of trucks rolled through the village to the rivers to remove mined material and cart it away into the Southeast Asian sand trade.

Suparno was born here in 1972; he completed secondary school at the state Islamic school a few minutes down the road.[45] When he was twenty, he married Anik from Banyiwangi, East Java. They lived in a two-bedroom house he inherited from his father, who had also lived his entire life in Keningar. After Suparno's father died in 2000, Yoni, Suparno's mother, lived with them. Suparno had three children; the eldest, Dewi, was attending the same secondary school that Suparno had attended. He rarely left Keningar and has never been outside of Java; a couple of times per year he will, as he put it, "descend" to the towns and cities in the lowlands. He has been to Jakarta only a handful of times. Suparno's neighbors were also born in Keningar or had married into Keningar families. During the day, he farmed rice and chilies on three parcels of land a short walk from his house. In the evenings, after dinner, he often hosted guests in his sitting room or went out to visit friends.

One evening he invited me into his sitting room to show me something. I arrived and was offered coffee by his mother while I waited for

Suparno to rummage through a cabinet and then return with his collection of polished stones and crystals. He emptied a black velvet bag onto the table. Some stones had not yet been fixed to their silver ring bands, and sometimes, he said, he spent leisure hours sanding down their edges to fit the backing. Some stones were milky white and smooth with different patterns; one was black and small with a matte finish. Some were jade, quartz, and agate. His jade, the most expensive, came from Borneo and cost Rp200,000, or the equivalent of roughly two weeks' earnings after feeding the family and paying bills. He explained that each stone held a different property; they affected health and could be used in meditation and prayer; some brought people closer or repelled others, and sometimes they created good luck. I pressed for more detail about their function, but he avoided answering and lowered his voice until it was a barely audible whisper. He said he was telling me secrets that I was unable to understand and, moreover, it was time to meet Santoso.

I finished my glass of bitter black coffee while Suparno circled his black Honda motorcycle around to the front of the house. I thanked his mother for the hospitality and joined Suparno on the motorcycle to ride through the paddy fields at night. Merapi was obscured behind silver clouds as we took the old brick roads too narrow for cars and descended through stands of bamboo and coconut palms into a river valley that passed the base of a national telecommunications tower. At that elevation, cellular data access on phones was irregular, and digital phones were rare until 2016. Almost no one had a personal computer. Televisions were common and showed local and national programs via a few rusted satellite dishes fixed to traditional red tile roofs. Radio was prevalent, too, and the first receiver was said to have arrived in the village when Somo Sitar, a farmer who had come into some money, bought a black and brown Galindra receiver in the 1960s, some thirty years after Babadan had broadcast a radio signal to the observatories in the lowlands.[46] Villages at that altitude, according to residents, were not permanently electrified until the 1980s, while Babadan, had electricity as early as 1931.[47] In this region, like many others around the volcano, the observatories were the first places to be electrified and connected with the lowlands.

As we descended toward Santoso's house, we merged with wider roads and the volume of traffic increased. Cars, small pickup trucks, and minivan buses rushed around us while motorbikes with racks fixed to their backs held fruits and vegetables from the lowlands for sale. Others passed us selling dumplings or fried rice. Frogs bellowed in the fields.

As we approached Santoso's in Talaman, we turned first into an alley, then into a narrow driveway in front of a green painted concrete house. Suparno opened the front door, said a few words, then gestured for me to follow.

I sat on a pink sofa with plastic wrapping on it in a sitting room with mint-green walls. A placemat with an aerial photo of the Kaaba was taped to one wall, another wall displayed a large oil painting of a goldfish. A bare light bulb hung from the middle of the room, and a bed sheet with cartoons on it was slung across a doorway, obscuring a person watching television news at a loud volume. Santoso's head appeared through the curtain, and he placed his phone on the coffee table and sat down. He wore a large, deep-red stone ring like one of the rings from Suparno's velvet bag.

Santoso was born in Sumatra and had moved to Talaman a decade ago, when he was in his fifties, together with his wife, Sutri. During the day, he was a cobbler at the market, a few minutes' drive away, where he made a few thousand rupiah a day to supplement his state pension from his twenty years working as a civil servant. His wife worked in the market, too, and his grown children still lived in Sumatra. In the evening, he provided fortune telling, spiritual guidance, and relationship counseling for his (mostly) male guests. Many came from nearby villages, were farmers like Suparno, miners, or civil servants working in local offices. Government employees were only slightly wealthier than farmers, but they retired with a pension, while farmers worked until they were supported by their children. Sometimes Santoso took telephone calls from his businessmen friends in Jakarta looking for advice. A few minutes after we arrived, Suparno's cousin Ade joined us; he was young, unmarried, and worked in a nearby sand mine operating large machinery.

Suparno told Santoso that I was interested in learning about Kejawen. It was common for local farmers and laborers in the region to claim that they practiced it; it was also often called mysticism, *kebatinan*, or *kearifan lokal* (local wisdom). In the village adjacent to Keningar there was a small personal Kejawen library, where Kejawen publications and divination manuals were consulted by reading groups. Elderly and young villagers, for instance, read *Puisi Kejawen* (Kejawen poetry) aloud together (it was published in Surakarta and contained poetry and spiritual mantras). Book stalls in Yogyakarta sold periodicals with titles such as *Kejawen: Jurnal Kebudayaan Jawa* (Journal of Javanese culture), a more recent, academic-oriented iteration of *Mawas Diri*. *Kitab Primbon* divination manuals, often derived from the *serat* and *babad* from Surakarta and Yogyakarta, also contained mantras, numerology, astrology, astronomy, traditional medicine, and calendars and were consulted by elderly rural Javanese men who practiced Kejawen. Monographs such as *Agama Jawa: Ajaran, Amalan, dan Asal-Usul Kejawen* (The religion of Java: Teaching, practices, and the origins of Kejawen), by Suwardi Endraswara at Gadjah Mada University, and *Manekung di Puncak Gunung: Jalan Keselamatan Kejawen* (Offerings on the mountain: The way of Kejawen), by Suhardi, also at Gadjah Mada University, explained the history and meaning of Kejawen as an intrinsically ethno-Javanese metaphysics and could be found in small local bookstores and larger chain stores. In Yogyakarta and Surakarta, small groups of Kejawen devotees met, sometimes buoyed by a local guru, to make pilgrimages to ancestral graves from the Mataram era. The group Kejawen Maneges published their own monograph, *Ajaran Kejawen Maneges: Agama Asli Jawa* (The doctrine of Kejawen maneges: A Javanese religion), detailing their genealogical connection to the pre-Islamic kingdoms of Majapahit.[48] It was not unusual in Keningar, or in other villages near Babadan, to meet men who proclaimed with varying degrees of commitment to practicing Kejawen. Santoso was one of them.

Santoso explained that his understanding of Kejawen was that it was a philosophy of communication and transmission. Everything communicated, he said, stones, volcanoes, people. What was important was to learn the "frequencies" of the person or object; frequencies were not material, they were waves of energy that moved through and animated material. He used the analogy of a radio station fifty kilometers away in Yogyakarta; the waves were always around us, we were immersed in them, but we could not hear them until we "tuned in to them." All beings broadcast, and we could learn to tune in to their signals. He explained that he knew that Suparno and I would arrive when we did without Suparno having to call him. Later, Suparno told me that he and Santoso often communicated this way, without the use of phones but by "tuning in."

I asked Santoso where communication comes from and what it is made of. He explained that energy is broadcast from the heart. He used the term *mata batin*, the "eye of the heart," but it also means feeling or intuition. By training himself to tune in to the hearts of his friends, they no longer needed to rely on state or private telecommunications infrastructure like the massive telecommunications tower Suparno and I passed on the way to Santoso's house. The red and white towers that transected the rice paddies and extended across the flanks of Java's volcanic spine were not there for him; they were not *his* infrastructure. The heart was its own, superior, independent device. With the "eye of the heart," he could know where Suparno was at any time of the day. Suparno mentioned that it was a habit of Santoso's to know what he had done the day before; he once explained that Santoso knew he was worried about his daughter's school fees without Suparno having spoken about it. Santoso could also apparently communicate directly with people at great distances, and friends in Jakarta and Sumatra could "tune in" to him. The "eye of the heart" could overcome distance and create new forms of proximity. Santoso's practices resonated with Kartosutedjo's rooster calls in that they were both fantasies of direct communication that nevertheless relied on communication mediums as their models. Tuning in was a radio metaphor for the body, just as the rooster call was a vision of the rooster as a telephone.

The heart, Santoso continued, did not broadcast in only one direction, though. In other words, it was not a radio show projected out over the airwaves. Rather, it was more like a call-in show. Such programs were often heard in the evenings in Keningar when people tuned their receivers or cell phones to them. Between American country music, Javanese gamelan, and Indonesian pop ballads, local callers would have brief discussions, make requests, or just call to say hello, mention their village, and send shout-outs to friends.

This was the model for Santoso's Kejawen mystical philosophy of communication, the call-in radio show. If one could tune in to the right frequency, hearts could converse. But in his model, tuning in was not a material, infrastructural process; it was *barely material*; but it had substance, it was a thing, it was energy, and it was made of bodies. It typified what people in Keningar often described as *mystical*, that which is at the edge of matter and space. Because communication was mystical, it was not restricted by the resistance and friction that space and time conventionally impose. Suparno and Santoso could contact each other without having recourse to mediation; they could bypass the technology and infrastructure that cost money they did not have and rely on their bodies alone. They did not need the pulse of the cell phone or the towers built by the state; they had autonomy and proximity, power over distance. Suparno and Santoso's mysticism overcame the material world through the very pulses that Einthoven Jr. and van Bemmelen attempted to register from the volcano.

Suparno was studying Santoso's techniques, and a month earlier, Santoso asked that he fast and meditate for grueling lengths of time. He spent the night in his rice field to learn how to tune in to the frequencies of the rice plants he had worked with for his entire life. This would give him a better understanding of their needs and, in turn, increase his yield. It would allow him to communicate with animals, including the rats and frogs that lived in his fields and who could sometimes become pests. One of the exercises included meditating with a Javanese scorpion; the purpose was to use the "eye of his heart" to subdue the scorpion and keep it at ease. He had a similar exercise with a rooster. For Suparno, tuning in was also a spiritual technology of self-control, focus, and empathizing with objects; it required a clarity and consistency of attention that became a way to draw distant objects and people close and showed that he was in control of himself and could transcend the material world. This mysticism was magical because it was extra-ordinary; in other words, at the frontiers of state infrastructure and technology, in highly volatile and vulnerable environments, it created intimacy.

WALKY-TALKIES · The presence of the observatory at Babadan, only a few kilometers away, was not insignificant. As mentioned previously, the volcano observatories were the first architectures to contain communication technologies such as telephones, telegraphs, radios, and electricity that became the very basis for the ideas that Suparno and Santoso had about communication. When van Bemmelen collaborated with Einthoven Jr. to use the string galvanometer to "hear" the distant crater, they were importing new technologies into an otherwise impoverished rural region. Observatories remained highly technological architectures throughout the twentieth century, increasing their number of scientific instruments and devices which, even by the twenty-first century, remained rare in nearby villages. This discrepancy did not go unnoticed by Suparno or Santoso: they understood that the observatories represented the state, and for them, the state was often associated with corruption and incompetence. State infrastructures such as radio and telephone networks were linked to crony capitalism that funneled capital to those with power in the lowland urban centers. Scientists were therefore representatives of the state and implicated in its corruption. Moreover, corruption led to incompetence; observatory scientists were often ineffective in predicting or managing eruptions, and their expertise was regarded with suspicion; observatories stood out as beacons of a broken system of governance. Kejawen promised to repair the failures of observatories by turning to ideas of tradition and Javanese ethnic purity. Mystical practices harkened back to the history of the sultanates while also promising a form of communication that circumvented the state and the observatory system; mystics could become their own observatories. Kejawen, therefore, was paradoxically modeled on observatories, yet undermined them; those who practiced Kejawen could create new forms of proximity and distance by remaking the observatories in the image of their own bodies.

Suparno's walky-talky rendered this paradoxical condition especially stark. During the eruption of 2010, residents of Keningar were forced to evacuate for nearly six weeks. This separated them from their fields, livestock, and livelihoods, and they were forced to live off donations in a refugee settlement in Muntilan. When the eruption subsided and they were permitted to return to Keningar, a local nongovernmental organization donated walky-talkies that were connected to the observatory at Babadan. One of the channels could tune in to a signal from the observatory that indicated the status of activity in the crater as a pattern of beeps. Other channels would permit the walky-talky holders to speak with each other or tune in to radio stations. The idea was that the villagers could communicate with each other or listen to the crater when they were out in their fields or at a distance from the village. Suparno explained to me that it was comforting to be able to tune in to the radio signal from the crater with the same ease that he tuned into music on the radio or to his friend Santoso. It allowed him to feel more directly connected to the crater. He relied on observatory infrastructure to feel connected and safe. Thus, his distrust of the observatory was not simple; its technologies were folded into the mysticism of Kejawen, but they were also used, through the walky-talky, to create proximity with the volcano. Architecture and technology operated in this thick, contradictory space: they did not simply monitor; they also provided means to work through a much broader bandwidth of what proximity and distance, togetherness and autonomy, meant. Technology reduced the spatial and temporal distance between the observatory and the lowlands, but it also created new metaphors through which the very meaning of subjectivity could be rethought.

EPISODE 3: METAXIAN'S WAVES

Everything makes a wave.—JEAN-PHILIPPE METAXIAN, 2015

I went to meet Jean-Philippe Metaxian, a French seismologist from the Institute for Research and Development (IRD), at the Center for Volcanology and Geological Hazard Mitigation in Bandung, where the coordination for

Indonesian volcano monitoring is overseen. He was directing a multiyear project called DOMErapi. The project's aim was to research the conduit and dome system of Merapi.[49] His team of volcano scientists and engineers were conducting their research, though, not in Bandung but in a messy, instrument-strewn office in the Merapi observatory in Yogyakarta. He explained that DOMErapi was a collaboration between the Indonesian and French governments and that their team would transfer their data to Indonesian volcano scientists in return for access to the volcano. The French government, he explained, saw Merapi as a living laboratory: it was unique because it was one of the most active volcanoes in the world with a dense population living on it. While there were no equivalent volcanoes in mainland France, there were many in French-governed overseas regions—departments and territories such as Soufrier, Pelée, and Piton de la Fournaise. But those volcanoes did not erupt often, so Merapi was their stand-in. The lessons they learned from Merapi, ideally, would later be transported and applied to those islands.[50]

The director of volcanology in Bandung asked that Metaxian direct the project from Bandung rather than from Yogyakarta, though, for reasons Metaxian did not understand (but he suspected the decision was the result of office politics). He explained this as he hosted me for dinner in his rented house in a wealthy colonial neighborhood in the hills of Bandung. The villa was of the typical tropical modernist 1920s style in which much of Bandung was built, the same style of house that van Bemmelen and Einthoven Jr. would have lived in. We ate lasagna and salad in the quiet, airy, dining room framed by curved glass and shutters that opened onto banyan and coconut trees in the back garden. Carefully trimmed boxwood hedges punctuated the tropical scene with the geometry of a modernist painting.

Metaxian explained that his work as a geophysicist in many of the world's volcano observatories had long been shaped by geopolitical forces. The fact that the French state monitored volcanoes outside of French borders meant that they were sometimes at the front lines of the politics of eruptions. In addition to advancing their own national scientific interests, French volcanology was also motivated by the politics of post–Cold War international development and aid, often in former European colonies. Metaxian described an example from Ecuador, in 1999, where he had been working in the state volcano observatory while the national banking system collapsed. The sucre was on the verge of hyperinflation, and bank deposits had been frozen; banks were shuttering, and President Jamil

Mahuad declared a state of emergency.[51] Mass demonstrations spilled onto the streets, and at the same time Pichincha, a volcano west of Quito, began to erupt. Metaxian explained that "trust in Mahuad was broken, but he was backed by the Americans." Concern began to emerge among the observatory staff and in the government that an eruption would further destabilize the country, in part because they were too underresourced to implement an effective disaster-management plan. The danger was that a failed evacuation could further enrage people and destabilize the country. Metaxian said that soon "shadowy Americans began to appear in the halls of the [state] observatory." François Goudard, the French ambassador, asked Metaxian to take him to the volcano for a survey. Metaxian drove the ambassador together with a French colonel and the director of the IRD to the volcano, and all the while (he suspected), they had been tailed by the American Secret Service. Soon after, French scientists were suddenly and bewilderingly shut out of scientific meetings about the eruption; only Americans and Ecuadorians could participate. There were explosions throughout 1999, but in the end, there was no massive eruption, and in January 2000, Mahuad fled his palace amid a military junta.[52] The change in government allowed for the venting of popular disdain for the United States and its history of backing puppet governments in the region; as a result, American military bases were soon forced to close and diplomats were repatriated.[53]

After being shut out of Quito, Metaxian moved to the scientific station at Darwin, in the volcanic Galapagos Islands. When one of the many volcanoes there erupted, he explained that scientists ran to the beaches to carry vulnerable turtles to safety: "They [had] to pick them up by hand, sometimes they [were] so heavy they require[d] two or three people." His purpose in the Galapagos Islands was to update the monitoring methods and to set up new seismic stations, but the observatory was, in his words, "full of spies."[54] The Americans, he thought, after having been kicked out of Ecuador, were using scientific espionage to reenter the region. United States military bases had been in the Galapagos Islands since the Second World War, but when they were forced out, they "destroyed the base, ripped up the tarmac, and shredded everything," rendering it useless to Ecuadorians. He suspected that United States and other aligned scientists were cooperating with intelligence agencies. He told me that an Australian scientist with administrative power had confronted him and questioned his presence in the Galapagos Islands, and soon after Metaxian's project was closed. The monitoring equipment on the island was never upgraded.

The day after Metaxian recounted this story, I sat in the passenger seat of his rented BMW on the way to the observatory headquarters in Bandung. We passed tennis courts and white villas protruding from lush hills, and it began to rain. As we crossed the Pasupati Bridge, we could see the shanty towns that filled the river valley below. Turning into the compound of white modernist buildings built when van Bemmelen was working in what was still the Netherlands East Indies, we entered the mission control center for Indonesian volcanology. I sat down on the leather sofa in Metaxian's office while he turned on the air conditioning unit beside a framed photo of former president Suharto shaking hands and giving an award to John Katili, former director of the Ministry of Mining and Resources, seismologist, champion of the legacy of van Bemmelen, and one of the first to apply the theory of plate tectonics to the Indonesian archipelago.

French scientists had long been present on Merapi's slopes, but they started appearing more frequently in the 1960s and 1970s under Suharto's New Order, when the government began to open in new ways to scientific collaborations with the United States and Western European democracies. Part of the reason for this was that Suharto had come to power through a violent attack on the Indonesian Communist Party and had murdered hundreds of thousands of people loosely associated with its membership between 1965 and 1966. The Communist Party was outlawed, which was seen as a victory in the Cold War battle against the spread of "Asian communism." The move realigned Indonesia's diplomatic relations toward capitalist democracies. These geopolitical realignments set the stage for new scientific (geological) collaborations and technological transfers between France and Indonesia. The work of Katili was crucial in this regard because he brokered the collaborations with US and European geologists; he invited Warren Hamilton from the United States Geological Survey (USGS) to Indonesia in 1970. International development agendas—premised as they were on supporting capitalist and not communist forms of political and economic development—brought French and other European volcanologists and geophysicists to the flanks of Merapi to share their skills and technologies with Indonesian scientists.

One important French scientist in this moment was Haroun Tazieff. He had begun his studies of Merapi's crater in the 1960s, and in 1966, only one year after Suharto had been in power and while the slaughter of communists was still unfolding. Tazieff wrote, "There is, at the moment, a lack of trained scientists"; there were only five scientists with degrees working in the observatory in Bandung with the responsibility for all Indonesia's volcanoes.[55] Tazieff returned to Merapi several times in the following years, becoming one of France's most famous scientists. Over the course of his career, he made nearly one hundred films and authored thirty books, most of them documenting his scientific work on volcanoes. He was the Jacques Cousteau of volcanoes. Elizabeth Inandiak, who grew up in France when Tazieff was active, explained Tazieff's celebrity: the French state did not have a space program to capture the public imagination in the Cold War; instead, they had volcanoes and the deep ocean. Jean-Luc Godard even praised one of Tazieff's films because of its rococo-like depictions of lava. In 1980, Tazieff made *Gunung Merapi* in a profile of his years of research on Merapi. He was fascinated, like Metaxian thirty-six years later, with studying the chemical and structural components of the dome.

In the 1970s and 1980s, Tazieff's former students Maurice and Katia Krafft were also seeking to become celebrity volcanologists, and they, too, visited Merapi and other Indonesian volcanoes on scientific expeditions. Their access was likewise predicated on sharing scientific information with Indonesian scientists, and over the course of 1971, they traveled across Java making films and taking scientific measurements that resulted in their book *A l'assaut des volcans: Islande, Indonésie* (The assault on volcanoes: Iceland, Indonesia) (figures 6.7 and 6.8). The Kraffts applied the new theory of plate tectonics, as articulated by Katili and Hamilton, to elaborate a vision of the earth as if it were in the violent throes of remaking itself (figure 6.9). When they undertook their ascent of Merapi to study the character of its crater, they called their project an "assault." They established their scientific camp on Pasar Bubar, the spirit market, for three days of measurements, the same plateau on which Metaxian would later establish his seismic signaling stations and on which he would even persuade Indonesian scientists to build another bunker to house digital seismographs and satellite internet ports.

The presence of French scientists on Merapi by way of the Cold War geopolitics of international development no doubt shaped the French public's appreciation for Merapi in a shifting conception of the earth. The Kraffts were explicit: for them, Merapi was the expression of an earth in violent turmoil. Its plates were defined by borders in conflict; volcanology was an assault; the earth was in a perpetual state of creative self-destruction. But this Cold War science also transformed Indonesian volcanology. Tazieff, for instance, helped establish a net of seismometers around Merapi to monitor earthquakes. Surono, the head of Pusat Vulkanologi dan Mitigasi Bencana Geologi (Center for Volcanology and Geological Hazard Mitigation) between 2006 and 2014, was trained as a seismologist at the Université de Savoie and had been supervised by Michel Halbwachs, who had also supervised Metaxian's doctoral work. Agus Budi Santoso, a seismologist at the observatory in Yogyakarta, also completed his PhD at the University Savoie Mont Blanc, while François Beauducel completed his PhD dissertation, in 1988, on ground deformation at Merapi at Université Paris-VII; Beauducel later advised the observatory on monitoring techniques. Since Tazieff's presence there, French geophysicists have regularly been included in scientific teams investigating the aftermath of major eruptions. When Surono published a scientific paper analyzing the eruption of Merapi in 2010, the most significant in a generation, five of his fourteen coauthors were from French universities.

Metaxian was unique, though, because unlike many others, he was a geophysicist who acknowledged this geopolitical history. He understood that volcano observatories were spaces through which foreign states operated via geophysical diplomacy, a form of geopolitics conducted through the dissemination of knowledge of the earth itself—in other words, shaping the narrative of how the earth worked and what its history was. When the Kraffts, for instance, assaulted Merapi, they were applying the (new to them) language of plate tectonics to the volcano, a theory that had been developed barely a decade earlier by Warren Hamilton and John Katili. In their analysis, monitoring an eruption on Merapi was linked with the new, broader conceptions of the earth's structure and evolutionary history. At the same time, the importation of new monitoring technologies such as wireless seismology was also becoming newly planetary, as it literally connected observatories on Merapi's flanks to international monitoring stations in USGS offices in Washington, DC, and at European universities. Earth theories flowed along the same paths created by post–Cold War geopolitical settlements, from the capitalist United States to the newly capitalist and recently invented "Third World" of Southeast Asia. While eruptions of Merapi were beginning to be monitored for the first time by Western satellites in orbit, the architecture of Merapi's observatories remained largely unchanged: Babadan was renovated to look like a comfortable Dutch colonial bungalow, even though it was sending signals

FIGURES 6.7 AND 6.8 (OPPOSITE AND ABOVE) Krafft Indonesia expedition.
Katia Krafft and Maurice Krafft, *A l'assaut des volcans: Islande, Indonésie* (Paris: Éditions G. P., 1976), 86–87.

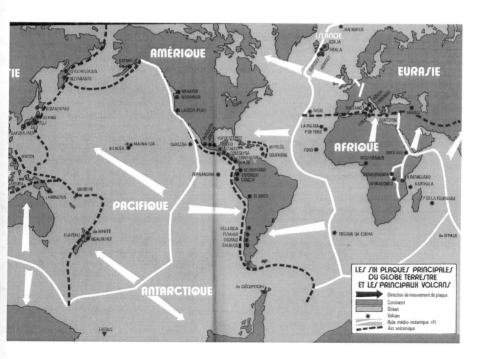

FIGURE 6.9 Plate tectonic diagram of the earth. Katia Krafft and Maurice Krafft, *A
l'assaut des volcans: Islande, Indonésie* (Paris: Éditions G. P., 1976), frontispiece.

to Washington, DC, via satellites. As the bunker became increasingly dilapidated in the 1980s and 1990s, and eventually fell into disuse, it was linked up to monitoring networks that sent its data directly to the Institut des Sciences de la Terre, Savoie, in the Alps; Merapi could now be monitored using data from the same dank bunker where van Bemmelen and Einthoven Jr. sought to sense the pulse of the crater, but at a desk in the Alps.

PICKING: FILTER THE NOISE · Metaxian understood more or less explicitly that volcano geophysics operated on the scales of the sensing human body, the geopolitics of states, and the earth itself. What was at stake in geophysics, in part, was the difficult negotiation of all these scales and that they were each implicated in the others. It was this implicit understanding that aligned his own work with the work of Einthoven Sr. and Jr., van Bemmelen, Santoso, and Suparno. As I sat beneath the photograph of Suharto with Katili, Metaxian explained to me how a geophysicist thinks of the earth as a medium; he said that his morning routine involved "picking," something he had instituted as a daily practice in Quito but that had not yet been taken up in Indonesia; it was "like tending a garden," he said, something one ought to do daily as a form of general maintenance and order.[56] To illustrate what he meant, he revealed the image from a seismograph on Merapi on his computer monitor; it consisted of a horizontal black scratch that looked like a sound wave. "Everything makes a wave," he said. When ocean waves crash on the beach, they propagate through land, sometimes even reaching seismographs located in the middle of continents, thousands of kilometers away. He explained that continents are mediums, as are volcanoes, which vibrate; they are neither stable nor solid; they hum, like the string on the galvanometer. The first step in reading a wave on a seismograph was to "pick" the information from the noise. On Merapi, the seismograph network—the grid of sensors covering an area almost 200 square kilometers and first established by Tazieff—surrounds the caldera and continues down to the Indian Ocean. When the readings from each point in the network were combined, they created a three-dimensional portrait of wave propagation through underground space. To understand how the volcano was moving, the origin of the wave needed to be identified: did it come from magma moving inside the conduit or from tectonic shifts farther afield? Picking identified the origin through the phase of the wave, its length and density in both the horizontal and vertical dimensions (every wave moves in three dimensions). Sometimes waves can even be created by people talking or walking, by rain or wind. The very sounds that van Bemmelen and Eintho-ven Jr. had been trying to tune into in the 1930s had, for Metaxian, become noise: if "the whole volcano is moving," as he put it, then it is important to identify the movements that really matter. As the sensitivity of the seismo-graph network increased, so too did the noise and, therefore, the impor-tance of picking, filtering out the junk. As Metaxian put it, "The mistake that beginners make is to not know the noise."

He isolated an earthquake wave on the screen and calculated its spec-trum, then looked at the frequency band. If it was above ten in amplitude, it was interesting. He checked the results from other stations to see if it registered. It did not: "not interesting."

CONCLUSION · Metaxian's practice of picking was conventional and rig-orous geophysics. His understanding that the earth was a medium for waves had been standard at least since the early twentieth century. Yet, what Metaxian brought to the fore was the social problem of what it meant to separate signals from noise. If picking reduced the problem to amplitude, it made it manageable. But Metaxian's narratives about geo-politics revealed something else: what differentiated signals from noise was more troubling. It was, after all, the geopolitics of the Cold War that made possible the very registering of seismic waves. Did geopolitics con-stitute noise that was "not interesting"? Or, was it the signal? Ought it be considered as intimately wrapped up in the very making of the sig-nal itself? When Santoso and Suparno claimed to tune in to each other, they were adopting the very language of waves that Metaxian would have recognized. But they foregrounded their own bodies, which many geophysicists would consider unreliable, even though scientists such as van Bemmelen and Einthoven Jr. and others tried to extend and manipu-late their bodies' capacities to sense with seismic instruments. What was radical was just how deeply Santoso and Suparno situated their pulsing bodies in the center of their Kejawen metaphysics. Their significance was to remind us that geophysics is, in fact, rooted in ideas of the human body as a communicating medium just as much as it is concerned with the earth as a communicating medium. This, indeed, was one of the impor-tant and unacknowledged functions of Kejawen mysticism: it widened the boundary of what could be considered noise; it was reliant on mod-ern communication technologies and sought to appropriate them to new, more inclusive ends. Their own repurposed mediumship was not a degraded or derivative form of geophysics; rather, it expanded who could participate in sensing the earth.

These three episodes, then, reveal that volcano observatories on Merapi were implicated in far more than the standard narratives of scientific modernization or rational volcano monitoring taking the place of local folk science. Observatories were, in fact, the result of negotiating fundamental problems of what it means to be close to or far from other people and the earth; they were bound up with questions of what constitutes a medium, and where to draw the line that differentiates a human body from the pulsing earth. Not only did observatories extend the state into its hinterlands; at the same time they created sites at which modern global geopolitical tensions played out, and they brought these scales together—the political, planetary, and bodily.

CONCLUSION

———

The Anthropocene is the Indonesian moment of the earth sciences. Scientists are understanding once again that geology is social. Modern political history is now visible in the rock record. We can make sense of this record with the help of the nearly one-century-long story we have just surveyed in this book. We have seen how volcanism, the history of the earth, its structure, the capacity of continents to move and crack and remake themselves were through and through a social process. The earth sciences we have just considered were a celebratory geology of radical uncertainty, a sensual geology, a geology that resisted becoming one thing or another; it was a geology that saw the sea on land, of chthonic underworlds to which we owed debts and obligations because our world emerged from it, a political geology of petrified heroes that remind us of the nearly mythical power we have to say no to unbearable conditions, a power of refusal so impressive it leaves a shape in the landscape to remind us the next time that we need inspiration; a geology that contained justice—geological justice—a justice so human and mortal and fragile and lithic; a social geology; a geology that was a mosque for deities to pray in, because deities also need to fall to their knees; a geology that recognized how the processes of our earth could conspire to form themselves in just such a way as to make a mosque for those deities; a geology that was cosmic and dangerously theological and mythical; a geology that knew the line between human bodies and stones was insecure; a geology that understood at its core that science told big stories about people and the earth; an unapologetically dandy geology, aesthetic, and always too much.

That is the geology that Anthropocene scientists are currently wondering if they can acknowledge. It is terrifying for some—some of my geologist friends still believe in the neat and naive separation of myth and science; some of them are still worried, they say that as scientists they don't "believe" something, instead they "know." But other geologists remember that they are in it because they have a place in their hearts for the earth sciences as a cosmic-mythic-religious project of making sense of where we live, telling stories and making impossible abstractions of this place called the earth. In that version of the earth sciences, we begin to glimpse just what can be learned from the history of volcanology in Java. Remember Umbgrove, wandering around in awe of the mist and peaks and sheer black volcanic stone on Borobudur. His vision was of a geology without restraint that could match the enormity, the complexity, of the cosmos, of crossing scales between the interior of the body and the rotations of the galaxy. It was a barely sober science that shaped how we now understand the earth system. Umbgrove's pulsing cosmos was ultimately polyphonic, a world in which everything produced more complexity by multiplying connections in the same way that a choral arrangement proliferates relationships when any new voice is added. Repetition in this polyphonic world was always at once the spread of difference, in deep time, from the interior of the earth to our beating hearts, out to the galaxy, a great, cosmic slow—but sometimes also unthinkably fast—differentiation. Thought itself was merely an expression, an extension, of this capacity because it was such an excellent tool for differentiation. Consciousness was another voice in the galactic fugue. The work of the dandy geologist was to help identify difference and connection, to labor on the undoing and redoing of what made the human lithic and the lithic inhuman. The danger and power and beauty of the work of volcanologists in Indonesia was on this very line, adding another voice to the chorus that would compound and multiply the zones of intercalation between ourselves and the earth. Such unashamed and naive affirmation was the essence of geopoetics, an undoing of the human through its diffraction into the *geos*, sending it deep into the earth and out into space, a narrative science, a refusal to understand the earth sciences as anything but modern myth-making. Geopoetics, made by the spiritual geographies of Java, transformed the modern understanding of the earth; it made the story of plate tectonics, created the understanding that the earth's surface drifts and folds and remakes itself; it made "our" Earth. Yet, this science has been mostly scrubbed out of our history texts. Indonesian spiritual geographies were partitioned into anthropology books and cataloged in the annals of "belief systems" and "worldviews." The Theosophists and occultists are uncomfortable reminders of the bad old days when the line between the earth sciences and beliefs had not yet been fully purified. But the volcano scientists that join ritual processions or pray in the mosque between taking measurements from their seismographs tangle up these partitions and remind us of how thoroughly theological it is to try to understand the earth.

It is *we*—this same *we* on our plate-tectonic, volcanic, self-differentiating earth—who inherit Javanese geopoetics, who have now to learn how to live with idols buried in slopes and revolutionary heroes jutting out of stone, ocean deities visiting us in our dreams, and the long-gone ghostly ancestors of our distant and unknown neighbors. We need to learn how our own material worlds are made from the deities of people we do not know, to welcome and harbor them, for they can teach us how to build a political geology in the Anthropocene, what it means to give offerings, how to pray again, how to know that geology is not a stable thing but fluid and tempestuous and made, in part, by us.

NOTES

PREFACE

1   Siegert, *Cultural Techniques*, 68–81.

CHAPTER 1. POLITICAL GEOLOGY AS METHOD

1   The Political Geology: Stratigraphies of Power conference was held at Lancaster University, June 2012, while the Political Geology: Active Stratigraphies and the Making of Life conference was held at Cambridge University, November 2017. See Bobbette and Donovan, *Political Geology*; Clark and Yusoff, "Geosocial Formations and the Anthropocene"; Clark and Szerszynski, *Planetary Social Thought*.

2   For a consideration of volume and materiality in the tradition of geopolitics, see Klinke, "On the History of a Subterranean Geopolitics"; Squire and Dodds, "Introduction," 4–16.

3   See Braun, "Producing Vertical Territory," 7–46; Elden, "Secure the Volume," 35–51; Yusoff, "Queer Coal," 203–29; Barry, *Material Politics*.

4   Schaffer et al., *Brokered World*; Delbourgo, "Knowing World," 373–99; Bashford, Kern, and Bobbette, *New Earth Histories*.

5   Yusoff, *Billion Black Anthropocenes*; Povinelli, *Geontologies*.

6   Rudwick, *Earth's Deep History*.

7   See Winchester, *Krakatoa*; D'Arcy Wood, *Tambora*.

8   Specialist literature on the sociology of volcanic risk is vast, with a tradition nearly as old as volcanology itself. Recent literature on "folk" and indigenous conceptions of volcanic risk is more limited. See K. Donovan, "Doing Social Volcanology," 117–26; Schlehe, "Cultural Politics of Natural Disasters," 275–99; Wessing, "Porous Boundaries," 49–82. Protchsky, "Disaster in Indonesia," 1–8.

9   See Oreskes, *Rejection of Continental Drift*; Oreskes, *Science on a Mission*, 139–93; Frankel, *Continental Drift Controversy*.

10   Pyenson, *Empire of Reason.*

11   Taylor, *Social World of Batavia.*

12   Mrázek, *Engineers of Happy Land.*

13   See, for instance, Kusumandinata, *Data Dasar Gunungapi* [sic] *Indonesia;* Sukamto, Soeradi, and Wikarno, *Menguak Sejarah Kelembagaan Geologi di Indonesia.*

14   Sudrajat, *Van Bemmelen.*

15   Sudrajat, *Prahara Gunung Galunggung.* For a merging of poetry, Sundanese cosmology, and volcanoes in West Java, see DW, *Manusia dan Gunung.*

16   Sudrajat, *Development of Volcanological Investigations in Indonesia.*

17   Katili, "Indonesia Eldorado Geologi, Bagian I," 23; Katili, "Indonesia Eldorado Geologi, Bagian II," 28.

18   For Katili's bibliography between 1951 and 2005 (he died in 2008), see Nusantara, *Harta Bumi Indonesia,* 324–54.

19   Katili and Sudradjat, *Galunggung.*

20   Vening Meinesz, "By Submarine through the Netherlands East Indies," 338–48.

21   Kuenen, *Kruistochten over de indische diepzeebekkens.*

22   Kemmerling, "De 'Piek van Ternate'"; Kemmerling, "Belimming van den G. Batoer," 55–65.

23   Ricklefs, *Polarizing Javanese Society,* 1–12; Ricklefs, *Seen and Unseen Worlds in Java;* Ricklefs, *Jogjakarta under Sultan Mangkubumi.*

24   Blaikie, *Political Economy of Soil Erosion.*

25   Blaikie's work was even directly applied to Mount Merapi by anthropologists Michael Dove and Bambang Hudayana. See Dove and Hudayana, "View from the Volcano," 736–46.

26   Van Bemmelen, *Mountain Building,* 2.

27   Umbgrove, *Symphony of the Earth,* 29.

28   Le Conte, "On Critical Periods in the History of the Earth," 556.

29   Selcer, "Holocene Is History."

30   "Soedjono dan 'Orde Dhawuh.'" See also Hannah, "Magical-Mystical Syndrome in the Indonesian Mentality, I," 1–12.

31   Hollie, "Indonesia," 9.

32   Friend, *Indonesian Destinies,* 260–63.

33   "Joko Piningit," 70–71.

34   Bubandt, "Haunted Geologies," G121–41.

35   Bubandt, "Haunted Geologies," G135.

36   For an overview of eruptions and profiles of individual volcanoes, see Kusumandinata, *Data Dasar Gunungapi* [sic] *Indonesia.*

37   See Goss, *Floracrats;* Li, *Will to Improve,* 1–31. On the Singapore context, see Barnard, *Nature's Colony.*

38   Geertz, *Agricultural Involution,* 39.

39   Winchester, *Krakatoa.*

40 Studies were immediately produced by volcanologists to come to grips with how the lake formed and exploded. See for instance, Kemmerling, "The Craterlake of Kelut Volcano."

41 Kemmerling, "De uitbarsting van den G. Keloet." Gruesome newspaper articles detailed the misery and devastation of the incident, of drowned children, houses flooded with mud, freak escapes. See for instance, "Miraculous Salvations during Kelut Volcano Eruption in 1919." See also Kemmerling, "The Outburst of the G. Kelut in 1919."

42 Kusumandinata, *Data Dasar Gunungapi [sic] Indonesia*, 798.

43 Kemmerling, "De uitbarsting van den G. Keloet," 112–13. See also Escher, "The Kelut"; van Bemmelen, *Geology of Indonesia*, vol 1.

44 This was established within the Dienst van de Mijnbouw (Department of Mines). See van Padang, "History of Volcanology in the East Indies," 24. For the proposal, see Visser, "Verslag van de werkzaamheden van de Commissie voor Vulcanologie," 159–65. Visser wrote, "The work of the Volcanological Service to be done in this volcanic country necessitates the establishment of a separate institution in all respects. Consider, first of all, the vastness of the region, and furthermore, our international obligation to science, the necessity to do everything in our power to determine through scientific research the methods for how to reduce disasters. Science and surveillance should go hand in hand, and success is only guaranteed by an independent body with permanent staff and ample scientific resources."

45 Kusumandinata, *Data Dasar Gunungapi [sic] Indonesia*, 798.

46 Protschky, "Military Responses to and Forms of Knowledge about Natural Disaster."

CHAPTER 2. THE ORIGINS OF JAVA IN FOUR MAPS

1 Verbeek, "Krakatoa Eruption," 10–15.

2 Verbeek, "Krakatoa Eruption," 10–15.

3 Verbeek and Fennema, *Description géologique*, 1:v–vii.

4 Verbeek, "Krakatoa Eruption," 10.

5 Verbeek and Fennema, *Description géologique*, 1:6–21.

6 Verbeek and Fennema, *Description géologique*,1:38. The Tertiary was further subdivided into the Old and Young. The Eocene and Oligocene belonged to the Old Tertiary, the Miocene to the Young Tertiary. The Quaternary was subdivided into the Pliocene.

7 Birchfield, "Age of the Earth," 137–43.

8 This was in the well-known section where Darwin sought to estimate the age of the Weald in the south of England. Darwin, *On the Origin of Species*, 251–52.

9 Thomson, "On the Secular Cooling of the Earth," 1–14. Thomson wrote, "It is quite certain that the whole store of energy in the solar system has been

greater in all past time than at present . . . It is probable that the secular rate of dissipation has been in some direct proportion to the total of the present order of things, and has been therefore very slowly diminishing from age to age." Thomson thought that the rate of energy dissipation and cooling of the earth was the basis on which to date it.

10 Rudwick, *Earth's Deep History*, 229.

11 Verbeek and Fennema, *Description géologique*, 2:928; Phillips, *Life on Earth*, 51.

12 Verbeek and Fennema, *Description géologique*, 2:941–44.

13 Verbeek and Fennema, *Description géologique*, 2:925.

14 Verbeek and Fennema, *Description géologique*, 2:1031; Suess, *Face of the Earth*, vol. 4, pt. 5, 294. Suess drew on Verbeek's evidence of folded mountains to make a broader claim about the youthfulness of Asian mountains:

> *Fore-deeps forming the boundaries of Asia:* The island world of the Pacific, although it only appears as isolated peaks and fragments rising out of the vast expanse of Ocean, yet claims on account of its wide distribution a prominent place in the plan of the earth's surface. The parts exposed to view are arranged in long and often arcuate lines; and it is becoming increasingly clear that most of these are the trendlines of recent mountain chains. We have already seen that in Java the beds with Lepidocyclina are folded, and Verbeek's description of Leitimor shows that in this island also very recent coral beds are carried up to a considerable height, inclined, and occasionally folded.

15 Verbeek and Fennema, *Description géologique*, 2:952–53, 1032.

16 Verbeek and Fennema, *Description géologique*, 2:953.

17 Verbeek and Fennema, *Description géologique*, 2:953.

18 Verbeek and Fennema, *Description géologique*, 2:1020.

19 Verbeek and Fennema, *Description géologique*, 2:1014.

20 Verbeek and Fennema, *Description géologique*, 2:1016.

21 Verbeek, *Oudheden van Java*, 1–6.

22 See Verbeek, *Oudheden van Java*. The accompanying map of antiquities was published as Verbeek, "Oudheidkundige kaart van Java."

23 Verbeek, *Oudheden van Java*, 7–14.

24 Verbeek and Fennema, *Description géologique*, 2:1037–50.

25 Verbeek and Fennema, *Description géologique*, 2:1037.

26 Verbeek and Fennema, *Description géologique*, 2:1031.

27 Kuitenbrouwer, "Dutch East Indies during the First World War," 28–31.

28 Verbeek and Fennema, *Description géologique*, 2:1031.

29 Van Aken, "Dutch Oceanographic Research in Indonesia," 36.

30 Boomgaard, "Making and Unmaking of Tropical Science," 209.

31 For an account of the emergence of metropolitan scientific cultures toward the end of the nineteenth century, see Taylor, *Social World of Batavia*, 114–58. For an account of the exact sciences from the late nineteenth century to the Indonesian revolution, see Pyenson, *Empire of Reason*, 83–125.

32   Pyenson, *Empire of Reason*, 126–28.

33   Vening Meinesz, "Gravity Anomalies in the East Indian Archipelago," 323.

34   Laudan, "Oceanography and Geophysical Theory," 656–57.

35   Vening Meinesz, *Gravity Expeditions at Sea*, 2:8, 9.

36   Laudan, "Oceanography and Geophysical Theory," 656–66.

37   Vening Meinesz, *Gravity Expeditions at Sea*, 1:5.

38   Vening Meinesz, "Gravity Anomalies," 323–24.

39   Vening Meinesz, "Gravity Anomalies," 324.

40   Vening Meinesz, "Gravity Anomalies," 324.

41   Visser, *On the Distribution of Earthquakes in the Netherlands East Indian Archipelago, 1909–1919*. See also Veldkamp, *History of Geophysical Research*, 69–81.

42   Vening Meinesz, "Gravity Anomalies," 329. As Kemmerling wrote in 1922, "Contrary to the popular opinion of lay people that 'volcanoes are the cause of earthquakes,' people are increasingly convinced that it is the contraction of the crust that causes disturbances of equilibrium and causes earthquakes, which then increases the activity of the volcanoes." Kemmerling, "De G. Keloet einde 1921," 94.

43   Vening Meinesz, "Gravity Anomalies," 329.

44   Wegener, *Origins of Continents and Oceans*.

45   Ashworth, "Scientist of the Day."

46   Vening Meinesz, *Gravity Expeditions at Sea*, 2:160.

47   Umbgrove, in Vening Meinesz, *Gravity Expeditions at Sea*, 2:146.

48   Kuenen, "Negative Isostatic Anomalies," 169–214.

49   Kuenen, "Negative Isostatic Anomalies," 171–72.

50   Vening Meinesz, *Gravity Expeditions at Sea*, 4:27.

51   Vening Meinesz, *Gravity Expeditions at Sea*, 4:38.

52   Vening Meinesz, "Origin of Continents and Oceans."

53   Vening Meinesz's vision was not concerned with the origin of water, which he explained was too complicated to add to this story.

54   Vening Meinesz, "Origin of Continents and Oceans," 373.

55   Oreskes, *Science on a Mission*, 142–51.

56   *Navy-Princeton Gravity Expedition to the West Indies*, 2.

57   *Navy-Princeton Gravity Expedition to the West Indies*, 2.

58   Ewing, "Marine Gravimetric Methods and Surveys," 47–70. Also, see Tomoda, "Gravity at Sea." Though Tomoda says the date of import was 1934, Ewing says the Japanese expeditions were in 1932 and 1935.

59   Tomoda, "Gravity at Sea," 771.

60   Worzel, *Pendulum Gravity Measurements at Sea*.

61   Oreskes, *Science on a Mission*, 164–211.

62   Le Pichon, "Fifty Years of Plate Tectonics," 2924.

63   Pyenson, *Empire of Reason*, 13–17.

64   Sudrajat, *Van Bemmelen*, 35–52.

65   See, for instance, the following, in which Brouwer considered the horizontal folding and stresses in the evolution of the Indies as departing from the tradition of focusing on the vertical stresses. He concluded: "It may be that the southeastern Indian Archipelago will in the future arrive at the same stage as was long before reached in the Alps. As the horizontal movements proceed, the sea basins will narrow, and eventually the masses of the deeper parts of the present rows of islands will be pushed over the present Australian continent and the Sahul shelf which extends its borders. For a judgment, whether the active force tending to produce movement is directed to the south-east or to the north-west, as would follow from the conceptions of Hobbs and Wegener, no sufficient data are available." Brouwer, "Horizontal Movement of Geanticlines," 577. Likewise, Molengraaff asked that geologists develop a sufficiently robust conception of large-scale folding to comprehend the shape of the Indies and, thus, invited theoretical crossovers with drift theories: "It is reasonable to surmise that a genetic connection must exist between the subsidence of the trough-shaped deep-sea basins and the elevation of the adjoining elongated islands; indeed, the common origin of these antagonistic movements, according to my opinion, has to be sought in one and the same crustal movement, viz. in a process of folding at a certain depth. If the question were raised as to what might be seen at the Earth's surface if an area were folded by crustal movement at a certain depth, I should be inclined to reply that its appearance would be similar to what obtains at present in the eastern portion of the Indian archipelago." Molengraaff, "Modern Deep-Sea Research in the East Indian Archipelago," 107.

66   Sudrajat, *Van Bemmelen*, 21.

67   Vickers, *History of Modern Indonesia*, 16–33.

68   Van Bemmelen, *Geology of Indonesia*, 1A:vii.

69   Van Bemmelen, *Geology of Indonesia*, 1A: foreword.

70   Van Gorsel, "Pioneers and Milestones of Indonesian Geology."

71   Holmes, *Age of the Earth*.

72   Van Bemmelen, *Geology of Indonesia*, 1A:723. The categories existed, the strata had been named, but it is unlikely that Verbeek and Fennema would have understood that they suggested such an age. Also, most fine-grained subdividing was accomplished on Java and Sumatra where the Netherlands Indies Geological Survey spent fourteen years surveying stratigraphy on Java between 1927 and 1940. See van Bemmelen, *Geology of Indonesia*, 1A:106.

73   Van Bemmelen, *Geology of Indonesia*, 1A:79.

74   On the theory of megaundations, see also van Bemmelen, "On Mega-Undations," 83–127.

75   Van Bemmelen, *Geology of Indonesia*, 1A:723.

76   He synthesized his system thus in the final pages of the first volume of the *Geology of Indonesia*: "The cosmic process of cooling of the earth causes a flow of free energy from the inner, hotter parts of our planet to the surface. However,

this cooling is not a simple thermal process. On its way to the surface, before the ultimate radiation and dissipation into the Universe, the free energy assumes all kinds of conditions. In the first place, the temperature gradients initiate exothermal chain reactions with a disperse, atomic and ionic flow of matter, bringing about geochemical adjustments in the composition of the earth's shells. Such physico-chemical processes cause changes in density, and as they are unevenly distributed, they result in a disturbance of the hydrostatic equilibrium. Therefore, the equilibrio-turbal effect of the physico-chemical process gives periodically rise to restorative reactions which have the character of more concentrated mass displacements. These equilibrio-petal movements in depth are accompanied by wavelike deformations or 'undations' of the earth's surface." Van Bemmelen, *Geology of Indonesia*, 1A:723.

77   Van Bemmelen, *Geology of Indonesia*, 1A:1–6.

78   Van Bemmelen attacked plate tectonics in a number of papers; see, for instance, van Bemmelen, "Plate Tectonics and the Undation Model," 145–82.

79   See Katili's biography edited but not solely authored by him. Nusantara, *Harta Bumi Indonesia*.

80   Katili and Hartono, "Van Bemmelen's Contributions," 107–16.

81   Hamilton, *Tectonic Map of Indonesia*, 21.

82   Hamilton, *Tectonic Map of Indonesia*, 8.

83   Hamilton, "Tectonics of the Indonesian Region," 31.

84   Ewing and Worzel, "Gravity Anomalies and Structure of the West Indies Part I," 165–74.

85   Hamilton, "Tectonics of the Indonesian Region."

86   Hamilton, "Tectonics of the Indonesian Region," 41.

87   Hamilton, "Tectonics of the Indonesian Region," 7.

88   Hamilton, "Convergent-Plate Tectonics," 37. See also Hamilton, "Tectonics of the Indonesian Region," 8.

89   See Hamilton, "Tectonics of the Indonesian Region," 39–44.

90   Hamilton, "Convergent-Plate Tectonics," 43.

91   Hamilton, "Convergent-Plate Tectonics," 43.

92   Nusantara, *Harta Bumi Indonesia*, 134–43.

93   Katili, *Sumberdaya Alam*, 83.

94   Katili and Reinemund, *Southeast Asia*, 44.

95   Katili and Reinemund, *Southeast Asia*, 46.

96   Katili, *Sumberdaya Alam*, 75–92.

97   Katili and Reinemund, *Southeast Asia*, 18.

CHAPTER 3. INTERCALATED

1   Snider, "Indian Ocean Expedition," 289. See also Snider, "International Indian Ocean Expedition," 113. He wrote, "Over the next four years, a fleet of ships carrying scientists with their highly specialized equipment will be sailing

in the Indian Ocean on new voyages of discovery, bringing one of the last unknown areas of the globe under intensive scrutiny."

2 Fischer, *Preliminary Report on the Expeditions* Monsoon *and* Lusiad, 36, 52–88.

3 Heezen and Tharp, *Physiographic Diagram of the Indian Ocean* (map), *Indian Ocean Floor* (map). See also [*Manuscript Painting of Heezen-Tharp "World Ocean Floor" Map by Berran*], [1977?], by Heinrich C. Berran, Bruce C. Heezen, and Marie Tharp, Library of Congress, Geography and Map Division, https://lccn.loc.gov/2010586277.

4 Hamilton, "Tectonics of the Indonesian Region," 28.

5 Katili and Reinmund, *Southeast Asia*, 44.

6 Veth, *Java*, 377.

7 Van Hien, *De javaansche geestenwereld en de betrekking*, 17.

8 Hamilton, "Tectonics of the Indonesian Region," 28.

9 For treatments of the history of Ratu Kidul's relationship with Central Javanese sultans, see Ricklefs, *Jogjakarta under Sultan Mangkubumi*, 13, 23. See the same text for a historical treatment of the foundation and divisions of the Mataram sultanate. For a view of the partition from inside the Surakarta *kraton*, see Ricklefs, "The Crisis of 1740–1 in Java," 268–90; and Carey, "Civilization on Loan," 711–34.

10 Ricklefs suggests Ratu Kidul is a much older indigenous animist deity, appearing as an avatar in stories about the founding of the Majapahit empire as early as the thirteenth century. It is probable that she first lived in a volcano "sand sea" such as the caldera desert at Mount Bromo before moving to the aquatic sea, where she established her kingdom. According to Ricklefs, she first appears as a hermit named Cemara Tunggal who was punished for refusing to marry. "She can be male or female, young or old, and will not die until the Day of Judgement." Ricklefs, *Seen and Unseen Worlds in Java*, 10. Ricklefs also suggests that Ratu Kidul is the reason for the erection of the Taman Sari water castle in the Jogja *kraton*, as a location of consort. See Ricklefs, *Jogjakarta under Sultan Mangkubumi*, 84–86.

11 Carey records that the sultan's and Yogyakarta elite visited Nyai Ratu Kidul and that Sultan Hamengkubuwono II built a small pavilion near her home. Carey, *Power of Prophecy*, 137–50.

12 Tirtakoesoema, "De verjaring van den verheffingsdag," 372–89.

13 Tirtakoesoema, "Anniversary of the Accession of His Highness the Sultan of Yogyakarta," 156.

14 Tirtakoesoema, "De verjaring van den verheffingsdag," 380. For a discussion of the origin of some place-names related to spiritual topographies of Java, see Adam, "Eenige historische en legendarische plaatsnamen in Jogjakarta," 150–62.

15 For Ricklefs's geography and genealogy of Sapu Jagad connected with Ratu Kidul, see note 10 above.

16 Wieringa, "Illusion of an Allusion," 199. Carey, *Power of Prophecy*, 493–99.

17 Carey, *Power of Prophecy*, 495–96.

18   Ricklefs, *Jogjakarta under Sultan Mangkubumi*, 404n88.

19   De Graaf, "De regering van Sultan Agung," 125.

20   Pigeaud, "Alexander, Sakèndèr en Sénapati," 354

21   Kemmerling, "Vulkanologische Berichten," 188–94.

22   Kemmerling, "Vulkanologische Berichten," 188.

23   Kemmerling, "Vulkanologische Berichten," 194.

24   Kemmerling, "Vulkanologische Berichten." 188–94.

25   See also Protschky and Morgan, "Historicising Sulfur Mining," 8–9.

26   Kemmerling, "Vulkanologische Berichten."

27   Triyoga, *Manusia Jawa dan Gunung Merapi*, 33.

28   Triyoga, *Manusia Jawa dan Gunung Merapi*, 45.

29   Schlehe, "Reinterpretations of Mystical Traditions," 395.

30   Schlehe, "Reinterpretations of Mystical Traditions," 396.

31   Prasetyo and Dono, *Lahirnya Kembali*, 243–45.

32   Prasetyo and Dono, *Lahirnya Kembali*, 243–45.

33   Pemberton, *On the Subject of "Java,"* 305–10. See also Friend, *Indonesian Destinies*, 260–263.

34   "Soedjono dan 'Orde Dhawuh.'"

35   This is a variation of Hannah's "Magical-Mystical Syndrome." See Hannah, "Magical-Mystical Syndrome in the Indonesian Mentality, I."

36   *Slamet* means "safety" and is the root word for the *selamatan*, a communal meal held for many occasions ranging from opening a business to circumcision. It is also the root for wishing someone safely on their way. Pemberton, *On the Subject of "Java,"* 1–27.

37   Triyoga, *Manusia Jawa dan Gunung Merapi*.

38   "Kisah Mbah Marijan dan 4 Kata Pantangan."

39   "Kisah Mbah Marijan dan 4 Kata Pantangan."

40   Inandiak, *Babad Ngalor-Ngidul*, 29.

41   Inandiak, *Babad Ngalor-Ngidul*, 29.

42   "Kisah Mbah Marijan dan 4 Kata Pantangan."

43   Inandiak, *Babad Ngalor-Ngidul*, 31.

44   Inandiak, *Babad Ngalor-Ngidul*, 91–97.

45   Inandiak, *Babad Ngalor-Ngidul*, 125–130.

46   Inandiak, *Babad Ngalor-Ngidul*, 130.

47   "Mbah Marijan Bertemu Wapres."

48   Marshall, "Gods Must Be Restless," 34.

49   Kurnia, "Surono Berdiri di Cincin Api," 36–47.

50   Inandiak, *Babad Ngalor-Ngidul*, 155.

51   Inandiak, "2010 Merapi Eruption Journals."

52   Inandiak, "2010 Merapi Eruption Journals."

53   "Highest Alert Issued for Indonesia's Merapi Volcano."

54   "Pesan Istana untuk Mbah Maridjan."

55   "Alasan Mbah Maridjan tak Mau Mengungsi."

56 O'Brien, "Science, Mysticism Meld."

57 Lang, "Spiritual Guardian of Indonesian Volcano Dies."

58 Resink, "Kanjeng Ratu Kidul," 314. See also the fascinating development of
    Ratu Kidul's aquatic hybridity by Trumbull, *Liquid World*, 105–6.

59 "Penuhi Hak Gunung Berapi."

60 "Penuhi Hak Gunung Berapi."

61 Syaifullah, "Labuhan Merapi."

62 Clark and Yusoff, "Geosocial Formations and the Anthropocene," 3–23.

CHAPTER 4. AD 1006 GEODETERMINISM

Epigraph: Suess, quoted by Wegener, in Wegener, *Origins of Continents and Oceans*, 9.

1   Couperus, *Hidden Force*, 151.

2   Couperus, *Hidden Force*, 151.

3   Vickers, *History of Modern Indonesia*, 18.

4   Vickers, *History of Modern Indonesia*, 18.

5   Vickers, *History of Modern Indonesia*, 18.

6   Hinloopen Labberton, "Oud-Javaansche gegevens omtrent de vulkanologie van
    Java."

7   Van Dijk, *Netherlands Indies and the Great War*, 275.

8   See for instance, Hinloopen Labberton, *Lajang Damar-woelan*.

9   Hinloopen Labberton, *Wayang, or Shadow Play*, 1.

10 The language and culture of Bali was also a direct descendent. See Hinloopen
    Labberton, "Mahabharata in Medieval Javanese," 1–3.

11 Hinloopen Labberton, "Mahabharata in Medieval Javanese," 1.

12 Kern, "Sanskrit-Inscriptie ter eere van den Javaanschen vost Er-Langa," 1–21.

13 It has not yet, at the time of this writing, been repatriated to Indonesia.
    Bullough and Carry, "Kolkata Stone (Calcutta Stone)," 4–5.

14 Kern, "Sanskrit-Inscriptie ter eere," 1–21.

15 Hinloopen Labberton, "Oud-Javaansche gegevens," 141.

16 Hinloopen Labberton, "Oud-Javaansche gegevens," 142–43.

17 Hinloopen Labberton, "Oud-Javaansche gegevens," 143.

18 Hinloopen Labberton, "Oud-Javaansche gegevens," 124–58.

19 Banner, *Romantic Java as It Was and Is*, 132. See also Scheltema, *Monumental Java*.

20 Raffles, *History of Java*, 32.

21 Raffles, *History of Java*, 32.

22 Besant and Leadbeater, *The Theosophical Society*.

23 Poller, "'Under a Glamour,'" 86.

24 Franklin, *Spirit Matters*, 185–211.

25 Sinnett, *Occult World*, 4.

26 Ramaswamy, *Lost Land of Lemuria*, 53–55.

27 See, for instance, Ryan, "Boro-Bodur, the Great Pyramid of Java," 482–85; Ryan, "Great Temples in Java," 225–36; Edge, "Age of the Earth," 77–148. Edge attempted to bring together Theosophy with modern geology: "The teachings of Theosophy are consistent and symmetrical; the idea that the earth during these vast ages was given over entirely to sedimentation and the lower forms of life, man being nowhere, does not enter into the Theosophical view. It is clear that we must not allow ourselves to be frightened by mere vastness. . . . The geological record shows many epochs of change in the distribution of land and water, and these mark the boundaries between the larger divisions of humanity" (80). Stratigraphy became human evolutionary history.

28 De Tollenaere, *Politics of Divine Wisdom*, 114–15.

29 He was the brother of the sultan of Surakarta, Pakubuwono X. See Brown, "Revival of Buddhism in Modern Indonesia," 47. The source text of the speech is from Hinloopen Labberton, "Riddle of Bhatara Kala to Sanghiang Vishnu," 156–58.

30 Hinloopen Labberton, "Riddle of Bhatara Kala to Sanghiang Vishnu," 156–58.

31 De Tollenaere, *Politics of Divine Wisdom*, 115–24.

32 Blavatsky, *Secret Doctrine*, 1:1.

33 Blavatsky, *Secret Doctrine*, 1:1.

34 See, for instance, Charles Leadbeater, who explained that "in our solar system there exist perfectly definite planes, each with its own matter of different degrees of density, and that some of these planes can be visited and observed by persons who have qualified themselves for the work, exactly as a foreign country might be visited and observed; and that, by comparison of the observations of those who are constantly working on these planes, evidence can be obtained of their existence and nature at least as satisfactory as that which most of us have for the existence of Greenland or Spitzbergen." Leadbeater, *Astral Plane*, 11. He explained that the populace of these lands includes living and dead humans, non-humans (including elements and minerals, astral bodies of animals, nature spirits), Hindu *devas*, and finally, human thoughts and feelings.

35 Blavatsky, *Secret Doctrine*, 2:46.

36 Blavatsky, *Secret Doctrine*, 2:1, 46. She says later of the age of the earth that "we are ready to concede the 100 millions of years offered by geology." However, she resists giving geological science authority until it has "traced man down to his primordial proto-plasmic form, then we will admit that it may know something of primordial man" (72). She also had to contend with the then-known fossil record to situate man as the first species. Rudwick, *Earth's Deep History*, 181–206.

37 Blavatsky, *Secret Doctrine*, 2:227.

38 Blavatsky, *Secret Doctrine*, 2: 266. See also Ramaswamy on Lemuria and the role of the lost continent in theosophy and Tamil postcolonial movements.

39 Blavatsky, *Secret Doctrine*, 2:274.

40   Blavatsky, *Secret Doctrine*, 2:332.

41   Blavatsky, *Secret Doctrine*, 2:314.

42   For travel dates see Tillett, "Charles Webster Leadbeater," 557; de Tollenaere, *Politics of Divine Wisdom*, 114.

43   Leadbeater, *Occult History of Java*, 16–18.

44   Van Bemmelen, [Untitled contribution], *Kogyo Jimusho Bandoeng Chishitsu-Chosajo*, 69–72.

45   Van Bemmelen, [Untitled contribution], *Kogyo Jimusho Bandoeng Chishitsu-Chosajo*, 69.

46   Sudrajat, *Van Bemmelen*, 90; Barzilay, "De ontwikkelingsgeschiedenis van Rein van Bemmelens (1904–1983) undatietheorie," 8–10.

47   Van Bemmelen, "On the Geophysical Foundations of the Undation-Theory," 338.

48   Van Bemmelen, [Untitled contribution], *Kogyo Jimusho Bandoeng Chishitsu-Chosajo*, 70.

49   Van Bemmelen, [Untitled contribution], *Kogyo Jimusho Bandoeng Chishitsu-Chosajo*, 69–74.

50   Van Bemmelen, [Untitled contribution], *Kogyo Jimusho Bandoeng Chishitsu-Chosajo*, 71.

51   Sudrajat, *Van Bemmelen*, 174.

52   Sudrajat, *Van Bemmelen*, 181.

53   Sudrajat, *Van Bemmelen*, 183.

54   Sukamto, Soeradi, and Wikarno, *Menguak Sejarah Kelembagaan Geologi di Indonesia*, 60.

55   Van Gorsel, "Pioneers and Milestones of Indonesian Geology."

56   Van Bemmelen, *VIII Report on the Merapi Eruption Cycle 2602–2603 (1943)*, 6.

57   Van Bemmelen, *VIII Report on the Merapi Eruption Cycle 2602–2603 (1943)*.

58   Mortimer, *Indonesian Communism under Sukarno*, 39.

59   Van Bemmelen, "Charles Edgar Stehn," 133; see also Sudrajat, *Van Bemmelen*, 186.

60   Thalmann, "Tan Sin Hok: 1902–1945," 25.

61   Van Bemmelen, *Geodynamic Models: An Evaluation and Synthesis*, 5.

62   Van Bemmelen, *Mountain Building*, 2.

63   Sudrajat, *Van Bemmelen*, 200.

64   De Neve, "Volcanological Investigations in Cooperation with the Auri," 34

65   Before the war, there had been seventy employees. De Neve, "Volcanological Investigations in Cooperation with the Auri," 34.

66   Hadikusumo, "Report on the Volcanological Research and Volcanic Activity," 34. De Neve. "Volcanological Investigations in Cooperation with the Auri," 36.

67   De Neve mentions Guntur, Galungung, and Telaga Bodas as subject to a reconnaissance mission on September 5 and 6, because of their political instability. De Neve, "Volcanological Investigations in Cooperation with the Auri."

68   Van Dijk, *Rebellion under the Banner of Islam*, 102.

69   Adnawidjaja et al., "Dari Redaksi," 1.

70   Petroeschevsky, "Volcanic Activity in Indonesia," 22.

71 Petroeschevsky, "Volcanic Activity in Indonesia," 22–23.

72 Hadikusumo, "Report on the Volcanological Research," 36.

73 Hadikusumo, "Report on the Volcanological Research," 37.

74 Hadikusumo, "Report on the Volcanological Research," 41.

75 Bloembergen and Eickhoff, "Conserving the Past," 405.

76 Hadikusumo, "Report on the Volcanological Research," 35.

77 Hadikusumo, "Report on the Volcanological Research," 15.

78 Hadikusumo, "Report on the Volcanological Research," 16.

79 Djajawinangun, "G. Merapi."

80 Leadbeater, *World Mother as Symbol and Fact*.

81 Bennett, *Witness*, 326.

82 Van Sommers, *Life in Subud*, 129.

83 The bank was sold in 1989 to the state bank Mandiri and renamed Bank Syariah Mandiri. It now belongs to one of the largest banking conglomerates in Indonesia.

84 Van Sommers, *Life in Subud*, 93–128.

85 Van Sommers, *Life in Subud*, 134.

86 Simanjuntak, *Archaeology*, 416. See also Andreastuti, Newhall, and Dwijanto, "Menelusuri Kebenaran Letusan Gunung Merapi 1006," 201–7.

87 Krafft and Krafft, *A l'assaut des volcans*.

88 Newman, "In Kringdjing, Java, the 'Glowing Cloud' Brings Rain of Death," 28.

89 Boechari argued throughout the 1960s and 1970s that Merapi had caused the destruction of classical Java. Tanudirjo, "Theoretical Trends in Indonesian Archeology," 73. See also Boechari, "Preliminary Report," 241–51.

90 Simanjuntak, *Archaeology*, 416.

91 Newhall et al., "10,000 Years of Explosive Eruptions," 47.

92 Mrázek, *Engineers of Happy Land*.

CHAPTER 5. GEOPOETICS

1 Last, "Fruit of the Cyclone," 57.

2 Last, "We Are the World?," 161.

3 Yusoff, *Billion Black Anthropocenes*.

4 Umbgrove, letter to his mother, January 8, 1929; see also the letter of July 15, 1929. In Umbgrove, letters to his mother, personal collection of Frederik van Veen, Groningen, Netherlands. All further citations of the letters refer to this collection.

5 Umbgrove, letter to his mother, August 29, 1928.

6 De Jongh, "On the Valency of the Chemical Atoms," 535–71.

7 Besant and Leadbeater, *Occult Chemistry*, 1–6.

8 Umbgrove, letter to his mother, May 15, 1928.

9 See Umbgrove's publications as follows: "Heterospira," 155–59; "Geological History of the East Indies," 1–70; "Madreporaria from the Bay of Batavia,"

1–64; "Origin of Deep-Sea Troughs," 73–80; "Periodicity in Terrestrial Processes," 573–76; "On Rhythms in the History of the Earth," 116–29; "A Second Species of Biplanispira," 82–89; *Structural History of the East Indies*; "Tertiary Foraminifera," 35–91; "Verschillende typen van tertiaire geosynclinalen," 33–43.

10   Sukamto, Soeradi, and Wikarno, *Menguak Sejarah Kelembagaan Geologi di Indonesia*, 136.

11   Umbgrove, *Symphony of the Earth*, 213.

12   See, for example, Umbgrove, letters to his mother, November 19, 1927, and March 14, 1927.

13   Umbgrove, letter to his mother, October 18, 1926.

14   Umbgrove, letter to his mother, November 29, 1926.

15   Umbgrove, letter to his mother, January 7, 1928.

16   Umbgrove's notes on this day were published as Umbgrove, "The First Days of the New Submarine Volcano near Krakatoa," 325–28. Umbgrove notes that Stehn published his account in *Vulkanologische Mededelingen*.

17   Umbgrove, letter to his mother, February 8, 1927; see also Fruin-Meese, *Geschiedenis van Java*.

18   Protschky, "Military Responses to and Forms of Knowledge about Natural Disaster," 67–91.

19   Umbgrove, letter to his mother, November 19, 1927.

20   Umbgrove, letter to his mother, November 19, 1927.

21   Umbgrove, letter to his mother, November 19, 1927.

22   See Tiffin, "Java's Ruined *Candis* and the British Picturesque Ideal," 525–58.

23   Umbgrove, letter to his mother, May 3, 1928.

24   Umbgrove, letter to his mother, May 3, 1928.

25   Umbgrove, letter to his mother, May 3, 1928. He is referring here to the book by the French geologist Termier, *La joie de la connaitre*.

26   Umbgrove, "Het ontstaan van het Diengplateau."

27   Umbgrove, "Het ontstaan van het Diengplateau."

28   Umbgrove, letter to his mother, May 3, 1928.

29   Goss, *Floracrats*.

30   See Umbgrove, *Pulse of the Earth*, 2.

31   Umbgrove, *Pulse of the Earth*, 2.

32   Dott, "Introduction to the Ups and Downs of Eustasy," 1–16. See also, Barrell, "Rhythms and the Measurements of Geologic Time," 745–904.

33   Umbgrove, *Pulse of the Earth*, 73–114.

34   Dott, "Introduction to the Ups and Downs of Eustasy," 1–16.

35   Gilbert, "Rhythms of Geologic Time," 1001–12.

36   Grabau taught at Peking National University and contributed to the Geological Survey of China and the golden age of Chinese geology. See Shen, *Unearthing the Nation*, 67–107; see also Mazur, "Amadeus Grabau in China," 51–94.

37   Johnson, "A. W. Grabau's Embryonic Sequence Stratigraphy," 43–54.

38 Johnson, "A. W. Grabau's Embryonic Sequence Stratigraphy," 43–54.

39 Umbgrove, "On Rhythms in the History of the Earth," 116.

40 Umbgrove, "On Rhythms in the History of the Earth," 116.

41 Umbgrove, *Pulse of the Earth*, 26.

42 Vening Meinesz, *Gravity Expeditions at Sea*, 2:163–82.

43 Umbgrove, *Pulse of the Earth*, 152. See also Umbgrove, *Symphony of the Earth*, 209–10. "In the history of our planet certain phenomena of a very heterogeneous nature have come to light; considerable upward and downward movements of the sea-level took place over long periods of time and with a rhythm which attracts attention by reason of its monotonous regularity, large continental ice-caps grew and melted again, basins and troughs appeared as dents in the outer covering of the earth, mountain-chains towered on high and were eroded away, granitic and other 'plutonic' rocks originated in the crust of the earth during certain periods. One day it becomes possible to see these heterogeneous phenomena in their relation to one another. There is found to be a definite mutual connection. They are no longer loose strains of music; they appear to be woven together as in one grand fugue. Thus, we can see the history of the earth before us as the score of a symphony. And we rejoice at this concord of harmonious sounds on account of the unity which enfolds the different parts."

44 Umbgrove, *Pulse of the Earth*, 146.

45 Le Conte, "On Critical Periods in the History of the Earth," 556.

46 Umbgrove, *Symphony of the Earth*, 29.

47 Umbgrove, *Symphony of the Earth*, 206.

48 Umbgrove, *Symphony of the Earth*, 147.

49 Umbgrove, *Leven en materie*, 118–23.

50 Umbgrove, *Leven en materie*, 122n2.

51 Deussen, *Philosophy of the Upanishads*.

52 Deussen, *Philosophy of the Upanishads*, 40–50.

53 Deussen, *Philosophy of the Upanishads*, 40–50.

54 Deussen, *Philosophy of the Upanishads*, 40.

55 Deussen, *Philosophy of the Upanishads*, 85–99, 180–201.

56 Umbgrove, *Symphony of the Earth*, 208–14.

57 Umbgrove, *Symphony of the Earth*, 211

58 Umbgrove, *Symphony of the Earth*, 211.

59 Gutenberg et al., "Colloquium on Plastic Flow," 498–543.

60 Gutenberg et al., "Colloquium on Plastic Flow," 535.

61 Gutenberg et al., "Colloquium on Plastic Flow," 530.

62 Hess, "History of Ocean Basins," 599–620.

63 Rudwick, *Earth's Deep History*, 258

64 Hess, "History of Ocean Basins," 599–620.

65 Ewing and Heezen, "Oceanographic Research Programs," 508–35.

66 Doel, Levin, and Marker, "Extending Modern Cartography," 608–10.

67 Doel, Levin, and Marker, "Extending Modern Cartography," 609–10.

68 Yusoff, *Billion Black Anthropocenes*; Povinelli, *Geontologies*.

CHAPTER 6. VOLCANO OBSERVATORIES

1 For an account of wealthy developments on Merapi, see Holst, "Terpisah Namun Cukup Dekat," 119–45.

2 Snellen, *Willem Einthoven*, 13.

3 Snellen, *Willem Einthoven*, 14–16.

4 Barron, *Development of the Electrocardiograph*, 9.

5 Burnett, "Origins of the Electrocardiograph," 62.

6 Einthoven, "Telecardiogram," 78.

7 Snellen, *Willem Einthoven*, 34.

8 Einthoven, "Telecardiogram," 602–15.

9 Einthoven, "String Galvanometer," 99. Burnett, "Origins of the Electrocardiograph," shows how the electrocardiogram was an assemblage of independently invented instruments. Part of the genius of Einthoven, according to Burnett was the capacity to assemble the instruments, combining their capacities.

10 Einthoven, "Telecardiogram," 81.

11 Einthoven, "Telecardiogram," 81.

12 Burnett, "Origins of the Electrocardiograph," 54.

13 Burnett, "Origins of the Electrocardiograph."

14 Snellen, *Willem Einthoven*, 73.

15 Mrázek, "Let Us Become Radio Mechanics," 3–4.

16 Mrázek, "Let Us Become Radio Mechanics," 3–33.

17 Snellen, *Willem Einthoven*, 49.

18 Snellen, *Willem Einthoven*, 49.

19 Snellen, *Willem Einthoven*, 50.

20 Snellen, *Willem Einthoven*, 50; Einthoven, "String Galvanometer," 99.

21 Einthoven, "String Galvanometer," 98.

22 Einthoven, "String Galvanometer," 98.

23 For more details on Petrochevsky, also spelled Petrushevsky or Petroechevsky, see Petrushevsky, "Diaries"; Belousov and Belousova, "First Russian Volcanologist."

24 Van Padang, "Measures Taken by Authorities," 188; van Padang, "De uitbarsting van den Merapi," 110–12.

25 Van Padang, "Volcanic Phenomena," 56.

26 Van Bemmelen, *V Report on the New Merapi Eruption Cycle of 2602 (1942)*.

27 Van Bemmelen, *V Report on the New Merapi Eruption Cycle of 2602 (1942)*, 4.

28 Van Bemmelen, *V Report on the New Merapi Eruption Cycle of 2602 (1942)*, 4.

29 Hadikusumo, "Report on the Volcanological Research and Volcanic Activity in Indonesia," 49.

30   Van Bemmelen, *V Report on the New Merapi Eruption Cycle of 2602* (1942), 4.

31   Van Bemmelen, *V Report on the New Merapi Eruption Cycle of 2602* (1942), 4.

32   Van Bemmelen, *Geology of Indonesia*, 1A:266.

33   Van Bemmelen, *Geology of Indonesia*, 1A:267.

34   Snellen, *Willem Einthoven*, 73.

35   Scott Petty, *Seismic Reflections*.

36   Kebun Lithos Foundation (@kebunlithos), "Robert H. Ray Company, 'The earth has *heartbeats*, too!'" (April 19, 1954), Instagram photo, July 13, 2021, https://www.instagram.com/p/CRRmy4FoR_h/.

37   On the links between Theosophy and Kejawen in the New Order, see Florida, "Reading the Unread" 3: "This early twentieth century move towards the construction of tradition has been repeated and intensified under the aegis of Suharto's self-proclaimed 'New Order' government. Following a differently constructed relationship with the past and with 'tradition' in the radically populist revolutionary and Sukarno eras, New Order *adiluhung* rhetoric is eerily reminiscent of the late colonial voice. Highlighting what is imagined as the super-refined and spiritualized ways of traditional priyayi and then contrasting them with those of the so-called coarse and material West, the New Order Javanese elite have invented a vision of their very own adiluhung heritage as the somewhat endangered pinnacle of cultural development, the preservation (and reservation) of which they see as a 'sacred duty.' One is tempted to call this dominant modern image of Javanese culture, based as it is on the adiluhung and extremely refined or halus, vision of life, the 'halusination' of Javanese culture."
     See also Endraswara, *Agama Jawa*, 28–31. Likewise, Suhardi, *Manekung di Puncak Gunung*, 214–23. On Suharto's spirituality, see also Ricklefs, *Islamisation and Its Opponents in Java*, 118–25. Paul Stange objected to a too strong link between Theosophy and Kejawen; personal communication with the author, June 2, 2019. See also Stange, "Deconstruction as Disempowerment," 51–71.

38   Ricklefs, *Islamisation and Its Opponents in Java*, 132–33.

39   Cited in Ricklefs, *Islamisation and Its Opponents in Java*, 132. See Subagya [Bakker], *Kepercayaan, Kebatinan, Kerohanian, Kejiwaan dan Agama*, 130–38. See also Ricklefs, *Islamisation and Its Opponents in Java*, 132–38.

40   Kartosutedjo, "Kokok Ayam," 5–13. The article appeared alongside a questioning article on the events of 1965 that brought Suharto to power. Other articles were titled, "Life Wisdom in Mysticism"; "Earth: The Place Where We Live," a description of earth from a geophysicist's point of view; and "Traditional Weapons of Revolution," which described physical and spiritual weapons used in the history of Indonesia's political struggles.

41   Kartosutedjo, "Kokok Ayam," 9.

42   Kartosutedjo, "Kokok Ayam," 12.

43   Kartosutedjo, "Kokok Ayam," 12.

44   Van Padang, "Volcanic Phenomena," 56; van Padang, "De uitbarsting van den Merapi," 108–12.

45   Suparno, interview by the author, Keningar, January 16, 2017.

46   Yehezkiel Sugiyono, WhatsApp communication with author, June 27, 2019.

47   Sukidi, interview by the author, Keningar, May 6, 2017. This history corresponds with dates of village electrification elsewhere. See also Moshin's argument linking mass village electrification in the 1980s with Suharto's New Order politics of patrimony. Moshin, "Wiring the New Order," 63–95.

48   See Aji, *Ajaran Kejawen Maneges*.

49   DOMErapi is a portmanteau of *dome* and *Merapi*.

50   Jean-Philippe Metaxian, interview by the author, Bandung, April 21, 2016.

51   Jácome, "Late 1990s Financial Crisis in Ecuador," 5; Cisternas, "Ecuador Faces Harsh Economic Measures."

52   Associated Press, "Day of Rebellion Ends."

53   Romero, "Ecuador's Leader Purges Military."

54   Jean-Philippe Metaxian, interview by the author, Bandung, April 21, 2016.

55   Tazieff, "Volcano Survey," 310.

56   Jean-Philippe Metaxian, interview by the author, Bandung, January 18–20, 2016.

BIBLIOGRAPHY

Adam, L. "Eenige historische en legendarische plaatsnamen in Jogjakarta." *Djåwå* 4–5, no. 10 (1929): 150–62.

Adnawidjaja, M. I., Djajadi Hadikusumo, G. A. de Neve, Moh. Slamet Padmokesumo, and Surjo. "Dari Redaksi." *Berita Gunung Berapi* 1, nos. 1–2 (1952): 1.

Aji, Rosa Mulya. *Ajaran Kejawen Maneges: Agama Asli Jawa.* Yogyakarta: Bening Pustaka and Dua Aksara, 2018.

"Alasan Mbah Maridjan tak Mau Mengungsi." *Tempo* (Jakarta), October 25, 2010. https://www.apakabarsidimpuan.com/alasan-mbah-maridjan-tak-mau-mengungsi/.

Andreastuti, Supriati Dewi, Chris Newhall, and Joko Dwiyanto. "Menelusuri Kebenaran Letusan Gunung Merapi 1006." *Jurnal Geologi Indonesia* 1, no. 4 (December 2006): 201–7.

Ashworth, William B. "Scientist of the Day." Linda Hall Library, July 30, 2019. https://www.lindahall.org/felix-vening-meinesz/.

Associated Press. "Day of Rebellion Ends with Ouster of Ecuador Leader." *New York Times,* January 22, 2000.

Banner, H. S. *Romantic Java as It Was and Is.* London: Seely, Service, 1927.

Barnard, Timothy P. *Nature's Colony: Empire, Nation and Environment in the Singapore Botanic Gardens.* Singapore: NUS Press, 2016.

Barrell, Joseph. "The Origin of the Earth." In *The Evolution of the Earth and Its Inhabitants,* 1–44. New Haven: Yale University Press, 1918.

Barrell, Joseph. "Rhythms and the Measurements of Geologic Time." *Bulletin of the Geological Society of America* 26 (December 1917): 745–904.

Barron, S. T. *The Development of the Electrocardiograph: With Some Biographical Notes on Prof. W. Einthoven.* London: Cambridge Instrument Company, 1952.

Barry, Andrew. *Material Politics: Disputes along the Pipeline.* Chichester: Wiley Blackwell, 2013.

Barzilay, Willemjan. "De ontwikkelingsgeschiedenis van Rein van Bemmelens (1904–1983) undatietheorie: Veertig jaar Nederlandse geologie." *Studium* 2 (2009): 8–10.

Bashford, Alison, Emily Kern, and Adam Bobbette, eds. *New Earth Histories: Geo-Cosmologies and the Making of the Modern World*. Chicago: University of Chicago Press, 2023.

Belousov, Alexander, and Marina Belousova. "The First Russian Volcanologist: Vladimir Petrushevsky." *Institute of Volcanology and Seismology, Far East Division of the Russian Academy of Sciences* (blog), accessed October 11, 2022. https://blogs.dickinson.edu/vapetrushevsky/files/2017/05/Priroda-article-final-translation.pdf.

Bennett, J. G. *Concerning Subud*. London: Hodder and Stoughton, 1959.

Bennett, J .G. *Witness: The Autobiography of John G. Bennett*. Tucson, AZ: Sufi Community Press, 1974.

Besant, Annie, and Charles W. Leadbeater. *Occult Chemistry: Clairvoyant Observations on the Chemical Elements*. London: Theosophical Publishing House, 1919.

Besant, Annie, and Charles W. Leadbeater, eds. *The Theosophical Society*. Supplement, *Theosophist* 41, no. 10 (July 1920).

Birchfield, Joe D. "The Age of the Earth and the Invention of Geological Time." In *Lyell: The Past Is the Key to the Present*, edited by Derek J. Blundell and Andrew C. Scott, 137–43. London: Geological Society, Special Publications, 1998.

Blaikie, Piers. *The Political Economy of Soil Erosion in Developing Countries*. London: Routledge, 1985.

Blavatsky, Helena P. *The Secret Doctrine: The Synthesis of Science, Religion, and Philosophy*, vol. 1: *Cosmogenesis*. Pasadena, CA: Theosophical University Press, 1952.

Blavatsky, Helena P. *The Secret Doctrine: The Synthesis of Science, Religion, and Philosophy*, vol. 2: *Anthropogenesis*. Pasadena, CA: Theosophical University Press, 1952.

Bloembergen, Marieke, and Matijn Eickhoff. "Conserving the Past, Mobilizing the Indonesian Future: Archeological Sites, Regime Change and Heritage Politics in Indonesia in the 1950s." *Bijdragen tot de Taal-, Land- en Volkenkunde* 167, no. 4 (2011): 405–36.

Bobbette, Adam, and Amy Donovan. *Political Geology: Active Stratigraphies and the Making of Life*. Cham: Palgrave, 2019.

Boechari, M. "Preliminary Report on the Discovery of an Old-Malay Inscription at Sodjomerta." *Madjalah Ilmu-Ilmu Sastra Indonesia* 2–3 (1966): 241–51.

Boomgaard, Peter. "The Making and Unmaking of Tropical Science: Dutch Research on Indonesia, 1600–2000." *Bijdragen tot de Taal-, Land- en Volkenkunde* 162, nos. 2–3 (2006): 191–217.

Braak, C. "Verslag omtrent den toestand en de werkzaamheden der Koninklijke Natuurkundige Vereeniging in Nederlandsch-Indië over het jaar 1920." *Natuurkundig Tijdschrift voor Nederlandsch-Indië* 71, no. 1 (1920) 13–20.

Braun, Bruce. "Producing Vertical Territory: Geology and Governmentality in Late Victorian Canada." *Ecumene* 7, no. 1 (January 2000): 7–46.

Brouwer, H. A. "The Horizontal Movement of Geanticlines and the Fractures near Their Surface." *Journal of Geology* 29, no. 6 (September–October 1921): 560–77.

Brown, Iem. "The Revival of Buddhism in Modern Indonesia." In *Hinduism in Modern Indonesia: A Minority Religion between Local, National, and Global Interests*, edited by Martin Ramstedt, 45–55. London: Routledge, 2004.

Bubandt, Nils. "Haunted Geologies: Spirits, Stones, and the Necropolitics of the Anthropocene." In *Arts of Living on a Damaged Planet: Ghosts and Monsters of the Anthropocene*, edited by Anna Tsing, Heather Swanson, Elaine Gan, and Nils Bubandt, G121–41. Minneapolis: University of Minnesota Press, 2017.

Bullough, Nigel, and Peter Carry. "The Kolkata Stone (Calcutta Stone)." *Newsletter* 74 (Summer 2016): 4–5.

Burnett, John. "The Origins of the Electrocardiograph as a Clinical Instrument." Supplement, *Medical History*, no. 5 (1985): 53–76.

Carey, Peter. "Civilization on Loan: The Making of an Upstart Polity: Mataram and Its Successors, 1600–1830." *Modern Asian Studies* 31, no. 3 (July 1997): 711–34.

Carey, Peter. *The Power of Prophecy: Prince Dipanagara and the End of an Old Order in Java, 1785–1855.* Leiden: KITLV Press, 2008.

Cisternas, Carlos. "Ecuador Faces Harsh Economic Measures." *Washington Post*, March 11, 1999.

Clark, Nigel, and Bronislaw Szerszynski, *Planetary Social Thought: The Anthropocene Challenge to the Social Sciences.* Cambridge: Polity, 2020.

Clark, Nigel, and Kathryn Yusoff. "Geosocial Formations and the Anthropocene." In "Geosocial Formations and the Anthropocene," edited by Nigel Clark and Kathryn Yusoff. Special issue, *Theory, Culture and Society* 34, no. 2–3 (2017): 3–23.

Crawfurd, John. *History of the Indian Archipelago, Containing an Account of the Manners, Arts, Languages, Religions, Institutions, and Commerce of Its Inhabitants*, 3 vols. Edinburgh: Archibald Constable, 1820.

Couperus, Louis. *The Hidden Force: A Story of Modern Java.* Translated by Alexander Teixeira de Mattos. London: Jonathan Cape, 1922.

D'Arcy Wood, Gillen. *Tambora: The Eruption That Changed the World.* Princeton, NJ: Princeton University Press, 2014.

Darwin, Charles. *On the Origin of Species by Natural Selection, or the Preservation of Favoured Races in the Struggle for Life.* New York: D. Appleton, 1861.

de Graaf, H. J. *De regering van Sultan Agung, vorst van Mataram 1613–1645 en die van zijn voorganger Panembahan Séda-ing-Krapjak 1601–1613.* The Hague: Martinus Nijhoff, 1958.

de Jongh, A. C. "On the Valency of the Chemical Atoms in Connection with Theosophical Conceptions concerning Their Exterior Form." *Theosophist* 35, no. 10 (July 1914): 535–71. http://iapsop.com/archive/materials/theosophist/theosophist _v35_n10_jul_1914.pdf.

Delbourgo, James. "The Knowing World: A New Global History of Science." *History of Science* 57, no. 3 (2019): 373–99.

de Neve, George A. : "Rentjana Pos Pendjagaan Gunung Api Untuk Dinas Gunung Berapi di 'Indonesia.'" *Berita Gunung Berapi* 1, nos. 1-2 (1952): 75–83.

de Neve, George A. "Volcanological Investigations in Cooperation with the Auri (1950–1952)." *Berita Gunung Berapi* 1, nos. 1–2 (September–December 1952): 34–64.

de Tollenaere, Herman A. O. "The Politics of Divine Wisdom: Theosophy and Labour, National, and Women's Movements in Indonesia and South Asia 1875–1974." PhD diss., Katholieke Universiteit Nijmegen, 1996.

Deussen, Paul. *The Philosophy of the Upanishads*. Edinburgh: T. and T. Clark, 1908.

Djajawinangun. "G. Merapi, kunjungan P. J. M. Drs Moh. Hatta dan Sultan Jogja IX di Pos Babadan. Tanggal 14–2-'52" (archival photograph). Balai Penyelidikan dan Pengembangan Teknologi Kebencanaan Geologi [Center for Research and Development of Geological Disaster Technology], Yogyakarta.

Doel, Ronald E., Tanya J. Levin, and Mason K. Marker. "Extending Modern Cartography to the Ocean Depths: Military Patronage, Cold War Priorities, and the Heezen-Tharp Mapping Project, 1952–1959." *Journal of Historical Geography* 32 (2006): 605–26.

Donovan, Amy, and Clive Oppenheimer. "Science, Policy and Place in Volcanic Disasters: Insights from Montserrat." *Environmental Science and Policy* 39 (2014): 150–61.

Donovan, Amy, and Clive Oppenheimer. "Volcanoes on Borders: A Scientific and (Geo)political Challenge." *Bulletin of Volcanology* 81, no. 31 (2019): 1–27.

Donovan, Katherine. "Doing Social Volcanology: Exploring Volcanic Culture in Indonesia." *Area* 42, no. 1 (2010): 117–26.

Dott, Robert H., Jr. "An Introduction to the Ups and Downs of Eustasy." In *Eustasy: The Historical Ups and Downs of a Major Geological Concept*, 1–16. Boulder, CO: Geological Society of America, 1992.

Dove, Michael, and Bambang Hudayana. "The View from the Volcano: An Appreciation of the Work of Piers Blaikie." *Geoforum* 39 (2008): 736–46.

DW, Pepep. *Manusia dan Gunung: Teologi, Bandung, Ekologi*. Yogyakarta: Djeladjah Pustaka, 2018.

Edge, H. T. "The Age of the Earth." *Theosophical Path* 2, no. 2 (February 1912): 77–148.

Escher, Berend George. "The Kelut." Translation from the Dutch original, "De Kloet." *Waterstaats-Ingenieur* 7 (1919): 1–18. Item E.19–9. Perpustakaan Direktorat Vulkanologi (archive), Bandung, Indonesia.

Einthoven, Willem, Sr. "The String Galvanometer and the Measurement of the Action Currents of the Heart." In *Nobel Lectures, Physiology or Medecine 1922–1941*, 94–111. Amsterdam: Elsevier, 1965.

Einthoven, Willem, Sr. "The Telecardiogram." Translated by F. A. L. Mathewson and H. Jackh. *American Heart Journal* 49, no. 1 (January 1955): 77–82.

Elden, Stuart. "Secure the Volume: Vertical Geopolitics and the Depth of Power." *Political Geography* 34 (2013): 35–51.

Endraswara, Suwardi. *Agama Jawa: Ajaran, Amalan, dan Asal-Usul Kejawen*. Yogyakarta: Narasi-Lembu Jawa, 2018.

Ewing, Maurice. "Marine Gravimetric Methods and Surveys." *Proceedings of the American Philosophical Society* 63, no. 1 (April 1938): 47–70.

Ewing, Maurice, and Bruce C. Heezen. "Oceanographic Research Programs of the Lamont Geological Observatory." *American Geographical Society* 46, no. 4 (October 1956): 508–35.

Ewing, Maurice, and J. Lamar Worzel. "Gravity Anomalies and Structure of the West Indies, Part I." *Bulletin of the Geological Society of America* 65 (February 1954): 165–74.

Fischer, Robert L. *A Preliminary Report on the Expeditions* Monsoon *and* Lusiad *1960–1963*. San Diego: Scripps Institution of Oceanography, 1964. https://escholarship.org/uc/item/2q24q7ss.

Florida, Nancy. "Reading the Unread in Traditional Javanese Literature." *Indonesia*, 44 (October 1987): 1–15.

Frankel, Henry R. *The Continental Drift Controversy*, 4 vols. Cambridge: Cambridge University Press, 2012.

Franklin, J. Jeffrey. *Spirit Matters: Occult Beliefs, Alternative Religions, and the Crisis of Faith in Victorian Britain*. Ithaca, NY: Cornell University Press, 2018.

Friend, Theodore. *Indonesian Destinies*. Cambridge, MA: Belknap, 2003.

Fruin-Meese, Willemine. *Geschiedenis van Java: Het hindoetijdpert*. Weltevreden: Commissie voor de Volkslectuur, 1919–20.

Fruin-Meese, Willemine. *Sedjarah Tanah Djawa: Zaman Hindoe Ditanah Djawa, Djilid I*. Weltevreden: Balai Poestaka, 1921.

Geertz, Clifford. *Agricultural Involution: The Processes of Ecological Change in Indonesia*. Berkeley: University of California Press, 1966.

Gieryn, Thomas F. "Boundary-Work and the Demarcation of Science from Non-science: Strains and Interests in Professional Ideologies of Scientists." *American Sociological Review* 48, no. 6 (December 1983): 781–95.

Gilbert, G. K. "Rhythms of Geologic Time." *Science* 11, no. 287 (June 29, 1900): 1001–12.

Goss, Andrew. *The Floracrats: State-Sponsored Science and the Failure of the Enlightenment in Indonesia*. Madison: University of Wisconsin Press, 2011.

Gutenberg, B., H. Benioff, J. M. Burgers, and David Griggs. "Colloquium on Plastic Flow and Deformation within the Earth." *Eos: Transactions American Geophysical Union* 32, no. 4 (August 1951): 498–543. https://doi.org/10.1029/TR032i004p00497.

Hadikusumo, Djajadi. "Report on the Volcanological Research and Volcanic Activity in Indonesia for the Period 1950–1957." *Berita Berkala Volkanologi/Bulletin of the Volcanological Survey of Indonesia for the Years 1950–1957*, no. 100 (1961): 3–122.

Hamilton, Warren. "Convergent-Plate Tectonics Viewed from the Indonesian Region." *Geologi Indonesia: Majalah Ikatan Ahli Geologi Indonesia* 12, no. 1 (1989): 35–88.

Hamilton, Warren. *Tectonic Map of Indonesia—A Progress Report*. US Geological Survey, Open File Report 1474. Washington, DC: US Department of the Interior, Geological Survey Project Report, Indonesian Investigations, 1970.

Hamilton, Warren. "Tectonics of the Indonesian Region." US Geological Survey Professional Paper 1078. Washington, DC: US Geological Survey, 1979.

Hannah, Willard. "The Magical-Mystical Syndrome in the Indonesian Mentality, I: Signs and Seers." *American Universities Field Staff Southeast Asia Series* 15, no. 5 (1967): 1–12.

Hannah, Willard. "The Magical-Mystical Syndrome in the Indonesian Mentality, II: Ka'Rachim and Other Initiates." *American Universities Field Staff Southeast Asia Series* 15, no. 6 (1967): 1–11.

Hannah, Willard. "The Magical-Mystical Syndrome in the Indonesian Mentality, III: The Rise and Fall of Mbah Suro." *American Universities Field Staff Southeast Asia Series* 15, no. 7 (1967): 1–14.

Hannah, Willard. "The Magical-Mystical Syndrome in the Indonesian Mentality, IV: Pak De Wadja and the Guides of Guided Democracy." *American Universities Field Staff Southeast Asia Series* 15, no. 8 (1967): 1–10.

Hannah, Willard. "The Magical-Mystical Syndrome in the Indonesian Mentality, V: Pak Harto; the Myth, the Man, and the Mystery." *American Universities Field Staff Southeast Asia Series* 15, no. 9 (1967): 1–19.

Heezen, Bruce C., and Marie Tharp. *Physiographic Diagram of the Indian Ocean: The Red Sea, the South China Sea, the Sulu Sea and the Celebes Sea.* New York: Geological Society of America, 1964.

Heezen, Bruce C., Marie Tharp, and Heinrich Berann. *Indian Ocean Floor* (map). *National Geographic Magazine* 132, no. 4 (October 1967): 600–601.

Hess, Harry H. "History of Ocean Basins." In *Petrologic Studies: A Volume to Honor A. F. Buddington,* 599–620. New York: Geological Society of America, 1962.

"Highest Alert Issued for Indonesia's Merapi Volcano." BBC News, October 25, 2010. https://www.bbc.com/news/world-asia-pacific-11617502.

Hinloopen Labberton, Dirk van. *Lajang Damar-woelan: Opnieuw bewerkt door D. van Hinloopen-Labberton.* Batavia: Visser, 1905.

Hinloopen Labberton, Dirk van. "The Mahabharata in Medieval Javanese." *Journal of the Royal Asiatic Society of Great Britain and Ireland* (January 1913): 1–22.

Hinloopen Labberton, Dirk van. "Oud-Javaansche gegevens omtrent de vulkanologie van Java." *Natuurkundig Tijdschrift voor Nederlandsch-Indië* 81 (1921): 124–58.

Hinloopen Labberton, Dirk van. "The Riddle of Bhatara Kala to Sanghiang Vishnu." *Theosophist* 41, no. 8 (May 1920): 156–58. http://iapsop.com/archive/materials/theosophist/theosophist_v41_n8_may_1920.pdf.

Hinloopen Labberton, Dirk van. *The Wayang, or Shadow Play as Given in Java.* Bandoeng: Be Uitgevers Trust Jamu Dvipa, 1912.

Hollie, Pamela G. "Indonesia: A Glut of Volcanoes and Many Rituals." *New York Times,* February 8, 1981.

Holmes, Arthur. *The Age of the Earth: An Introduction to Geological Ideas.* London: Ernest Benn, 1927.

Holst, Paoletta. "Terpisah Namun Cukup Dekat: Disconected but Close Enough." In *Hal-hal Yang Dikatakan oleh Bungalow* [What bungalows can tell], edited by Mira Asriningtyas, Paoletta Holst, and Brigita Murti, 119–45. Printon: Onomatopee, 2021.

Inandiak, Elisabeth D. *Babad Ngalor-Ngidul.* Jakarta: Gramedia, 2016.

Inandiak, Elisabeth D. "2010 Merapi Eruption Journals." Yogyakarta. In possession of the author.

Jácome, Luis I. "The Late 1990s Financial Crisis in Ecuador: Institutional Weaknesses, Fiscal Rigidities, and Financial Dollarization at Work." IMF Working Paper No. 4/12, International Monetary Fund, January 2004.

Jasanoff, Sheila. *Science at the Bar: Law, Science, and Technology in America.* Cambridge, MA: Harvard University Press, 1995.

Johnson, Markes E. "A. W. Grabau's Embryonic Sequence Stratigraphy and Eustatic Curve." *Eustasy: The Historical Ups and Downs of a Major Geological Concept*, 43–54. Boulder, CO: Geological Society of America, 1992.

"Joko Piningit: Satria pembela mahluk lemah." *Misteri*, January 5, 1991, 70–71.

Junghuhn, Frans. *Java, zijne gedaante, zijn plantentooi, en inwendige bouw*, vol 1. The Hague: C. W. Mieling, 1854.

Junghuhn, Frans. *Java-album: Landschafts-ansichten von Java*. Leipzig: Arnoldische Buchhandlung, 1856.

Kartosutedjo, K. "Kokok Ayam Sebagai Indikator Adanya Hotline." *Mawas Diri* 9, no. 19 (September 30, 1990): 5–13.

Katili, John A. "A Review of the Geotectonic Theories and Tectonic Maps of Indonesia." *Earth-Sciences Review*, 7 (1971): 143–63.

Katili, John A. *Geotectonics of Indonesia: A Modern View*. Jakarta: Directorate General of Mines, 1980.

Katili, John A. "Indonesia Eldorado Geologi, Bagian I." *Mimbar Indonesia*, December 8, 1951, 10–11.

Katili, John A. "Indonesia Eldorado Geologi, Bagian II." *Mimbar Indonesia*, December 15, 1951, 27–29.

Katili, John A. *Sumberdaya Alam untuk Pembangunan Nasional* [Natural resources for national development]. Jakarta: Ghalia, 1983.

Katili, John A., and H. M. S. Hartono. "Van Bemmelen's Contributions to the Growth of Geotectonics and the Present State of Earth-Science Research in Indonesia." *Geologie en Mijnbouw* 58, no. 2 (1979): 107–16.

Katili, John A., and John A. Reinemund. "Southeast Asia: Tectonic Framework, Earth Resources and Regional Geological Programs." *International Union of Geological Sciences* 13 (1984): 167–237.

Katili, John A., and Adjat Sudradjat. *Galunggung: The 1982–1983 Eruption*. N.p.: Volcanological Survey of Indonesia, 1984.

Kemmerling, Georg L .L. "Belimming van den G. Batoer." *Natuurkundig Tijdschrift voor Nederlandsch-Indië* 78 (1919): 55–65.

Kemmerling, Georg L. L. "The Craterlake of Kelut Volcano." 1921. Item E.21–2. Perpustakaan Direktorat Vulkanologi (archive), Bandung, Indonesia.

Kemmerling, Georg L. L. "De G. Keloet einde 1921." *Natuurkundig Tijdschrift voor Nederlandsch-Indië* 82 (1922): 93–105.

Kemmerling, Georg L. L. "De 'Piek van Ternate.'" *Natuurkundig Tijdschrift voor Nederlandsch-Indië* 80 (1920): 37–49.

Kemmerling, Georg L. L. "De uitbarsting van den G. Keloet in den nacht van den 19[den] op den 20sten Mei 1919 door den tijdel." *Vulkanologische Mededeelingen* 2 (1921): 1–120.

Kemmerling, Georg L. L. "The Outburst of the G. Kelut in 1919." Translation from the Dutch original, "De uitbarsting van den G. Kelut in den nacht van den 19[den] op den 20sten Mei 1919," 1922. Item E.19–2. Perpustakaan Direktorat Vulkanologi (archive), Bandung, Indonesia.

Kemmerling, Georg L. L. "Vulkanologische Berichten." *Natuurkundig Tijdschrift voor Nederlandsch-Indië* 82, no. 2 (1922): 188–94.

Kemmerling, Georg L. L. "Wedus Gembel: A Few General Considerations on the G. Merapi and Its Eruption Character." Translation from the Dutch original, "De hernieuwde werking van den vulkaan G. Merapi (midden Java) van begin Augustus 1920 tot en het einde Februari 1921," 1921. Item E.21–3. Perpustakaan Direktorat Vulkanologi (archive), Bandung, Indonesia.

Kern, Johan. "Sanskrit-Inscriptie ter eere van den Javaanschen vost Er-Langa." *Bijdragen tot de Taal-, Land- en Volkenkunde van Nederlandsche-Indië* 34 (1885): 1–21.

"Kisah Mbah Marijan dan 4 Kata Pantangan." *Detik News*, May 15, 2006. https://news.detik.com/berita/d-595121/kisah-mbah-marijan-dan-4-kata-pantangan.

Klinke, Ian. "On the History of a Subterranean Geopolitics." *Geoforum* 127 (2019): 356–63. https://doi.org/10.1016/j.geoforum.2019.10.010.

Krafft, Katia, and Maurice Krafft. *A l'assaut des volcans: Islande, Indonésie*. Paris: Éditions G.P., 1976.

Krafft, Katia, and Maurice Krafft. *Objectifs volcans*. Paris: Éditions de la Martinière, 1992.

Krafft, Katia, and Maurice Krafft. *Volcano*. New York: Harry N. Abrams, 1975.

Krafft, Katia, and Maurice Krafft. *Volcans et éruptions*. Paris: Hachette, 1985.

Kuenen, Philip. H. "Contributions to the Geology of the East Indies from the Snellius Expedition." *Leidse Geologische Mededelingen* 7, no. 1 (1935): 273–331.

Kuenen, Philip. H. *Kruistochten over de indische diepzeebekkens: Anderhalf jaar als geoloog aan boord van Hr. Ms. Willebrord Snellius*. The Hague: H. P. Leopolds Uitgevers Mij N.V, 1941.

Kuenen, Philip. H. "The Negative Isostatic Anomalies in the East Indies (with Experiments)." *Leidse Geologische Mededelingen* 8, no. 2 (January 1937): 170–214.

Kuitenbrouwer, Vincent. "The Dutch East Indies during the First World War and the Birth of Colonial Radio." *World History Bulletin* 31, no. 1 (2015): 83–103.

Kurnia, Atep. "Surono berdiri di cincin api." *Geomagz: Majalah Geologi Populer* 4, no. 1, (March 2014): 36–47.

Kusumandinata, K., ed. *Data Dasar Gunungapi [sic] Indonesia*. Bandung: Departamen Pertambangan dan Energi, Direktorat Vulkanologi, 1979.

Lamar Worzel, J. *Pendulum Gravity Measurements at Sea, 1936–1959*. Lamont Geological Observatory Contribution No. 807. New York: Wiley, 1965.

Lang, Olivia. "Spiritual Guardian of Indonsian Volcano Dies." BBC News, October 27, 2010. https://www.bbc.com/news/world-asia-pacific-11634824.

Last, Angela. "Fruit of the Cyclone: Undoing Geopolitics through Geopoetics." *Geoforum* 64 (August 2015): 56–64. https://doi.org/10.1016/j.geoforum.2015.05.019.

Last, Angela. "We Are the World? Anthropocene Cultural Production between Geopoetics and Geopolitics." *Theory, Culture and Society* 34, nos. 2–3 (2017): 147–68.

Laudan, Rachel. "Oceanography and Geophysical Theory in the First Half of the Twentieth Century: The Dutch School." In *Oceanography: The Past*, edited by Mary Sears and Daniel Merriman, 656–66. New York: Springer-Verlag, 1980.

Leadbeater, Charles. *The Astral Plane: Its Scenery, Inhabitants, and Phenomena*. 3rd ed. London: Theosophical Publishing Society, 1900.

Leadbeater, Charles. *The Occult History of Java*. Adyar, India: Theosophical Publishing House, 1951.

Leadbeater, Charles. *The World Mother as Symbol and Fact*. Adyar, India: Theosophical Publishing House, 1928.

Le Conte, Joseph. "On Critical Periods in the History of the Earth, and Their Relation to Evolution: On the Quaternary as Such a Period." *American Naturalist* 11, no. 9 (September 1877): 540–57.

Le Pichon, Xavier. "Fifty Years of Plate Tectonics: Afterthoughts of a Witness." *Tectonics* 38, no. 8 (2019): 2919–33. https://doi.org/10.1029/2018TC005350.

Li, Tanya Murry. *The Will to Improve: Governmentality, Development, and the Practice of Politics*. Durham, NC: Duke University Press, 2007.

Lyell, Charles. *Principles of Geology: Being an Inquiry How Far the Former Changes of the Earth's Surface Are Referable to Causes Now in Operation*, 4th ed. 4 vols. London: John Murray, 1835.

Mahaguru Merapi (Part I). Kementerian ESDM, BPPTKG Channel, May 16, 2018, video, 15:20. https://www.youtube.com/watch?v=7LauJtksUCc.

Marshall, Andrew. "The Gods Must Be Restless: Living in the Shadow of Indonesia's Volcanoes." *National Geographic Magazine* 213, no. 1 (January 2008): 35–57.

Mazur, Allan. "Amadeus Grabau in China: 1920–1946." *Carbonates and Evaporites* 21, no. 1 (2006): 51–94.

"Mbah Marijan Bertemu Wapres." *Detik News*, April 15, 2007. https://news.detik.com/berita/d-767533/mbah-marijan-bertemu-wapres.

"Miraculous Salvations during Kelut Volcano Eruption in 1919." Translation from the Dutch original, "Wonderbaarlijke Reddingen, Kedirische Courant (1919)": 1–4. Item E.19–7a. Perpustakaan Direktorat Vulkanologi (archive), Bandung, Indonesia.

Molengraaff, G. A. F. "Modern Deep-Sea Research in the East Indian Archipelago." *Geographical Journal* 57, no. 2 (February 1921): 95–118.

Mortimer, Rex. *Indonesian Communism under Sukarno: Ideology and Politics 1959–1965*. Jakarta: Equinox, 1974.

Moshin, Anto. "Wiring the New Order: Indonesian Village Electrification and Patrimonial Technopolitics (1966–1998)." *Sojourn: Journal of Social Issues in Southeast Asia* 29, no. 1 (2014): 63–95.

Mrázek, Rudolf. *Engineers of Happy Land: Technology and Nationalism in a Colony*. Princeton, NJ: Princeton University Press, 2002.

Mrázek, Rudolf. "'Let Us Become Radio Mechanics': Technology and National Identity in Late-Colonial Netherlands East Indies." *Comparative Studies in Society and History* 39, no. 1 (January 1997): 3–33.

Mus, Paul. "Barabudur: Les origines du stupa et la transmigration, essai d'archéologie religieuse comparée." *Bulletin de l'École française d'Extrême-Orient* 32, no. 1 (1932): 269–439.

Navy-Princeton Gravity Expedition to the West Indies in 1932. Washington, DC: Government Printing Office, 1933.

Newhall, C. G., S. Bronto, B. Alloway, N. G. Banks, I. Bahar, M. A. del Marmol, R. D. Hadisantono, et al. "10,000 Years of Explosive Eruptions of Merapi Volcano, Central Java: Archaeological and Modern Implications." *Journal of Volcanology and Geothermal Research* 100 (July 2000): 9–50. https://doi.org/10.1016/S0377 -0273(00)00132-3.

Newman, Barry. "In Kringdjing, Java, the 'Glowing Cloud' Brings Rain of Death." *Wall Street Journal*, May 23, 1979, 1, 28.

Nusantara, A. Ariobimo, ed. *Harta Bumi Indonesia*. Jakarta: Gramedia, 2007.

O'Brien, Miles. "Science, Mysticism Meld in Predicting Mount Merapi's Deadly Eruptions." *PBS News Hour*, December 2, 2010. https://www.pbs.org/newshour /show/science-mysticism-meld-in-predicting-mount-merapis-deadly -eruptions.

Oreskes, Naomi. *The Rejection of Continental Drift: Theory and Method in American Earth Science*. New York: Oxford University Press, 1999.

Oreskes, Naomi. *Science on a Mission: How Military Funding Shaped What We Do and Don't Know about the Ocean*. Chicago: University of Chicago Press, 2021.

Pemberton, John. *On the Subject of "Java."* Ithaca, NY: Cornell University Press, 1994.

"Penuhi Hak Gunung Berapi." *Tempo* (Jakarta), May 25, 2015. https://majalah.tempo .co/read/wawancara/148253/penuhi-hak-gunung-berapi .

"Pesan Istana untuk Mbah Maridjan." *Tempo* (Jakarta), October 22, 2010. https:// nasional.tempo.co/read/286449/pesan-istana-untuk-mbah-maridjan.

Petroeschevsky, W. A. "The Volcanic Activity in Indonesia during the Period 1942–1948." *Berita Gunung Berapi* 1, 1–2 (1952): 9–31.

Petrushevsky, Vladimir. "Diaries." *Vladimir Petrushevsky: An Archive* (blog), accessed October 19, 2022, https://blogs.dickinson.edu/vapetrushevsky/category/diary/.

Phillips, John. *Life on Earth: Its Origin and Succession*. Cambridge, UK: Macmillan, 1860.

Pigeaud, Theodore. "Alexander, Sakèndèr en Sénapati." *Djåwå* 7, no. 1 (1927): 321–61.

Pigeaud, Theodore. *De tantu panggelaran: Een Oud-Javaansch prozageschrift, uitgegeven, vertaald en toegelicht*. The Hague: H. L. Smits, 1924.

Pigeaud, Theodore. *Javaanse volksvertoningen: Bijdrage tot de beschrijving van land en volk*. The Hague: Martinus Nijhof, 1938.

Poller, Jake. "'Under a Glamour': Annie Besant, Charles Leadbeater and Neo-theosophy." In *The Occult Imagination in Britain, 1875–1947*, edited by Christine Ferguson and Andrew Radford, 77–93. London: Taylor and Francis, 2018.

Povinelli, Elizabeth. *Geontologies: A Requiem to Late Liberalism*. Durham, NC: Duke University Press, 2016.

Prasetyo, Elisabeth D., and Heri Dono. *Lahirnya Kembali Beringin Putih* [The white banyan]. Yogyakarta: Babad Alas, 1998.

Protchsky, Susie. "Disaster in Indonesia: Along the Fault Line toward New Approaches." *Indonesia* 113 (April 2022): 1–8.

Protchsky, Susie. "Military Responses to and Forms of Knowledge about Natural Disaster in Colonial Indonesia, 1865–1930." *Indonesia* 113 (April 2022): 67–91.

Protschky, Susie, and Ruth Morgan. "Historicising Sulfur Mining, Lime Extraction and Geotourism in Indonesia and Australia." *Extractive Industries and Society* 8, no. 4 (December 2021): 10081. https://doi.org/10.1016/j.exis.2021.02.001.

Pyenson, Lewis. *Empire of Reason: Exact Sciences in Indonesia, 1840–1940*. Leiden: Brill, 1989.

Raffles, Stamford. *The History of Java*. London: Black, Parbury and Allen, 1817.

Ramaswamy, Sumathi. *The Lost Land of Lemuria: Fabulous Geographies, Catastrophic Histories*. Berkeley: University of California Press, 2004.

Resink, G. J. "Kanjeng Ratu Kidul: The Second Divine Spouse of the Sultans of Ngayogyakarta." *Asian Folklore Studies* 56, no. 2 (1997): 313–16.

Ricklefs, M. C. "The Crisis of 1740–1 in Java: The Javanese, Chinese, Madurese and Dutch, and the Fall of the Court of Kartasura." *Bijdragen tot de Taal-, Land-en Volkenkunde* 139, nos. 2–3 (1983): 268–90. https://doi.org/10.1163/22134379-90003445.

Ricklefs, M. C. *Islamisation and Its Opponents in Java: A Political, Social, Cultural and Religious History, c. 1930 to the Present*. Singapore: NUS Press, 2012.

Ricklefs, M. C. *Jogjakarta under Sultan Mangkubumi 1749–1792: A History of the Division of Java*. London: Oxford University Press, 1974.

Ricklefs, M. C. *Polarizing Javanese Society: Islamic and Other Visions*. Honolulu: University of Hawai'i Press, 2007.

Ricklefs, M. C. *The Seen and Unseen Worlds in Java, 1726–1749: History, Literature, and Islam in the Court of Pakubuwana II*. Honolulu: University of Hawai'i Press, 1998.

Romero, Simon. "Ecuador's Leader Purges Military and Moves to Expel American Base." *New York Times*, April 21, 2008.

Rudwick, Martin. *Earth's Deep History: How It Was Discovered and Why It Matters*. Chicago: University of Chicago Press, 2014.

Ryan, C. J. "Boro-Bodur, the Great Pyramid of Java." *Theosophical Path* 13, no. 5 (November 1917): 482–85.

Ryan, C. J. "Great Temples in Java." *Theosophical Path* 26, no. 3 (March 1924): 225–36.

Schaffer, Simon, Lissa Roberts, Raj Kapil, and James Delbourgo. *The Brokered World: Go-Betweens and Global Intelligence, 1770–1820*. Sagamore Beach, MA: Watson Publishing International, 2009.

Schaffer, Simon, and Steven Shapin. *Leviathan and the Air-Pump: Hobbes, Boyle, and the Experimental Life*. Princeton, NJ: Princeton University Press, 1985.

Scheltema, J. F. *Monumental Java*. London: Macmillan, 1912.

Schlehe, Judith. "Cultural Politics of Natural Disasters: Discourses on Volcanic Eruptions in Indonesia." In *Culture and the Changing Environment: Uncertainty, Cognition, and Risk Management in Cross-Cultural Perspective*, edited by M. J. Casimir, 275–99. Oxford: Berghahn, 2008.

Schlehe, Judith. "Reinterpretations of Mystical Traditions: Explanations of a Volcanic Eruption in Java." *Anthropos* 91, nos. 4–6 (1996): 391–409.

Scott Petty, O. *Seismic Reflections: Recollections of the Formative Years of the Geophysical Exploration Industry*. Houston: Geosource, 1976.

Selcer, Perrin. "The Holocene Is History." In *New Earth Histories*, edited by Alison Bashford, Emily Kern, and Adam Bobbette. Chicago: University of Chicago Press, forthcoming.

Shen, Yen Grace. *Unearthing the Nation: Modern Geology and Nationalism in Republican China*. Chicago: University of Chicago Press, 2014.

Siegert, Bernhard. *Cultural Techniques: Grids, Filters, Doors, and Other Articulations of the Real*. New York: Fordham University Press, 2015.

Simanjuntak, Truman, ed. *Archaeology: Indonesian Perspective: R. P. Soejono's Festschrift*. Jakarta: Indonesian Institute of Sciences, International Centre for Prehistoric and Austronesian Studies, 2006.

Sinnett, Alfred Percy. *The Occult World*. London: Trubner, 1884.

Snellen, H. A. *Willem Einthoven (1860–1927): Father of Electrocardiography; Life and Work, Ancestors and Contemporaries*. Dordrecht: Kluwer Academic Publishers, 1995.

Snider, Robert G. "The Indian Ocean Expedition—An International Venture." *Transactions: American Geophysical Union* 42, no. 3 (September 1961): 289–94. https://doi.org/10.1029/TR042i003p00289.

Snider, Robert G. "The International Indian Ocean Expedition 1959–64." *Discovery* 22, no. 3 (March 1961): 114–17.

Stange, Paul. "Deconstruction as Disempowerment: New Orientalisms of Java." *Bulletin of Concerned Asian Scholars* 23, no. 3 (1991): 51–71.

"Soedjono dan 'Orde Dhawuh.'" *Tempo* (Jakarta), February 4, 2008. https://majalah.tempo.co/read/laporan-utama/126289/soedjono-dan-orde-dhawuh?

Squire, Rachael, and Klaus Dodds. "Introduction." In "Subterranean Geopolitics," edited by Rachael Squire and Klaus Dodds. Special issue, *Geopolitics* 25, no. 1 (2020): 4–16.

Subagya, Rahmat [Jan Bakker]. *Kepercayaan, Kebatinan, Kerohanian, Kejiwaan dan Agama*. 1973; repr., Yogyakarta: Penerbitan Yayasan Kanisius, 1976.

Sudrajat, Adjat. *The Development of Volcanological Investigations in Indonesia*. Bandung: Universitas Padjadjaran Press, 2009.

Sudrajat, Adjat. *Prahara Gunung Galunggung*. Bandung: Badan Geologi, 2013.

Sudrajat, Adjat. *Van Bemmelen: Kisah di Balik Ketenarannya*. Bandung: Badan Geologi, 2014.

Suess, Eduard. "Are Great Ocean Depths Permanent?" *Natural Science: A Monthly Review of Scientific Progress* 2 (March 1893): 180–99.

Suess, Eduard. *The Face of the Earth*, 4 vols. Oxford: Clarendon Press, 1909.

Suhardi. *Manekung di Puncak Gunung: Jalan Keselamatan Kejawen*. Yogyakarta: Gadjah Mada University Press, 2018.

Sukamto, Rab, Tjoek Soeradi, and Dan Wikarno. *Menguak Sejarah Kelembagaan Geologi di Indonesia: Dari Kantor Pencari Bahan Tambang Hingga Pusat Survei Geologi*. Bandung: Badan Geologi, 2006.

Surjo. "The Merapi Guarding System." 地 学 雑 誌 Chigaku Zasshi [Journal of geography] 67, no. 4 (1958): 31–37.

Surjo. "Volcanic Activities in Indonesia during the 1950–1957 Period." *Berita Berkala Volkanologi/Bulletin of the Volcanological Survey of Indonesia for the Period 1950–1957*, no. 100 (July 18, 1961): 17–101.

Swann Lull, Richard. "The Pulse of Life." In *The Evolution of the Earth and Its Inhabitants*, 109–46. New Haven: Yale University Press, 1819.

Syaifullah, M. "Labuhan Merapi, Cara Warga Mensyukuri Gunung Berapi." *Tempo* (Jakarta), May 9, 2016. https://tekno.tempo.co/read/769424/labuhan-merapi -cara-warga-mensyukuri-gunung-berapi/full&view=ok.

Tanudirjo, Daud A. "Theoretical Trends in Indonesian Archeology." *Theory in Archaeology: A World Perspective*, edited by Peter Ucko, 62–76. London: Routledge, 1995.

Taverne, N. J. M. "The G. Kelut." Translation from the Dutch original, "De G. Kelut" (1923): 1–17. Item E.23–1a. Perpustakaan Direktorat Vulkanologi (archive), Bandung, Indonesia.

Taylor, Jean Gelman. *The Social World of Batavia: Europeans and Eurasians in Colonial Indonesia*. Madison: University of Wisconsin Press, 1983.

Tazieff, H. "Volcano Survey." *Earth-Science Reviews* 1 (1966): 299–355.

Ter Horst de Boer, T. "A Legend of Kelut." Translation from the Dutch original, "Een legend van den Kloet," 1919. Item E.19–6. Perpustakaan Direktorat Vulkanologi (archive), Bandung, Indonesia.

Termier, Pierre. *La joie de la connaitre: Souvenirs d'un géologue*. Paris: Brouwer, 1925.

Thalmann, Han E. "Tan Sin Hok: 1902–1945." *Micropaleontologist* 3, no. 4 (October 1949): 25.

Thomson, William. "On the Secular Cooling of the Earth." *London, Edinburgh, and Dublin Philosophical Magazine and Journal of Science* 25, no. 165 (1863): 1–14.

Tiffin, Sarah. "Java's Ruined *Candis* and the British Picturesque Ideal." *Bulletin of SOAS* 72, no. 3 (2009): 525–58.

Tillett, Gregory John. "Charles Webster Leadbeater: A Biographical Journey." PhD diss., University of Sydney, 1986.

Tingkat Aktivitas Gunungapi. BPPTKG Channel, December 1, 2016, video, 15:20. https://www.youtube.com/watch?v=Ek-n9al6tPA.

Tirtakoesoema, R. Soedjana. "The Anniversary of the Accession of His Highness the Sultan of Yogyakarta (Tingalan Panjenengan)." In *The Kraton: Selected Essays on Javanese Courts*, edited by Stuart Robson, 143–68. Leiden: KITLV Press, 2003.

Tirtakoesoema, R. Soedjana. "De verjaring van den verheffingsdag van Z. H. den Sultan van Jogjakarta (Tingalan Pandjenengan)." *Djåwå* 12, 2–3 (1933): 372–89.

Tomoda, Yoshibumi. "Gravity at Sea: A Memoir of a Marine Geophysicist." *Proceedings of the Japan Academy, Series B: Physical and Biological Sciences*, 86, no. 8 (2010): 769–87. https://doi.org/10.2183/pjab.86.769.

Triyoga, Lucas Sasongko. *Manusia Jawa dan Gunung Merapi: Persepsi dan Kepercayaannya*. Yogyakarta: Gadjah Mada University Press.

Trumbull, Raissa DeSmet. "A Liquid World: Figuring Coloniality in the Indies." PhD diss., University of California, Santa Cruz, 2013. https://escholarship.org /content/qt6fm7v1d2/qt6fm7v1d2.pdf.

Umbgrove, Johannnes H. F. "The First Days of the New Submarine Volcano near Krakatoa." *Leidsche Geologische Mededelingen* 2, no. 1 (January 1926): 325–28.

Umbgrove, Johannes H. F. "Geological History of the East Indies." *Bulletin of the American Association of Petroleum Geologists* 22, no. 1 (1938): 1–70.

Umbgrove, Johannes H. F. "Heterospira: A New Foraminiferal Genus from the Tertiary of Borneo." *Leidse Geologische Mededelingen* 8, no. 1 (1936): 155–59.

Umbgrove, Johannes H. F. "Het ontstaan van het Diengplateau." *Leidsche Geologische Mededelingen* 3, no. 1 (1928): 131–49.

Umbgrove, Johannes H. F. Johannes Umbgrove's letters to his mother (June 24, 1926–July 30, 1929). 173 letters. Personal collection of Frederik van Veen, Groningen, Netherlands.

Umbgrove, Johannes H. F. "In Memoriam, Prof. Dr G. A. F. Molengraaff." *Geologie en Mijnbouw* 4, no. 3 (May 1942): 33–38.

Umbgrove, Johannes H. F. *Leven en Materie.* The Hague: Martinus Nijhoff, 1943.

Umbgrove, Johannes H. F. "Madreporaria from the Bay of Batavia." *Zoologische Mededelingen* 22, no. 1 (1939): 1–64.

Umbgrove, Johannes H. F. "On Rhythms in the History of the Earth." *Geological Magazine* 76, no. 3 (1939): 116–29.

Umbgrove, Johannes H. F. "The Origin of Deep-Sea Troughs in the East Indies." Reprinted in International Geological Congress, *Report of the Eighteenth Session, Great Britain, 1948,* Part 8 (1948): 73–80.

Umbgrove, Johannes H. F. "Periodicity in Terrestrial Processes." *American Journal of Science* 238, no. 8 (1940): 573–76.

Umbgrove, Johannes H. F. *The Pulse of the Earth.* The Hague: Martinus Nijhoff, 1942.

Umbgrove, Johannes H. F. "A Second Species of Biplanispira from the Eocene of Borneo." *Leidse Geologische Mededelingen* 10, no. 1 (1938): 82–89.

Umbgrove, Johannes H. F. *Structural History of the East Indies.* Cambridge: Cambridge University Press, 1949.

Umbgrove, Johannes H. F. *Symphony of the Earth.* The Hague: Martinus Nijhoff, 1950.

Umbgrove, Johannes H. F. "Tertiary Foraminifera." *Leidse Geologische Mededelingen* 5, no. 1 (1931): 35–91.

Umbgrove, Johannes H. F. "Verschillende typen van tertiaire geosynclinalen in den Indischen Archipel." *Leidse Geologische Mededelingen* 6, no. 1 (1933): 33–43.

van Aken, Hendrik M. "Dutch Oceanographic Research in Indonesia in Colonial Times." In "The Indonesian Seas." Special issue, *Oceanography* 18, no. 4 (December 2005): 30–41.

van Bemmelen, Reinout W. [Untitled contribution]. *Kogyo Jimusho Bandoeng Chishitsu-Chosajo (Kwazan Chosabu)/Bulletin of the East Indian Volcanological Survey for the Year 1941,* nos. 95–98 (1943): 69–72.

van Bemmelen, Reinout W. "Charles Edgar Stehn." *Bulletin Volcanologique* 8, no. 1 (1949): 133–37.

van Bemmelen, Reinout W. "De physisch-chemische ontwikkeling der aarde." *Geologie en Mijnbouw* 11, no. 1 (January 1949): 1–21.

van Bemmelen, Reinout W. "VIII Report on the Merapi Eruption Cycle 2602–2603 (1943)." Typescript, 1956. Perpustakaan Pusat Volkanologi (Archive), Bandung, Indonesia.

van Bemmelen, Reinout W. "V Report on the New Merapi Eruption Cycle of 2602 (1942)." Typescript. Perpustakaan Pusat Volkanologi (Archive), Bandung, Indonesia.

van Bemmelen, Reinout W. *Geodynamic Models: An Evaluation and Synthesis.* Amsterdam: Elsevier, 1972.

van Bemmelen, Reinout W. *The Geology of Indonesia,* 3 vols. The Hague: Government Printing Office, 1949.

van Bemmelen, Reinout W. "The Geophysical Contrast between Orogenic and Stable Areas." *Geologie en Mijnbouw,* n.s., 16e (August 1954): 326–34.

van Bemmelen, Reinout W. *Mountain Building: A Study Primarily Based on Indonesia Region of the World's Most Active Crustal Deformations.* The Hague: Martinus Nijhoff, 1954.

van Bemmelen, Reinout W. "On Mega-undations: A New Model for the Earth's Evolution." *Tectonophysics* 3, no. 2 (1966): 83–127.

van Bemmelen, Reinout W. "On the Geophysical Foundations of the Undation-Theory (Communicated by G. A. F. Molengraaff)." *Proceedings of the Royal Academy Amsterdam* 36 (1933): 322–42.

van Bemmelen, Reinout W. "On the Origin of Igneous Rocks in Indonesia." *Geologie en Mijnbouw* 12, no. 7 (July 1950): 207–20.

van Bemmelen, Reinout W. "Plate Tectonics and the Undation Model: A Comparison." *Tectonophysics* 32 (1976): 145–82.

van Bemmelen, Reinout W. "Report on the Volcanic Activity and Volcanological Research in Indonesia during the Period 1936–1948." *Extrait du Bulletin Volcanologique, organe de l'Association de volcanologie de l'Union géophysique internationale,* series II, vol. 9 (1949): 3–29.

van Bemmelen, Reinout W. "The Scientific Character of Geology." *Journal of Geology* 69, no. 4 (July 1961): 453–63.

van Dijk, C. *Rebellion under the Banner of Islam: The Darul Islam in Indonesia.* Leiden: Koninklijk Instituut voor Taal-, Land- en Volkenkunde, 1981.

van Dijk, Kees. *The Netherlands Indies and the Great War.* Leiden: KITLV Press, 2007. http://library.oapen.org/handle/20.500.12657/34639.

Van Gorsel, J. T. "Pioneers and Milestones of Indonesian Geology." Biography of Indonesia Geology, accessed August 1, 2021. https://vangorselslist.com/pioneers.html.

Van Hien, H. A. *De Javaansche geestenwereld en de betrekking, die tusschen de geesten en de zinnelijke wereld bestaat,* vol. 1: *Primbon's.* Semarang: G. C. T. Van Dorp, 1896.

van Padang, M. Neumann. "De uitbarsting van den Merapi (Midden Java) in de jaren 1930–1931." *Vulkanologische en Seismologische Mededeelingen* 12 (1933): 110–12.

van Padang, M. Neumann. "History of Volcanology in the East Indies." *Scripta Geologica* 71 (1983): 1–76.

van Padang, M. Neumann. "Measures Taken by Authorities to Safeguard Volcanic Outbursts." *Bulletin Volcanologique* 23 (1960): 181–92.

van Padang, M. Neumann. "Volcanic Phenomena during the Months of May and June 1931." *Bulletin of the Netherlands East Indies Volcanological Survey 1927–1931*, nos. 45–46 (1931): 55–62.

Van Sommers, Raymond. *A Life in Subud*. Northbridge, Australia: Dawn Books, 2003. https://ia903102.us.archive.org/22/items/Subud/subud_book.pdf.

Veldkamp, J. *History of Geophysical Research in the Netherlands and Its Former Overseas Territory*. Amsterdam: North-Holland Publishing, 1984.

Vening Meinesz, Felix A. "By Submarine through the Netherlands East Indies: A Paper Delivered at the Evening Meeting of the Society on 17 November 1930." *Geographical Journal* 77, no. 4 (1931): 338–48.

Vening Meinesz, Felix A. "The Earth's Crust Deformation in the East Indies (Provisional Paper)." *Koninklijke Nederlandsche Akademie van Wetenschappen*. Reprint from *Proceedings of the Royal Netherlands Academy of Arts and Science* 43, no. 3 (1940): 278–93.

Vening Meinesz, Felix A. "Gravity Anomalies in the East Indian Archipelago." *Geographical Journal* 77, no. 4 (April 1931): 323–32.

Vening Meinesz, Felix A. *Gravity Expeditions at Sea 1923–1930*, 4 vols. Delft: N. V. Technische Boekhandel en Drukkerij J. Waltman Jr., 1932–1948.

Vening Meinesz, Felix A. "The Origin of Continents and Oceans." *Geologie en Mijnbouw* 14, no. 11–1 (1952): 373–84.

Vening Meinesz, Felix A. "A Third Arc in Many Island Arc Areas." *Koniklijke Nederlandsche Akademie van Wetenschappen*. Reprint from *Proceedings of the Royal Netherlands Academy of Arts and Science Series B* 54, no. 5 (1951): 432–42.

Vening Meinesz, Felix A., and Veikko A. Heiskanen. *The Earth and Its Gravity Field*. McGraw-Hill: New York, 1958.

Verbeek, Rogier D. M. *Krakatau: Album*. Brussels: Institut National de Géographie, 1886.

Verbeek, Rogier D. M. "The Krakatoa Eruption." *Nature* 30 (May 1, 1884): 10–15.

Verbeek, Rogier D. M. *Oudheden van Java: Lijst der voornaamste overblijfselen uit den hindoetijd op Java met eene oudheidkundige kaart*. Batavia: Landsdrukkerij, 1891.

Verbeek, Rogier D. M. "Oudheidkundige kaart van Java." *Bataviaasch Genootschap van Kunsten en Wetenschappen* 46 (1891): five maps.

Verbeek, Rogier D. M. *Rapport sur les Moluques: Reconnaissances géologiques dans la partie orientale de l'archipel des indes orientales néerlandaises, atlas*. Batavia: Imprimerie de L'État, 1908.

Verbeek, Rogier D. M., and Reinder Fennema. *Description géologique de Java et Madoura*, 2 vols. Amsterdam: Joh. G. Stemler, 1896. https://archive.org/details/descriptiongeo01fenngoog.

Verbeek, Rogier D. M, and Reinder Fennema. *Description géologique de Java et Madoura*, vol. 3: *Atlas: Cartes géologique de Java et Madoura, et feuilles annexes*. Amsterdam: Joh. G. Stemler, 1896.

Veth, Pieter J. *Java: Geographisch, ethnologisch, historisch*. Haarlem: De Erven F. Bohn, 1882.

Vickers, Adrian. *A History of Modern Indonesia*. Cambridge: Cambridge University Press, 2005.

Visser, S. W. *On the Distribution of Earthquakes in the Netherlands East Indian Archipelago, 1909–1919; with a Discussion of Time Tables*. Batavia: Javasche Boekhandel en Drukkerij, 1921.

Visser, S. W. "Verslag van de werkzaamheden van de Commissie voor Vulcanologie en het ontworpen plan voor de vulkaanbewaking." *Natuurkundig Tijdschrift voor Nederlandsch-Indië* 81 (1921): 159–65.

Wegener, Alfred. *The Origins of Continents and Oceans*. New York: Dover, 1966.

Wessing, Robert. "Porous Boundaries: Addressing Calamities in East Java, Indonesia." *Bijdragen tot de Taal-, Land- en Volkenkunde* 166, no. 1 (2010): 49–82.

Wieringa, Edwin. "The Illusion of an Allusion: A Soothing Song for the Exiled Prince Dipasana (d. ca. 1840) in Ambon." *Journal of the Royal Asiatic Society* 10, no. 2 (2000): 244–63.

Winchester, Simon. *Krakatoa: The Day the World Exploded, August 27, 1883*. New York: HarperCollins, 2003.

Yusoff, Kathryn. *A Billion Black Anthropocenes or None*. Minneapolis: University of Minnesota Press, 2018.

Yusoff, Kathryn. "Queer Coal: Genealogies in/of the Blood." *philoSOPHIA: A Journal of Continental Feminism* 5, no. 2 (2015): 203–29.

INDEX

Page numbers in italics refer to figures.

differentiation, 9, 115, 116, 133, 134; cosmic, 90, 176; primordial, 95–96; signals and noise used in mapping, 172–73

Dipasana, Prince, 60

distance, 142–44, 150, 162; between observatories and craters, 151, 153, 164; of the universe to ourselves, 123, 129

Djåwå journal, 59

Dutch colonialism. *See* Netherlands East Indies

Dutch East India Company, 58, 60

Dutch Royal Navy, 31

earth sciences, xi, xvi, 5, 8, 140, 175–77. *See also* geological sciences

earth's crust, 23, 139, 185n76, 193n43; bulging of, 95; compression of, 133; contraction of, 183n42; cooling and shrinking of, 26, 41, 46, 184n76; folding of, 34–36, 184n65; fragmentation of, 48; periodicity and, 131, 134; primordial differentiation of, 95–96. *See also* plate tectonics

earthquakes, 11, 23, 56, 61, 69, 118; at Dieng Plateau, 128; measuring and monitoring of, 33, 73, 169, 173; Merapi eruption of 2010 and, 73–74; origins of, 33–34, 37, 72, 183n42

East Indian archipelago. *See* Indonesian archipelago

East Indies, 22, 29, 32, 37, 38, 88. *See also* Netherlands East Indies

economic geology, 44, 46, 117

Ecuador, 165–66

Edge, H. T., 189n27

Einthoven, Willem Frederik, Jr., 148, 150, 162, 163, 165, 172, 173; short-wave seismograph and, 153–54

Einthoven, Willem, Sr.: electrocardiograph and, 147–48, 149, 154, 194n9; string galvanometer and, 148, 150–51, *151*

electrocardiograph, 147–48, 149, 154, 194n9

energy, earth's, 42, 44, 185n76

Eocene epoch, 26, 47, 181n6

eruptions, volcanic: clouds and, 151; creation of modern Java and, 26–27, 48, 182n14; cycles of, 94–98, 111; in the Galapagos Islands, 166; of Krakatoa, 11, 12, 22, 27, 125; of Merapi in AD 1006, xviii, 83, 92, 94, 110; of Merapi in 1930, 14–15, *16–17*, 98; of Merapi in 2006, 67–68; of Merapi in 2010, 73–75, 164, 169; mud from, 10–11; of Pichincha, 166; significant Indonesian, 11–12, *13*, 14–15

Ethical Policy (1901), 81, 82, 127

Eurasian plate, 48, 54, 57

eustasy, 131

evacuations, xii, 68, 73–74, 104–5, 164

Ewing, Maurice, 38, 46, 47

extractivism, 1–4, 28–29, 117; national development and, 49

Fennema, Rinder: map of East Indian Archipelago, 29, *30*, 33; map of Java and Madoura, 21, 23–26, *24*, 42, 98; theory of volcanoes as ruins, 26–28, 126, 127

fieldwork, 7, 61–62, 63, 123–29, 151

folded mountains, 26–27, 182n14

folk culture, xv, 5, 81, 157

fossils, 26, 27, 28, 41, 126

Frankel, Henry, 5

French scientists, 164–68, 169

Fruin-Mees, Willemine, 125, *126*, 128

Galapagos Islands, 166

Galunggung, 6, 101

gatekeeper, function of, 65. See also *juru kunci*; Maridjan (gatekeeper of Merapi)

Geertz, Clifford, 12

geodeterminism, 82, 83, 111, 128, 134

geological knowledge, x, xvi–xvii, 2–3, 8, 19

geological sciences, x, 8, 19, 79, 189n36; aesthetics and, 117, 123; histories, xvi–xvii, 1–4, 5; institutions, 45, 72. *See also* earth sciences

Geological Survey (Geologische Opsporingsdienst), 117, 118, 128

geological time, xi, 2, 4, 44, 88, 176; earth
cycles and periodicity and, 18, 118,
130–34; human evolution and, 91,
189n36; measuring or dating of, 24–26,
41, 83, 181n9. *See also* stratigraphy
Geology of Indonesia, The (van Bemmelen),
38–42, *43*, 44, 99, 184n72, 184n76
geophysics, x, 41, 116, 172, 173–74; French,
169; geopoetics and, 138, 139, 140, 141; oil
and gas prospecting and, 154. *See also*
Metaxian, Jean-Philippe
geopoetics, 176–77; colonial geology and,
117–18, 122–23; cosmic rhythms and,
130–31, 135; origins and contemporary
usage of, xviii, 114–16, 140–41; plate
tectonics and, 137–39, 176
geopolitics, 103, 116, 140, 148, 174; Cold
War and, 167, 168, 173; of East Indies
and Netherlands, 150; France-Indonesia
collaborations and, 165, 167, 168; *geos*
and, 1, 8; geophysical diplomacy and,
169, 172; spiritual, 67, 68, 79
geos. See bios and *geos*
geosynclinists, 46–47
German Idealism, 135–36
Gilbert, G. K., 131
Glissant, Édouard, 116
Golkar, 70
Goss, Andrew, 129
Grabau, Amadeus William, 132–33, 134,
140, 192n36
gravity measurements, 30–34, *33*, 41, 72,
138; ocean expeditions and, 37–38, 46,
51, 52, 140
Griggs, David T., 35
Gurdjieff, George, 108

Haarmann, Erich, 95
Halbwachs, Michel, 72, 169
Hamilton, Warren, 167, 168, 169; "Tectonics
of the Indonesian Region" map, 45–46,
46, 54, 66; on the drifting of Java, 47–49;
on intercalations, 56–57, 75; rejection of
predecessors by, 46–47
Hatta, Mohammad, 89, 104–5, 112

heartbeats, 147–48, 150, 154, 176
Heezen, Bruce, *53*, *55*, 140
Hess, Harry H., 37, 116, 138–40
Hidayat, Irwan, 69–70
Hinduism, 84, 88, 92, 118, 155; caste system
in, 93–94; cosmology of, 4, 130, 189n34;
culture and traditions of, 89, 97, 98, 127,
130; decline and revival of, 82–83, 99, 100,
112; and the *Mahabharata*, 60, 192n30; philosophy and, 135, 141; *pralaya* concept in,
85, 90, 110; temples and ruins of, 86, 103,
111, 126; and the *Upanishads*, 4, 135–37
Hinloopen Labberton, Dirk van, 93, 96,
123; interpretation of the Calcutta Stone
by, 84–86, 90, 94, 110; retirement of, 107;
Theosophist membership of, 87, 88–89
Holmes, Arthur, 41
Holocene epoch, 9
honorifics, 60, 74
human body, 131, 174, 175; geophysics and,
172, 173; heart and heartbeat in, 147–48,
150, 154, 161–62; volcano observatories
and, xviii, 142–43, 164
human evolution, 90–93, 189n36

immeasurability, 130–31, 135
Inandiak, Elisabeth, 66, 68, 69–71, 73, 168;
The White Banyan, 63–64
Indian Ocean, 29, 42, 49, 60, 172; earthquakes and, 61, 69, 91; expeditions in,
52–54, *53*, 185n1; Opak Fault in, 75; volcano
connection with, 62–63, 64–65, 75, 78–79.
See also Nyai Ratu Kidul; ocean floor
Indo-Australian plate, 48, 54, 56–57
Indonesia, 64, 87, 99; culture of, 7, 103;
decolonization of, 100, 103–4, 112;
geology and, 38–42, *43*, 44; geopolitics
and, 167; independence celebrations
in, 112; Japanese occupation of, 39, 40,
98–99; national identity and, 155; plate
tectonic theories and, 45–46, *46*, 48,
50, 66; political transformation of, 76;
volcanology of, 4–7
Indonesian archipelago, 4, 7, 21, 54,
184n65; gravity anomalies and, 32–33,

Magelang, *17*, 99, 104

magic, xvi, 60; science *vs.*, , 74, 75

magma, 18, 48, 54, 72, 75, 78

Mahabharata, 60, 192n30

Mahuad, Jamil, 165–66

Majapahit kingdom, 161, 186n10

malaria, 12

Mangkubumi kingdom, 58

mantle, 35, 95, 131, 138, 139

mantris, 61

maps and cross sections, xvii, 20–22, 140; of the East Indian archipelago, 29, *30*; of the geology of Indonesia, 38–42, *43*, 44; of the geology of Java and Madoura, 24, *24–26*; of gravity anomalies, 30–33, *33*; of Krakatoa, 23–24, *25*; of Mount Merapi, 96, *97*, 98

Maridjan (gatekeeper of Merapi): eruption of 2010 and death of, xii–xiii, 73–74, 75, 78; fame and criticism of, 69–72; recounting his dream, 63–64; relationship with the sultan, 66–69; son Asih, 76

mata batin (eye of the heart), 64, 161–62, 163

Mataram sultanate, 58, 65, 105, 161, 186n9

matter, 90, 99, 142, 143, 147, 162; geological, 1, 57, 126; life and, 3–4, 136, 140

Mawas Diri, 155–57, *156*, 195n40

Maximin, Daniel, 116

meditation, 156, 159, 162–63; *latihan* (group), 107, 108

mediumship, 162, 172, 173–74

Merapi: aerial photos of, 15, *17*, 100–101, *101*; avalanches at, 103; deities and ritual offerings to, 59–60; development projects and, 67, 70; DOMErapi project and, 165; eruption cycles of, 94–98, *97*, 102–3; eruption of AD 1006, xviii, 83, 92–93, 110–11; eruption of 1930, 14–15, *16–17*, 98, 143; eruption of 2006, 67–68; eruption of 2010, 73–75, 164, 169; executions at, 65; French scientists on, 165–68, 169, *170–71*; ocean connection with, 62–63, 64–65, 66; potential eruption of 1943, 152–53; seismograph network at, 172–73; spiritual geography of, 61–62,

75; stories about, xiii–xiv; unpredictability of, xi–xii; warning system at, 104–5, *105*, *106*, 107. *See also* observatories; Maridjan (gatekeeper of Merapi)

Metaxian, Jean-Philippe, 72, 164–68, 169, 172–73

mineral deposits, 29, 44, 49–50, 158

mining companies, 39–40, 81, 108

Miocene epoch, 26, 28, 34, 47, 48, 181n6

modern science, 3, 4, 14, 104, 136–37, 139; geopoetics and, 115, 130; local knowledge and, 5, 72, 76; religion and, 87–88, 108, 137

molecular structures, 117, *120–22*

Molengraaff, Gustav A., 39, 95, 184n65

monitoring, volcano, 73, 100, 144, 174, 181n44; Bandung office for, 73, 164–65; French, 165–66; in the Galapagos Islands, 166–67; at Maron hill, 14–15, *16*, 143, 151; via satellites, 169, 172; warning system and, 104–5, *105*, *106*, 107. *See also* observatories

Monsoon (ship), 140; samples collected by, 52–54, 56, 59, 62, 75, 78; tracks covered by, *53*

Morse code, 150, *151*

mountain building, 14, 18, 47, 95, 100, 134; compression and, 133; creation of modern Java and, 26–27; transgressions and, 132

Mrázek, Rudolf, 5, 112, 148

mud eruptions, 10–11, 12, 181n41

mysticism, xiii, xv, xvi, xvii, 8, 68, 74; communication technologies and, 156–58, 161–63; Islamic, xvi, xviii, 8, 108, 155; silent, 80–81, 83. *See also* Kejawen (Javanism); occultism; spirits

National Geographic, 53, 62

nationalism, 83, 84, 93, 112, 155; postcolonial ruling and, 103–4; publications and, 101–2; Theosophist movement and, 89, 99

natural resources, 1, 44, 49

nature: control of, 93, 112, 141; cycles of, 131; disorder of, 66; respect for, 76;

society and, xii, 10; spirits and, 63; as a sultanate, 64; transformation of, 1, 85, 116; unknowability of, 136

Netherlands, 21, 22, 31–32, 99; communication with East Indies, 148, 150

Netherlands East Indies: exports and trade of, 11, 12, 58, 81; geological exploration and mining in, 39–40, 44; Japanese occupation of, 98–99, 130; Javanese culture and, 80–82, 84, 93, 112; laborers and, 117, 122–23, 124; maps of, 21; modernization in, 127, 128, 148; photography studios in, 15; postcolonialism and, 103–4; residencies in, 24, 41; scientists in, 31, 61–62, 112, 128–29; telecommunications and, 148, 150; Theosophists and, 87–88; volcanology and, xviii, 4–6, 14, 18, 98, 99

New Order government, 10, 21, 49, 65, 167, 196n47; *adiluhung* rhetoric of, 195n37; spiritual geographies and, 62–63

Newman, Barry, 110

Ngepos observatory, 151–52

Nietzsche, Friedrich, 135

Nyai Ratu Kidul (deity), 57, 65, 79, 186n10; Kyai Sapu Jagad and, 60, 75; offerings to, 10, 54, 56, 59, 76, 78; relations with sultans, 58–59, 104, 186n11

observatories, xvi, 174; in Babadan, 15, 104–5, *106*, 146, 151–54, 164, 172; in Batavia, 33, 39; in Ecuador, 165–66; electrification of, 159; in the Galapagos Islands, 166–67; Kejawen mystics and, xviii, 158, 163–64; locations and architecture of, 100, 142–44, *145*–46; at Maron hill, 14–15, *16*, 143, 151; seismographs and string galvanometer technology at, 151–53, 172–73; in Yogyakarta, 68, 73, 104, 107, 165

Occult History of Java, The (Leadbeater), 92

occultism, 87–90; chemistry and, 117, *119–22*

ocean floor, 7, 21, 22, 23, 38, 44; continents and, 36–37, 51, 140; expansion of, 116, 138–39; fold in, 30, 33–36, *36*, 42; low-

ering of, 133; mapping the, 31–32, 140; Merapi and, 66; samples collected from, 52–54, 56; telegraph cables and, 29, 30; volcanic eruptions and, 48–49

ocean trenches, 7, 41, 138. *See also* Java Trench

oil and gas prospecting, 10–11, 22, 23, 29, 154; companies, 39–40, 45, 81, 117; exploitation and, 44; plate tectonics and, 46, 49–50

Oligocene epoch, 28, 42, 44, 48, 181n6

Opak River, 67, 75

Oreskes, Naomi, 5

origin stories, ix, 20, 30, 39, 44; of continents, 36–37, 41, 139; of human evolution, 90–91; of modern earth, 57; of plate tectonics, 48; of the universe, 90

orogeny. *See* mountain building

Ouspensky, Pyotr, 108

Pacific Science Congress, 12, 128–29

palm plantations, 12, 111

Pasar Bubar, 61–62, 144, 168

Pelée, 116

Pemberton, John, 65–66

periodicity, 99, 131, 132, 134

Phillips, John, 26

Pigeaud, Theodore, 61

pilgrimages, xii, 56, 62, 76, 79, 161

plantation economy, 3, 11–12, 14, 18, 23, 128

plate tectonics, 2, 5, 21, 66, 185n78; diagram of the earth's, 168, *171*; earth narratives and, ix, xi, 20, 50–51; earthquakes and, 72; geopoetics and, xviii, 123, 137–38, 141, 176; Hamilton's map and theory of, 45–48, *46*, 54; Indian Ocean floor and, 52, 54, *55*; Katili's application of, 44, 45, 49–50, 51, 56, 168; Merapi and, xiii, 168, 169; spiritual geographies and, xvii, 56–57, 75–76, 78–79; Surono's plumbing system for, 75, 78; undation theory and, 44, 45; US geologists and, 37, 38, 140. *See also* continental drift

Plawangan, 61, 65, 96, 144

Pliocene epoch, 26, 48, 181n6

poetics. *See* geopoetics

political geology, xv, 19, 63, 79, 175; Anthropocene and, xvi–xvii, 177; extractivism and, 1–3; political ecology and, 8–9; volcano-ocean connection and, 64, 69

Povinelli, Elizabeth, 3, 140

Prambanan temple, 10, 85, 86, 92, 103, 111, 129

Prasetyo, Elisabeth. *See* Inandiak, Elisabeth

praying, 74, 103, 175, 177

Protchsky, Susie, 15

Psychozoic, 9, 134

Pulse of the Earth, The (Umbgrove), xviii, 9, 126, 130–31, 133–34; influence on geologists of, 114, 137–38, 140

pulses/pulsations, 41, 134, 142–43, 153, 162, 172; deep time and, 18; electrical, 147–48, 157; human body and, 173, 174; oceanic, 132, 140

Pyenson, Lewis, 5, 31

Quaternary period, 26, 181n6

racialized hierarchies, 118, 123

radio, 129, 159; volcano observatories and, 104, 105, 107, 144, 151. *See also* Kejawen

Raffles, Stamford, 84–85, 86, 125

Ramaswamy, Sumathi, 87

Ramayana, 130

reality, universe and, 136–37

religion, 7, 76, 82–83, 90; geological time and, xi, 91; philosophy and, 136; science and, 87–88, 108, 137. *See also* occultism; *and specific religions*

Republic of Indonesia. *See* Indonesia

Resink, G. J., 75

revivalisms: cultural, 82, 112; Hindu-Buddhist, 82–83, 99, 100, 104

rhythms, xviii, 3, 18, 131; earth or planetary, 99, 116, 133–35, 193n43; undations as, 96

Ricklefs, Merle, 7–8, 186n10

risk, volcanic, 5, 179n8

ritual offerings, 62, 66, 155, 161, 177; to the earth (*sedekah bumi*), 76; flowers as, 126;

to Nyai Ratu Kidul, 10, 54, 56, 59, 76, 78; to volcanoes, 11, 92–93

Robert H. Ray Company, 154

rooster calls, 155–57, 162

rotations, earth and galactic, 18, 118, 131, 132, 133, 176

Royal Dutch Shell, 81, 117

rubber products, 12

Rudwick, Martin, 4, 139

ruins, 26–28, 42, 92, 111–12, 118; of Atlantis, 91; Dieng plateau, 85, 125, 126, 127–28, 129; earthly evolution and, 139–40; of Javanese culture, 82, 85–86, 98, 125–27

safety (*slamet*), 66, 187n36

Salam (village), 111–12

sand mining, xiv–xv, 67, 69, 70, 160

Santoso (Kejawen practitioner), 159–64, 172, 173

Santoso, Agus Budi, 169

Schlehe, Judith, 63, 65

Scripps Oceanographic Institute, 46, 50, 52

sea level, 24, 131, 132, 193n43

Secret Doctrine, The (Blavatsky), 90–91

seismographs, 74, 144, 157–58, 177; in Babadan bunker, 15, 103, 152–54; human body and, 173; for Merapi, 172–73; for monitoring earthquakes, 33, 73, 169; new technology, 168, 169

seismologists, xiv, 37, 61, 72, 164, 169, 172

Senopati, Susuhunan, 58, 65, 76

Siegert, Bernard, xvi

single-celled organisms, 26

Sinnett, Alfred Percy, 87

Snellius Expedition, 7, 35, 40

Snider, Robert G., 52, 185n1

society, geology and, x, 1, 9–10, 175

sovereignty, 10, 61

spirits, xv, 64, 67, 144, 147, 175, 189n34; communication with, 156–57; as guardians, 112; hauntings by, 11, 65; hierarchies and, 63; possession by, 107, 108; as volcano and ocean deities, 9–10, 56,